D1327428

# HUMAN RIGHTS / HUMAN WRONGS

# HUMAN / HUMAN RIGHTS / WRONGS

## ART AND SOCIAL CHANGE

Essays by members of the faculty of The University of Iowa

EDITED BY ROBERT HOBBS & FREDRICK WOODARD

*With an Afterword by*

ROBERT HUGHES

MUSEUM OF ART
THE UNIVERSITY OF IOWA

1 9 8 6

*Photo credits:* Color photography by C. Randall Tosh. Photographs for the University of Iowa Museum of Art by Mark Tade and Gerald Davey.

*Figure credits:*

*Becker: Fig. 1:* Museum of Modern Art, New York; *Fig. 2:* Kittel, Quedlinburg; *Figs. 3–4:* Andreas Feininger; *Fig. 5:* Museum of Modern Art, New York.

*Andrew: Figure 2:* Courtesy of the University of California Press, Berkeley; *Fig. 8:* Reprinted from Donald C. Crafton, *Before Mickey* (Cambridge: M.I.T. Press).

*Waite: Figure 1:* Jane Boller and L. W. Ward, *Cedar Rapids Gazette; Figs 2–3:* Reprinted from *The World of Atget* by Berenice Abbott, Copyright 1964, by permission of the publisher, Horizon Press, New York; *Fig. 4:* Molzohn-Foto, Altheim; *Fig. 5:* Baker, New York; *Fig. 6:* Alinari/Art Resource; *Figs. 7–8:* Copyright 1985 by R. Crumb; *Fig. 9:* Reprinted from *Pioneers of Soviet Photography,* ed. Grigory Shudakov, Olga Suslova, and Lilya Ukhtomskaya, trans. Paul Keegan (Paris: Philippe Sers, 1983).

*Kuenzli: Figure 1:* George Karger, PIX: *Fig. 2:* Museum of Modern Art, New York; *Fig. 3:* Don Myer, San Francisco Museum of Modern Art.

Copy Editor: Gail Parson Zlatnik
Composition: Annie Graham & Co., Iowa City
Design: Norman Sage

**Library of Congress Cataloging-in-Publication Data**

Human rights/human wrongs.

Exhibition catalog.
Includes bibliographies.
1. Art–Political aspects–Exhibitions.
2. Art and society–Exhibitions.
3. Art–Psychology–Exhibitions.
I. Hobbs, Robert Carleton, 1946–
II. Woodard, Fredrick.
III. University of Iowa. Museum of Art.
N72.P6H86    701'.03    86-50147
ISBN 0-87414-046-3

The title of this catalogue, *Human Rights/Human Wrongs: Art and Social Change*, represented a challenge to University of Iowa professors from nine different academic disciplines: to view art and politics from the perspective of their own fields of expertise.

Three works of art from the permanent collection of the University of Iowa Museum of Art were chosen for analysis. Each exhibits a different degree of social commitment: Robert Arneson's *Minuteman* borders on propaganda; Lyonel Feininger's *In a Village Near Paris* uses forms and ideas common to the artist's political cartoons, and Jackson Pollock's *Mural* appears to be unrelated to the artist's leftist views.

The artists, all Americans, lived and worked at different times and in different places. Feininger was an American expatriate living in Germany in the early twentieth century; Pollock was a leader of the New York School during World War II; and Arneson is a postwar California Bay Area ceramicist.

Together these studies provide a picture of three significant American artists and an overview of three important developments in twentieth-century art. They also demonstrate the value and practicability of bringing the knowledge and methods of the scientific and humanistic disciplines to bear on the visual arts.

# CONTENTS

# ACKNOWLEDGMENTS

The exhibition and catalogue *Human Rights/Human Wrongs: Art and Social Change* developed out of a series of important conversations with Dorothy Schramm. The late C. Maxwell Stanley responded to the idea of an exhibition focusing on the relationships between art and politics, and he encouraged the Stanley/University of Iowa Foundation Support Organization to underwrite the exhibition and catalogue.

The project was endorsed by Dorothy Paul, Dorothy Schramm, and Burns Weston, who together with Robert Hobbs organized the symposium "Human Rights in the Global Community" (April 4–5, 1986), sponsored jointly by the Iowa Division of the United Nations Association of the United States of America, the University of Iowa College of Law, the Iowa Humanities Board, the Stanley Foundation of Muscatine, and the Museum of Art. This was the first human rights colloquium to view art as a significant force for human rights.

Museum staff members who have been integral to the realization of this project include Jo-Ann Conklin, Leonard Curtis, Nancy DeDakis, David Dennis, Honee A. Hess, Eva Huber, Karen Hueftle, James Lindell, and Ellen Ramsey.

Gail Parson Zlatnik has been a thoughtful copy editor. Lawrence Gelfand and Carl Brosseau provided essential assistance with research, Joan Kellogg and Suzanne Richerson with proofreading, and Judith Pendleton with typesetting. Tim Mosman lent his aesthetic eye, and Jane Miller hers, and David Salisbury and Mary Stefaniak their keyboarding skill, to the catalogue project.

The members of the University of Iowa faculty who have contributed pieces to this book have been immensely helpful and supportive throughout the entire project. From the outset they were enthusiastic about considering works of art from the perspective of their individual disciplines; the extent of their interest is clearly evident in the quality of their essays and the importance they have all placed on their repeated contacts with the three works of art featured in this exhibition.

We believe that this project charts an important course for university museums, which can become ideal forums for interdisciplinary studies and the intelligent dialogue that is a central component of any vital culture. We hope the approaches used by the various scholars will suggest new possibilities of inquiry to art historians and critics. We hope in addition that this project will prove useful to those artists who wonder who their real audience is and who wish to know more about how professionals in other fields look at a work of art.

ROBERT HOBBS
*Director, Museum of Art*

FREDRICK WOODARD
*Associate Dean of the Faculties*

# PREFACE

Fredrick Woodard

At the opening of a recent exhibition, *Jean Metzinger in Retrospect,* at the University of Iowa Museum of Art, I found myself drawn into the paintings and drawings of this noted Cubist and full of reflections upon literature. The images, the lines, and the light (but mostly the varieties of the light) mesmerized me with a kind of motion that I had heretofore associated only with certain sections of poetry from the works of LeRoi Jones (Baraka), Eliot, Stevens, and Pound, and the prose of Gertrude Stein, Ralph Ellison, James Joyce, and Albert Murray. Near the end of my tour of the artworks, I realized, and said to a friend, that so many of the seminal and critical works of literature dearest to me were in the Cubist mode and that my own mode of logic, of thinking, had not yet transcended that essentially blues/jazz medium. Eager to test this revelation, I engaged another patron in a discussion of Wallace Stevens's "The Man with the Blue Guitar." As I did so, I convinced myself and him that the subtle, though incremental, shifts and repetitions of rhythms in the poem have the cumulative effect of the lines and light of the Picasso painting for which the poem is named.

Certainly, in my teaching of several literary pieces I had sensed what had been made so clear by the works of Metzinger. I had, for example, taught Stein, particularly *Three Lives,* with practically the library's entire collection of Cubist art books as exhibitions for the students. I had also discussed in detail the failure of Sherwood Anderson's art in terms of his inability to conceptualize in the art of the novel—*Dark Laughter*—the intellectual roots of his essentially Cubist vision. So it was not as if I had had no experience with the subject

---

Fredrick Woodard is Associate Dean of the Faculties.

matter. It was that I had not heretofore *experienced* the subject matter, and that made all the difference.

"In the museum," Cézanne remarked once, "the painter learns to think." One sees the result of Cézanne's thinking, in, say, *The Basket of Apples,* as one becomes witness to his thoroughly realized apples spilling across a table whose top is speculatively tilted upward on the right, tipping the surface until, in real life, the fruit would be rolling off. The painting forces the spectator to think about the gravitational fields of vision that appear to warp the plate and the other objects. Cézanne's thinking makes the execution of the painting possible; it is our thinking which makes us experience the implicit human suffering there, even in the absence of human figures. But the point I wish to make here has to do with the value of art and the museum in an environment where thinking is the all-consuming preoccupation. Perhaps the single greatest lesson to be taught by museums and their treasures in such an environment is that art expresses the conditions of man in time. In that regard, art is history; it is also science, and social science, and the humanities. And yet the museum and its programs can also demonstrate that art may go far beyond the modernity of the traditional disciplines to share common ground with the most elemental, creative forces: the traditional disciplines provide much of the substance of our harmony with the world; art disturbs, it fractures, it throws things out of joint.

My experience with Metzinger was not the source of the experiment that makes this volume possible. However, it contributed to my belief that the project of this experiment was worth pursuing for what it would reveal about the impact of art upon the scholars' imaginations, as well as the impact of the scholars' disciplinary imaginations upon thinking about and discussing art.

The essays collected here were written for the occasion of a special exhibition, *Human Rights/Human Wrongs,* and as part of an experiment to integrate the Museum of Art more finely into the total life of the university and the community. The writers of these selections are known, nationally and internationally, for their work in the disciplines of dermatology, neurology, political science, poetry, film studies, comparative literature, rhetorical theory, photojournalism, and English literature. Their venture into art was by invitation. It was in response to a collegial curiosity: what would be the results if scholars in disciplines other than art history were to write about art from their experiences with it or from the perspectives of their own disciplinary interests?

The project was easy enough to formulate in so rich an interdisciplinary environment as we enjoy at The University of Iowa. For, to be sure, each of the writers has had broad interdisciplinary experience in research and teaching, traditionally related to his or her discipline – in seminars speculating on the bridging of epistemologies, in conferences on medical humanities, in team-taught courses on law and literature, in studies of the rhetoric of the social sciences, and many others. So the interdisciplinary activity, qua intellectual exploration, was not in itself far removed from their current scholarly interests. Nevertheless, art as object, or as a division of history, was for each of them an interest approached *en passant.* Museums of art and art per se were, for the most part, outside their ordinary, everyday preoccupations. By all accounts, therefore, the scholars selected were perfectly suited for the experiment.

What merit the experiment may have can spring only from the task that each of the writers set for himself or herself – to study one of the three pieces of twentieth-century art and the literature written about the piece and then to interpret the piece according to his or her experience or according to the lights of his or her discipline. The givens in the task, of course, were the constraints of the "assignment," over which the writers had little control. Beyond the givens, however, was their mastery of disciplines that they were free to manipulate toward a coherent discourse on the work of art. The domain that was theirs to mold as they willed should be the domain of interest to us as readers, for it is there that they will convince us of the magnitude of their subjects and also of the limitations of the experiment. If, in their essays, they have been able to stimulate further interest, provoke questions, and pose some major problems, they shall have done quite enough to demonstrate that art is a vital resource for perspectives on virtually every discipline in the academy.

It is essentially this openness, this accessibility of institutional and intellectual resources to promote change, that lies at the heart of the experiment. And, though in itself the experiment grew out of an intellectual curiosity, the climate which makes such experiments successful is a trademark of The University of Iowa. For it was the farsightedness of the university over a half-century ago that opened the way to the creative arts in an academic environment once reserved for the "traditional disciplines." By appointing artists and writers to its faculty and by offering degrees to students in fields never before recognized as part of the academy, the university inaugurated a principle in education of promoting exploration in the arts as in all other areas of knowledge. This openness, this free and easy access to intellectual re-sources, places the faculty contributions in this volume in a historical context that is not easily matched in the history of any other major re-search institution in the world.

Yet, even for The University of Iowa, there are aspects of this proj-ect which are new. As with many such inventions, the impetus that gave rise to the idea was an outgrowth of a need: to explore possibil-ities for the integration of the university's Museum of Art and its pro-grams into the total life of the university and the community. If, as Robert Hobbs points out in his introductory essay, it is culturally and intellectually irresponsible to maintain a museum as a mausoleum, how does one effectively challenge the old perceptions and assump-tions about the role of art in the world, and thus evolve toward an orientation that invites thought about and discussion of art as history, as object, but also as a kind of liberty of the mind?

The very portability of art suggested one possibility. That is, by anal-ogy we sought to bring the scholars to the art or, to be precise, to bring the art of the scholars to the need at hand. We asked them to be voyeurs through the eyes of their own experiences or disciplinary preoccupations. Their visions as represented in this volume surpass by far the results we had imagined, for they have opened a window to art, and to the Museum of Art, which we are committed to keep open and to widen.

# HUMAN RIGHTS/HUMAN WRONGS:
*Museums and Their Objects*

ROBERT HOBBS

Although museum staff members and the general public often accept the conventions of exhibiting art and producing catalogues as norms which are beyond question, I believe these conventions need to be challenged. I wish to begin this book by questioning assumptions about the inherent goodness of art, the great benefits to be derived from going to museums, the satisfying knowledge currently available about art, and the separation of art from the power struggles that seem to pervade all other aspects of life. Rather than providing answers, this introduction will suggest ways that certain beliefs can and should be questioned.

Museums and their publications often constitute a way of looking that is superimposed upon the visions of an individual artist to become the societal work of art that we call culture. If we are to free art from the current mode of museum practice—which seems intent on embalming it in a mausoleum—and allow it to be a deeply felt reaction to the world by a sensitive individual, then we have to look critically at museums and assess their attitudes about the role of art in contemporary life.

## THE MUSEUM AS MAUSOLEUM

Largely a late eighteenth- and early nineteenth-century creation, the art museum has been viewed as an arbiter of taste, a legitimizer of vanguard experiments, and a repository for art where one can go and look and be suspended in time. Many art museums cultivate the feeling of a world outside time by mixing works of different periods and by emphasizing the universal appeal of art's formal qualities. To enter

---

Robert Hobbs is the Director of the University of Iowa Museum of Art.

the hallowed marble halls of some institutions, or the pure white spaces of others, is to be removed from the mundane and situated in a rarefied atmosphere conducive to meditation. The idea is a brilliant one, but unfortunately it is an approach geared to look at all art as sensuous surface and design, and not to see that art is historical as well.

Many artists have remarked on the problems of this approach, which makes art precious and prevents it from functioning as a historical indicator of a particular time, place, and sensibility. In *News from Nowhere,* the nineteenth-century Utopian William Morris described the British Museum as irrelevant to the future, when people would wear their art and live with it daily in the form of beautiful and significant tools and furniture. In the twentieth century, Dadaist artist Marcel Duchamp suggested that museums were the repositories for objects that had ceased to be art. He stated that an art object has a life span of approximately forty years (a little over a generation), during which time it is the subject of discussion and inquiry. After that time, its content ceases to be controversial and significant, and it comes to be prized primarily for its formal qualities. More recently, in a note titled "Some Void Thoughts on Museums," the sculptor Robert Smithson wrote:

> Visiting a museum is a matter of going from void to void. Hallways lead the viewer to things once called "pictures" and "statues." Anachronisms hang and protrude from every angle. Themes without meaning press on the eye. Multifarious nothings permute into false windows (frames) that open up onto a verity of blanks. Stale images cancel one's perception and deviate one's motivation. Blind and senseless, one continues wandering around the remains of Europe, only to end in that massive deception "the art history of the recent past." Brain drain leads to eye drain, as one's sight defines emptiness by blankness. Sightings fall like heavy objects from one's eyes. Sight becomes devoid of sense, or the sight is there, but the sense is unavailable. Many try to hide this perceptual falling out by calling it abstract. Abstraction is everybody's zero but nobody's nought. Museums are tombs, and it looks like everything is turning into a museum. ("Some Void Thoughts on Museums," in *The Writings of Robert Smithson,* ed. Nancy Holt [New York: New York University Press, 1979], 58.)

When a museum sanctions vanguard work, Smithson implies, it removes the art from its original context and universalizes it as significant form. The museum is therefore a void because it eliminates discussion about art by making it absolute. Using many display techniques common to Tiffany's window dressers, museum staff members have a tendency to turn works of art into products.

At the University of Iowa Museum of Art, we hope to challenge some museum assumptions about the rarefied nature of art. This exhibition and catalogue represent a university-wide search for ways to approach art so that it remains a piece of history, so that other orientations besides the formalist approach prevail, and so that art will serve as the basis for discussion and thought.

## THE MUSEUM'S CONTROL: THE CULTURAL LINE-UP

Our culture is so used to seeing art as a positive creative outlet, and museums as essential ingredients of culture, that we forget that modern museums originated in the eighteenth century, when such institutions as asylums, hospitals, and prisons were being formed on the theory of control through constantly exposing the insane, the ill, and the criminal elements to supervising eyes. Although French critic Michel Foucault has not written about museums as such, his analyses of asylums and prisons in *The Birth of the Clinic: An Archeology of Medical Perception* and *Discipline and Punishment: The Birth of the Prison* provide a new means for comprehending the significance of the origins of museums in the eighteenth century. Foucault is concerned with the ways that power operates in a given society. Instead of regarding power as the prerogative of an individual ruler, Foucault suggests that in the modern world it operates through specific systems. Exemplary models of the power base created by systems include prisons and asylums, which in the eighteenth century used visibility as a means of control. If criminals and the insane could be watched, then their actions might provide clues to understanding their deviancy and ultimately suggest methods for reforming them.

Emphasizing visibility as rationality put into practice, Foucault provides concepts useful for understanding how museums serve to extend the power base of a society by controlling its creative sector. If the art of a people can be gathered together and lined up in galleries, just as criminals and the insane were lined up, it can be periodically reviewed the way a general reviews his troops, and order and reason can be maintained. Such an approach is particularly important in controlling any recently produced art because it allows people to see what deviations from the norm are being created and how the norm itself is becoming changed over time.

Individual works of art have always wielded power. But before the establishment of museums, and before art was assembled in a line-up according to style, art's illusion seemed more mysterious and remarkable. Before museums, people could not readily compare works, study compositional devices, and review individual developments; they had to respond to the art images in front of them and to the feelings these images evoked. From their beginning, museums functioned like the *Encyclopédie* of Diderot and d'Alembert, which leveled the distinctions between different craft guilds and robbed craftspeople of both dignity and secrets by vesting authority in a written account of the trade rather than in the craftsperson.

Museums changed the concept of what art should be and promoted the assumption that only those objects that could be easily housed in galleries, such as prints, drawings, paintings, and sculpture, were art. Painting, the form most accommodating to the museum concept, came to be regarded as the most significant art. Over time museums have robbed art of much of its spiritual function by creating displays that encourage rapid consumption, and by de-emphasizing the miraculous feat of creating a believable illusion in a single object. Museums have developed during an era dominated by such historicist movements as Neoclassicism, Pre-Raphaelite art, the Gothic Revival, and primitivism, during an era when style seemed so easily assumable that an entire culture could try to clothe itself in the garments and manners of another time and place. The avant-garde came into being soon after museums went public and appears to have developed as a critique of the official art housed in museums. First the avant-garde served as a self-critical element of the art world; at the turn of the century it came to be an expected irritant; and in the late twentieth century it has become an established institution.

The term "art for art's sake" gained currency in France and England only fifty years after the first public museums were established in those countries. The concept of "art for art's sake" was first elaborated by Théophile Gautier in 1835 in his introduction to his novel *Mademoiselle de Maupin,* and it was soon adopted by artists who used it to promote what they thought were fundamental artistic freedoms. The freedom of "art for art's sake," of course, is severely limited because it separates art from life. What these artists regarded as freedom was, in actuality, a new way of exhibiting art, a new norm that stripped art of many of its mysteries and provided it with a public forum. Probably the first truly important museum-oriented artist was Edouard Manet, who created self-conscious works of art that alluded to known masterpieces in public collections. In works such as his *Déjeuner sur l'herbe,* he played with common preconceptions about the propriety of classical nudes and the impropriety of contemporary female nude models, even when they assumed the same postures as figures in well-known Renaissance paintings.

Although the University of Iowa Museum of Art has few works from the time when museums were first changing public attitudes toward art, the majority of its paintings reflect these changes. The Jawlensky *Spanierin* in the museum's collection [*Fig. 1*], for example, makes clear reference to the Spanish paintings of Manet. Jawlensky's is a cultivated and knowing art, a public discourse on art in the mod-

*Figure 1.*
ALEXEJ VON JAWLENSKY
*Spanierin* [Spanish woman], 1910.
Oil on canvas on board.
38¼ x 25½ in. (97.3 x 64.9 cm.).
University of Iowa Museum of Art.
*Gift of Owen and Leone Elliott.*

ern world as a closed system that signifies its own formal means—paint, color, and canvas—and its own conventions, in this case, equivalence between the idea of the exotic and the Spanish woman.

For better or worse, over the past two centuries the museum has become an institution that is destined to mirror itself. And the art that has been made since the origin of the museum concept also reflects the museum's role: lining up paintings and sculpture for systematic review. The museum levels distinctions so that art loses much of its power to communicate distinct new sensibilities. It tends to turn art into decontextualized masterworks that elicit awe and appreciation of universal qualities that are usually left undefined. Museums have turned art into objects, primarily into painted, printed, drawn, and sculpted objects that are portable. The art that has been made for museums is an art subject to manipulation by being sequestered in storerooms or by being exhibited as an example of a particular species. The museum work of art is in danger of becoming either a decoration or an isolated masterpiece that evokes aesthetic pleasure and speaks to universally relevant human values that have little to do with the problems of living in a specific time and place.

Even works not intended for the museum fall under its influence. African fetishes are exhibited as sculpture, North American Indian rattles become *objets d'art;* thus, sacred objects are secularized, and everyday objects such as ceramic bowls and silver cups are turned into merely beautiful forms. The meaning of the work of art as an integral symbol in a social network is lost, and the object becomes "Art" with a capital "A."

There are, of course, advantages as well as disadvantages to the museum line-up, for it does insure that works of art are preserved, studied, and exhibited with some regularity. Museums make works of art available to large numbers of people, and they provide people who are especially open to the language of these forms with an opportunity to understand the sensibilities of another place, another time, perhaps another individual, in a special way.

In coordinating the exhibition *Human Rights/Human Wrongs,* we are fully aware of the limitations of the museum setting and the profound influence it has had on the viewing of art. Museum buildings in themselves provide a form of social control over the creative human spirit by giving art a ponderous and official quality that may never have been intended. A sketch exhibited in a museum no longer can be considered casually. In a museum it becomes official, and it is usually backed up with solid masonry, theatrical lighting, and galleries so constructed as to muffle sounds.

Although the art of the museum becomes accepted art, it does not have to cease being provocative. If viewers wish to come to terms with the art in itself, they must understand how this institution has changed art. They must try to comprehend the ways our society tends to institutionalize and contain knowledge so that ambiguity is lessened, and freedom—another form of ambiguity—is curtailed.

## ART'S POWER

Approximately two centuries after the establishment of museums, which have emphasized the formal properties of art at the expense of its content, we are again coming to appreciate the power of art.

We need to set aside the notion that art is concerned only with decoration or with ineffable pleasures, with pure delectation of the senses, and with all those refinements that make it rarefied and separate from daily existence. And we need to focus on what art does: it establishes identity, whether that identity be personal, societal, or political, and it also endows groups with power. The Israelites of the Old Testament understood the power of art when they made the Ark of the Covenant into a symbol so forceful that only a few could come near it. And Solomon certainly comprehended the power of art to confer high status on Jerusalem when he lavished the riches of his burgeoning empire on the temple. Similarly Native North Americans knew the power of art when they carved effigies and put them in their sacred bundles; when they lost their bundles to others, they were demoralized and felt that they had lost their source of strength.

So important is the power of art that it is worth examining its premises more fully to see how specific styles of art have established identities for Iowa and New York.

When Grand Wood painted *American Gothic* in 1930, he established an identity for the Midwest and for Iowa. Fully aware of the impace of the Depression, Wood sought an image which would communicate the enduring strengths of the Midwest and at the same time poke fun at the Puritan work ethic and the rigor with which ascetic people approached life, leading them in the nineteenth century to use the Gothic church style for even their simple homes. Wood used Late Gothic painting of fifteenth-century Flanders as a basis for his art. By creating an interesting interplay of Gothic arches that encompasses the rickrack of the woman's apron, the farmer's overalls, his pointed head, and his pitchfork, Wood referred indirectly to the religious devotion that permeated the lives of the people he depicted. The success of his image can be measured by the parodies of it that recur with surprising regularity on the editorial pages of newspapers, on greeting cards, and even on calendars. His *American Gothic* has become a well-loved cliché of American life, and it has also become a way of instantly categorizing the Midwest and Iowa.

It is no accident that Grant Wood chose to immortalize the humble birthplace of Iowa-born President Hoover, who was still in office in the early years of the Depression. Both men believed in the truisms of their youth. Both were intent on ignoring the problems of the Great Depression. Just as Hoover refused to create large-scale relief programs for the masses of hungry, unemployed Americans because he believed that a dole would rob them of their dignity, so Grant Wood refused to portray contemporary problems and instead created cartoon-like renditions of American clichés in *The Birthplace of Herbert Hoover* (the rise of a powerful man from a humble background) and in *Parson Weems' Fable* (the honesty of the first President). The problem with the approach of both Grant Wood and Herbert Hoover is that they believed humor could be an antidote for overwhelming problems. They trivialized present-day concerns and they appeared to the world to be unfeeling. Hoover misconstrued the Depression, seeing it as a psychological state rather than the economic calamity that it actually was. He told newsman Raymond Clapper in February 1931: "What the country needs is a good big laugh. There seems to be a condition of hysteria. If someone could get off a good joke every ten days, . I think our troubles would be over."

Although *American Gothic* and *The Birthplace of Herbert Hoover* are important works of art, and Grant Wood was without question a brilliant artist, his work has come to be regarded as emblematic of the Midwest. The result is that many people have become distrustful of it; they regard both Wood and the region as the embodiment of an alien world view.

In the 1930s, when most Americans were confronted by the difficulties of the Depression, a number of wealthy New Yorkers were patronizing European contemporary art and at the same time supporting a grandiose concept of colonial America. It is highly ironic that the Rockefeller Foundation gave money for the establishment of Colonial Williamsburg on the eve of the Great Crash. Colonial Williamsburg represents an ostentatious, baroque phase of American art; it illustrates the taste of the Tories more than it does that of the colonists, and it clearly establishes a basis for believing the American colonies to be elegant, refined, and highly cultivated. It suggests that the colonists might give up their tea, but they would never relinquish their love of fine earthenware, opulent damasks, and polished mahogany.

About the same time the Rockefellers funded Colonial Williamsburg, they also helped to establish and support the Museum of Modern Art, which opened its doors in New York City during the fateful year 1929. The Rockefellers, along with a few other well-placed New Yorkers, embraced European modern art. They wished to free themselves from the hegemony of older moneyed collectors, such as J. Pierpoint Morgan, who built the Morgan Library to house old master drawings and manuscripts, the Mellons, who also collected old masters and who helped to fund the National Gallery of Art, and Henry

Clay Frick, who viewed the art of Whistler as the culmination of his superb collection of Renaissance bronzes, old master European paintings, and other treasures. The Rockefellers wished to patronize a different artistic trend, one which was mostly French and avant-garde. In the thirties they commissioned Matisse and Léger to decorate their apartment, and the ascendancy of their financial empire was heralded by the creation of that great Art Deco masterpiece, Rockefeller Center. They allied themselves with Europe, and in their commissioned art they made a clear-cut statement about their international allegiances. Interestingly, their patronage of contemporary art went far beyond that evident at the time in Europe, where avant-garde artists were greatly respected by only a small group of intellectuals.

In the 1930s the American art world became separated into several camps and polarized into two main groups: the international progressive group, representing the new money of the Rockefellers, and the conservative Midwestern Regionalists, who rejected modernism and attempted with the grace of folk humor to reinvigorate the art of the old masters. Although Grant Wood may not have been consciously aware of his role in this power play between the isolationists and the internationalists, he certainly benefited from the almost overnight exposure his art received.

The practice of using art as a means for establishing power has continued in the second half of the twentieth century. Soon after World War II the U.S. government sent to Europe an exhibition of work by a small group of New Yorkers known as the Abstract Expressionists. Most members of this loosely formed group, which included Jackson Pollock, were considered politically suspect during the years of the McCarthy trials; they were known disdainfully as "Greenwich Village liberals" because they had sympathized with the Communists in the 1930s. Their art was perfect, however, for sending on international tours because it demonstrated to the world that even dissenting individual opinions were respected in the United States.

Grant Wood's Regionalism was not revived, even though some of its conservative ideas were continued by Andrew Wyeth. In the late 1940s and 1950s Wyeth became the spokesperson for a postwar generation that wanted to return home to live comfortably in ranch-style homes filled with solid rock maple furniture. And Wyeth has continued to find favor because he has been able to suggest nostalgia without giving in to it. His most famous work, *Christina's World,* pictures a crippled New Englander who is crawling toward her ancestral home.

The old homeplace is in shambles, indicating symbolically a sense of hopelessness in the American attempt to return home.

In postwar America, internationalism won out over regionalism, and New York has since become the artistic as well as the financial capital of the world. The combination of art and power is not a coincidence but a recurring phenomenon. It happened in Athens in the fifth century B.C.; it occurred again in fifteenth-century Florence and in sixteenth-century Rome, when Pope Julius II used Raphael and Michelangelo to aggrandize the papacy, provide Rome with a new point of view, and make the Vatican a center for international political intrigue. During the Counter Reformation, when Rome attempted to fight the Protestants, several popes found the Baroque style of the devout sculptor Bernini a perfect form of propaganda. In France in the late seventeenth and early eighteenth centuries Louis XIV, the Sun King, used art to limit the power of the nobles. He built the stolid, Neoclassical Versailles and made of himself a significant work of art that had to be courted, dressed, and honored. He later helped to stimulate the seemingly benign, frivolous style of art and life known as Rococo, which to his great political advantage kept his nobles entertained in enormously expensive but harmless diversions while he and his cardinals ran the country. One has only to compare the light-hearted work of the mid-eighteenth-century Rococo artist Boucher, who created for the nobility, with the painstaking realism of Chardin, who made works for the small middle class, to understand how effective a political tool frivolity was in controlling the court by keeping it immersed in an unreal world.

Although no one fully understands why art has so much power, everyone knows that cities in the world become great because of their cultural resources, and that a style of art can confer enormous power upon a group. Probably this power goes far back in the memory of humankind to a time when art was magic, and an image of an animal on a cave wall appeared to be the animal itself, when the creator of that image possessed it and symbolically killed it before going out on a hunt. Dictators frequently overthrow the art of a former regime and then commission artists to create a style for them. Napoleon had his Jacques Louis David; Hitler his Albert Speer; and Mao Tse Tung the Cultural Revolution. All felt the need to impose an art, a style, and a way of living upon their subjects. They used art as an ultimate form of propaganda because art manifests a system of beliefs and values only hinted at by advertising. As symbols, works of art communicate both consciously and unconsciously. Instead of imitating life, art directs it.

Art provides us with models, with attitudes and, most important, with distinct sensibilities that become new ways of seeing, touching, hearing, and even smelling and tasting the world around us. Art instills in us a unique vision and new possibilities. It provides us with believable and intriguing identities.

## MUSEUMS, ART, AND CULTURAL IDENTITY

Museums are usually described as being engaged in collecting, preserving, and interpreting works of art. The responsibilities of "collecting," "preserving," and "interpreting" are now so self-evident as to seem almost unimportant. Of course, museums are involved in finding works of art, keeping them in good condition, and making certain that the humidity and temperature control is constant, that people don't touch the art, and that it is cared for by conservators. Catalogues about particular collections or exhibitions are published periodically, and the museum education department organizes special tours and slide programs that focus on the collection. These activities are so firmly ingrained in the concept of a museum that few of us ever stop to think about what a museum really is and how it helps establish a cultural identity.

In the United States we have had continuing education in cultural identity since the nineteenth century, when Thomas Cole reflected in his art and writings on the beauties and the passing of the American wilderness, and when the Philadelphia Centennial of 1876 served to revive interest in our colonial cultural heritage. In the twentieth century our identity has been secured by the Williamsburg restoration, by Time-Life books focusing on the innovations of "this fabulous century" of ours, by American Heritage books, by Griffith's film *The Birth of a Nation,* and even by films like *Sunset Boulevard,* which give us a feeling of the recent past and the passing of time. Our music also fortifies us with a security about our world. Frank Sinatra, Elvis Presley, the Talking Heads, and Tina Turner all give us confidence in ourselves. No matter where we are in the world, we feel at home when we turn on the radio because the music is often our own.

In a more subtle and less direct manner, works of art in museums reinforce our identity as citizens of a particular place and time. George Rickey's sculpture *Four Rectangles Oblique, Variation II* [*Fig. 2*], which stands outside the University of Iowa Museum of Art, can be used as an example. We might examine briefly the values this sculpture assumes and attempts to reinforce in us. We don't even have to

*Figure 2.* GEORGE RICKEY. *Four Rectangles Oblique, Variation II,* 1972–75. Stainless steel. 99 x 108 in. (251.4 x 274.3 cm.). University of Iowa Museum of Art. *Museum purchase.*

become acquainted with Rickey's personality, with his likes and dis-likes, in order to understand some profound aspects of this work.

Probably the first aspect of this sculpture that one notices is that it is industrially fabricated. The sculpture looks like a machine; conceived in polished metal, it rotates with the wind, and in the process it shimmers in the sunlight and radiates a positive attitude toward modern technology. Because this technological sculpture does not manufacture any product and cannot be used to make anything, its function is obviously aesthetic. We do not have to concern ourselves with its possible obsolescence as a machine; all we have to do is enjoy it. We can relax as we examine it and simply savor the beauties of technology; we do not need to be threatened by the fact that machines might replace us on the job, separate us from the world, or overwhelm nature with a mechanized and polluted atmosphere. *Four Rectangles Oblique* and the landscape in which it is located look compatible and suggest to us that a machine can be a work of art, that it can be the real fruit of the land, that perhaps we did not veer in a totally wrong direction when we chose to become a technological society and in the process polluted our waterways and strip-mined our land. Rickey presents us with the technological ideal, and his importance rests in his ability to make this ideal believable again after almost two centuries of industrialization and one-third of a century of high technology. If we can enjoy the work of Rickey, we might begin to look appreciatively at other accomplishments of technology such as power lines, electric circuits, television aerials, and computer chips. Rickey's sculpture thus comforts and perhaps soothes us; it helps us to look positively at high technology and to appreciate its beauties; it enables us to accept our role in the last quarter of the twentieth century; and it provides a way for us to identify ourselves positively in the present.

Museums are important and necessary to us because they enable us to look at art in neutral settings and accept ideas on the aesthetic level – that is, on the emotional and intellectual level. We can come to terms with the past through seeing, thinking, and feeling its glories, and we can also start dealing with the present when we pause to enjoy the technology of *Four Rectangles Oblique*. The art museum is not about decoration, mere objects, or facts; it is concerned with identity, with identities in the past and in the present, with confirming in us what is real. The best artists don't necessarily set out to create beautiful objects; they set out to confirm a specific feeling or hunch they might have about reality. Rickey has confirmed an optimistic point of view and therefore his work elicits a pleasurable response. The Ger-

*Figure 3:* MAX BECKMANN. *Karneval,* 1943. Oil on canvas. Triptych: 75 x 116¾ in. (190.5 x 296.5 cm.). University of Iowa Museum of Art. *Purchased through the aid of the Mark Ranney Memorial Fund.*

man Expressionist Max Beckmann is not quite so optimistic in *Karneval* [*Fig. 3*], another work in this museum's collection. He presents us with an aspect of humanity that is unsettling, and his work may be less beautiful in the sense of being less pleasurable and harmonious, but it is no less real or significant.

A museum should deal with concepts of reality – and all the collecting, preserving, and interpreting that it does should in some way keep this goal in mind. Museums can help people to recognize through art who they are and what humans are capable of being. A museum can provide touchstones with reality; it can help people to achieve workable identities.

## The Purpose of Art

Of what use is a work of art? If this question had been asked a few years ago, most people would have responded that a work of art is of little or no practical use. The correct answer, they then believed, is that a work of art is primarily aesthetic. They would have emphasized that art is unique and provides viewers with a special experience that they could feel but not really describe. If prodded further, they might have spoken of art as a secular religion, as the essence of a feeling, as rarefied objects that could take them away from the mundane workaday world and give them a lift. If it had been pointed out that their "lift" was not exactly gratuitous but might be as practical and necessary as a cool drink or a comfortable chair, they would have insisted that art was special and different, not mundane, not repeatable, and not exactly inherent in the object, even though it depended on the object for its very existence.

This not-so-imaginary dialogue has a great deal to do with a desire to circumvent the materialism of the modern world while still affirming it. Art has been turned into the ultimate commodity that transcends the everyday at the same time that it hints at the spiritual. In other words, people have believed an abstract painting to be about shape, line, and color even though they thought it somehow something more than mere shape, line, and color. And painting has been regarded as only paint and canvas and also as more than its constituent materials; it is pure and universal and yet full of unassigned meanings.

If one asked the same question today, the response might well be different. Many people today would not think of discussing the gratuitous aspects of art. Instead, they would dwell on the context of art, that is, they would talk about the art's referents, its historical period, and its maker's political, religious, and social attitudes. They would regard art as an arrow that points away from itself and directs one to a specific time. To these respondents art is a function of all the non-art elements giving birth to it.

Obviously, both past and present responses to the question of art's function exhibit some difficulties. We use art as decoration, and yet we don't want to succumb to the purely decorative; we use art as a time machine to plunge us into another dimension, and yet we really don't want to accept the realities of another world. We do not ask enough of our art. We are still attempting to assume styles of the past and yet we don't really want to be tied to only one style: we wish to be universal. In the nineteenth century people developed a range of historical styles so that they could imaginatively live in Greece or Rome or the Middle Ages or the Renaissance – in any time but their own. In twentieth-century abstract art we have similarly attempted to circumvent both the mundaneness of day-to-day life and the upsetting changes that constantly besiege us by finding an imaginative realm in the unchanging and comforting materialism of such formal values as color, shape, and form.

Art can be merely decorative if we choose to minimize its quotient

*Figure 4.* REMBRANDT VAN RIJN. *Christ Preaching,* circa 1652. Etching with engraving and drypoint. 6⅛ x 8⅛ in. (15.6 x 20.7 cm.). University of Iowa Museum of Art. *Gift of Owen and Leone Elliott.*

of feeling and personally intuited truth and emphasize its form. But it can be a useful tool for coming to understand ourselves through careful inspection of how artists marshal their compositions, their figures, and their narrrative devices to appeal to a specific type of viewer. In our society art continues to have the capacity to function; it still can cast us in a specific role that we must play if we are to understand it. The Jackson Pollock *Mural* in this museum surrounds us with dancing figures that are evocative, not clearly defined, and appeal as much to our subconscious as to our conscious mind, while the Rembrandt etchings in the Elliott Collection draw us into an intimate world and cause us to caress velvety inks with our eyes and reconstitute figures that are only summarily rendered. [*Fig. 4*] As we look, we turn white paper into light, and we empathize with those ideas that can best be communicated through the print medium and, by analogy, through the privacy of books. The Pollock painting is a private event made public. Created for the foyer of Peggy Guggenheim's townhouse in New York City, Pollock's *Mural* places an intuitive vision in a semi-public space. The Rembrandt etching inverts this approach, turning religious scenes into private meditative experiences and making portraits – often a public form of art – private and revealing of thoughtful personalities.

Just as African masks serve the important functions of providing dead ancestors an entry into the world and manifesting earth spirits, so Western art serves the function of revealing aspects of our spiritual world to ourselves. Art is a mask which unveils reality; it is a conduit through which we can feel – if we're willing to take the chance – as someone else has felt. It's a mask that we wear when we wish truly to understand what it is like to see as another sees.

Although art is always enriching, it is not always uplifting. To see with the eyes of Pollock or Rembrandt is to see profoundly, but also to see at times negatively and despondently. Pollock manifested in his art many of the difficulties of his period, and Rembrandt certainly understood many of the problems of his own time. The beauty of their art is to be found in their acceptance of humanity and their refusal to gloss over what they perceived to be reality. The beauty of their art lies in the truth and perspicacity of their vision rather than in the richness of their colors and the harmony of their compositions. Their art functions as an emotional/intellectual barometer of their time; it is useful as an instrument of truth, and its beauty depends on its faithfulness to a specific vision. Beauty is not the goal of art: it is the captivating force that causes one to look; it entices one to understand and to come to terms with truth.

## A Word about the Project

The three works of art featured in *Human Rights/Human Wrongs: Art and Social Change* were selected because they span the twentieth century and provide three very different views of American culture. One of the three works is overtly political, but the other two works of art are not, and consequently they have served as excellent test cases for seeing how art in general relates to fundamental concerns and to broad-based political and social issues.

Lyonel Feininger's *In a Village Near Paris (Pink Sky)* (1909) represents the art of an American expatriate who became involved first with late Art Nouveau illustrations and political cartoons and later with the European avant-garde styles of Fauvism, Cubism, and German Expressionism. Jackson Pollock's *Mural* (1943) was created at a time when European avant-garde artists representing Surrealism, Cubism, Purism, and De Stijl were all gathered in New York because World War II had forced them to leave Europe. His painting reformulates several of these trends, particularly Surrealism, Cubism, and the all-over approach of the De Stijl painter Piet Mondrian, and provides the basis for the large-scale paintings that have come to be associated with the New York School. The ceramics of California artist Robert Arneson mark a dramatically new direction in American art, for they parody the seriousness of the New York School and embrace a new funk sensibility that joins lowbrow and highbrow elements and dares to be tasteless. In his recent political pieces inspired by his own bout with cancer and his concerns about an ultimate nuclear holocaust for all humankind, Arneson continues the process of debunking certain elevated art clichés such as Jackson Pollock's drips, which he used to cover one side of the face of his *Minuteman*. At the same time he elevates cartoons and graffiti, using tick-tack-toe configurations, scratched-out drawings of piled-up bodies, and words that become commands and wounds scarring the *Minuteman*'s head, which closely resembles the heads Leonardo used for his *Battle of the Anghiari*.

In this project Fred Woodard and I were interested in the ways in which people from divergently different fields would look at works of art. This study provides an opportunity to see how non-art historians approach art and how a work of art can subtly change into a different work of art, depending on what questions are asked and what information is marshalled for an interpretation. Looking at a Feininger painting from the point of view of a journalist is very different from regarding it from the point of view of a specialist in German literature; similarly, approaching Pollock as a neurologist is very different from regarding him from the perspective of a poet.

Although the various approaches in this book represent the orientations of nine different disciplines, the works of art, to a certain extent, presuppose a certain kind of viewer — or, perhaps, a distinct sensibility that is a necessary prerequisite to their being understood. The Feininger demands a new understanding of highbrow and lowbrow culture in the forms of fine art and illustration. It also demands an acceptance of the painting as a highly artificial construct of abstract colors and shapes that distances viewers from the scene; it forces them to become alienated from the characters portrayed in the painting and to accept these figures as types rather than as the nineteenth-century individuals they first appear to be. Similarly, the Pollock mural plays on assumptions about the public and private nature of the self when it blows up to mural scale intimations of unconscious understandings. And the Arneson mixes up tragedy and graffiti to create a disturbing image of nuclear holocaust as one horribly tragic bad joke. Its mixture of horror and humor makes viewers uncomfortable because it provides them with contradictory scripts for reacting.

Each of these works presupposes a view of the world that is distinctly new, and these new world views, in my opinion, provide one of those remarkable ways through which art becomes a vehicle for social change. Rather than converting viewers through its subject matter, art makes new approaches to the world possible by indirectly choreographing its viewers so that they are forced to look from a new perspective. And it is from this new perspective, be it positive or negative, that art orients people to fundamental human concerns.

In this essay I have attempted to undermine the myth of pure vision by pointing out how museums alter seeing so that one looks at art through an institutional lens. The essays in this catalogue demonstrate that one sees art from distinct perspectives that depend on one's knowledge and field of expertise, as well as on the vantage point of the work of art in question.

To look at art is to think about an aspect of the world from a special point of view. It is my hope that this book will encourage people to take more time looking at individual works of art and to use their own experiences and knowledge of the world in forming their own conclusions about its meaning.

# LYONEL FEININGER

American, 1871-1956

# A SOCIAL HISTORY OF A PAINTING:
## Charting the Clouds That Have Crossed Feininger's *Pink Sky*

An intimidating task lies before me—to stretch the borders of my discipline to venture onto a terrain that is usually circumscribed by the field of art history, in order to offer some fresh insights into a painting by a man clearly established as a great artist, with the expectation that my venture into this foreign domain will somehow enrich humanistic inquiry into the relationship between art and social change. It is not my task alone, since others have been given the same assignment. The insights will come, not so much from the individual pieces each of us produces, but from the differences among us, and how we, as members of diverse disciplines, each interpret the same object. Despite the dissolution of traditional disciplinary boundaries and the cross-fertilization of paradigms and vocabularies among our fields—movements which each of us has been actively involved in—are we not still nagged by the suspicion that one should really be grounded in a knowledge of art history before presuming to speak about a work of art?

*In a Village Near Paris (Pink Sky),* * which Lyonel Feininger painted on

Karin E. Becker is an Associate Professor in the School of Journalism and Mass Communication.

* Feininger is not known to have given a title to the painting now catalogued by the University of Iowa Museum of Art as *In a Village Near Paris.* In the earliest known publication of this painting, it appears as an illustration with the title *In a Village Near Paris* accompanying an article by Charlotte Teller, "Feininger—Fantasist," *The International Studio* 63 (November 1917), xxv–xxx. On the reverse side of the stretcher, bearing the title *Street in Paris,* is a label possibly affixed when the Buchholz Gallery of New York bought or borrowed the painting from Julia Feininger, the artist's wife, for a 1941 exhibition of Feininger's work. Several labels affixed in succeeding years use both *Pink Sky* and *Street in Paris.* By 1959, when Owen and Leone Elliott purchased the painting for their collection from the Willard Gallery of New York (which had cosponsored Feininger exhibitions with the Buchholz Gallery), *Pink Sky* had become the primary title in gallery documents, *Street in Paris* an alternate title. The museum now considers

two Sundays late in the spring of 1909, was my choice of the three works included in this project. It was the only one of the three that I could place in some rough context related to my other work. Lacking the "proper" art historical framework, I could nevertheless grasp a thread that might anchor me to a period and an artist I recognized. Although I had never seen *Pink Sky*, I knew Feininger had been a master in the graphics workshop at the Bauhaus during the years of Germany's exciting and turbulent Weimar Republic. I had seen reproductions of a few of his paintings, and knew that he was among the scores of artists and intellectuals who escaped National Socialism by emigrating to the United States in the 1930s. I did not know that Feininger was in fact a U.S. citizen, born in New York in 1871, who had been sent to Germany by his German-American parents to study when he was sixteen years old. In 1937, at the age of sixty-five, Feininger returned to New York with his wife Julia. It was his first time back in nearly fifty years.

In my studies of photography in the mass media, I have focused on the German press during the Weimar Republic.[1] The popular picture magazines of that period were institutions where a style and pattern of professional routines developed that were carried out of Germany by the photographers and editors leaving the country in the wave of emigration that included Feininger. These magazines provided me with a small window into the society where Feininger had made his home, raised his family, established his career, and created his art.

The mass media typically do not provide much coverage of current art movements, however. Specialized publications do cater to particular interests and tastes, and in this capacity, journals and magazines on the arts reflect and shape the status of artists and their work. Reviews of Feininger's exhibited work, as they appeared in such publications at different points in his life, offered significant indications of the artist's reputation and evaluations of specific works.

The more popular media, those of general public interest, exist in a complex relationship to their society. They do not clearly follow nor do they lead the public's tastes and interests. Rather, they reflect and interact with other cultural institutions and are vehicles for expressing cultural issues and themes within the constraints and patterns that evolve in the process of media production. They are thus an invalu-

---

the earliest known title, *In a Village Near Paris*, to be the primary title, and *Pink Sky* an alternate title. See Geoffrey Waite, "Truckin' Under a Pink Sky, Seeing Red," in the present volume, for further discussion of the title of this work.

able resource for simply seeing what people at the time were seeing as topics of current interest.

The content of the media, their surface manifestation, is only one side of viewing the media as cultural expression, however. The production process itself offers another sort of window into the culture. The status of a magazine, the people who work for it, and the patterns of power and influence that create each number of the magazine are all thoroughly embedded in cultural practice. This framework is relevant to Feininger's work as a magazine illustrator, a career he pursued for many years immediately prior to painting *Pink Sky*. His status as an illustrator and the type of magazines that employed him at that time provide one way of understanding the work that preceded and thus laid a foundation for this painting.

The view of mass media production as unavoidably a cooperative or collective enterprise can be extended to other forms of work, including the work of art.[2] First, we must assume that the production of works defined as "art" occurs in a network of social and historical relationships. The materials used to create the art and the forms that define the limits and content of the work are never constructed by a lone individual. The person must rely on tools and media and forms of expression, parts of which are always created and used by others for other purposes, but nevertheless, in the hands of this person, satisfy conventions of what art is. An audience must be familiar with or educated into the language of expression the individual is using. Pushing the conventional boundaries of materials, forms, and expressive language is of course an important attribute of being an artist—but when the boundaries are stretched too far, the accusations arise: "*That's* not art!" A work cannot be considered art, nor a person an artist, except through the creation of a social world which admits such works and those who create them.

When art worlds are explained as arising through the process of establishing (and destroying and re-creating) social conventions, we can no longer base our explanation of a work as "art" on its transcendent, timeless, or universal value. If it survives as a great work of art, it is not because of any qualities inherent in the work itself, but because a social world has persisted which continues to hold the piece in high regard.

To explain the success of a work or its artist *within* that social world requires a knowledge of its language, that is, an intimate understanding of the medium and its range of techniques and expressions. One must, in other words, be a *member* of the art world before one can offer an insightful or even adequate account of how and why a piece "works" within that sphere. The member's knowledge is clearly important to a full and rich account of the work's form and execution.

It is not necessary to be a member, however, in order to chart the rise and fall of a work as "art." The traces a work leaves in reviews, in exhibitions, in the letters and documents of the artist's life, allow us to examine its social history—how it has been treated by its artist and its audience of critics and others. This perspective directs us toward a critical examination of the social world in which the work lives.

First, I will turn to the painting itself, to describe my untutored impressions of *Pink Sky*, and how someone like myself, with limited knowledge of art as a discipline, would nevertheless recognize *Pink Sky* as a work of art. I will then examine the range and status of the work Feininger did prior to painting *Pink Sky*, to learn how these precedents guided his and his audience's evaluation of the career that led to this painting. The break that occurred during the time this painting was done launched Feininger into a new "career" in oil painting. The art world in which he then became established precluded consideration of *Pink Sky* as part of Feininger's major work—for reasons that are then discussed. In the conclusion, I argue that after Feininger's death, a broadened definition of art in the 1960s recovers *Pink Sky*, moving the painting again closer to what the social world of fine art might call the center of this artist's serious work.

Remember that I had not seen *Pink Sky* before being intrigued by the prospect of participating in this project. It was with some trepidation that I walked into the gallery where the painting was hung. I quickly realized which painting it was—the name fits—and was at once delighted and relieved by what I saw. I realize now that I had expected a Feininger more like the paintings which followed *Pink Sky*, closer to abstraction, farther removed from the conventions of representation with which I am most familiar.

Here is a painting that shows a village street near dusk in the early spring. The high buildings are cast in shadows of blue and green. A few of the crooked windows glow with the warm pink-gold of the lit rooms behind them. The high garret windows catch the deep orange reflecting the last sun of the day. The sky is indeed an intense pink, as if heavily overcast, with its underside now warmed for the last moments before the sun slips away. The few trees are bare and jagged against the buildings. The outline of the chimneys is also rough and angular against the sky. And the cobblestoned street is full of people, all shapes and sizes, hurrying, alone and in pairs; one is leaning against a tree, another peers into a window. They are all bundled up in colorful attire, their hats are askew, and they, too, are rough and angular, full of movement and in crazy proportions up the space and depth of the crooked street.

Obviously, my initial delight in *Pink Sky* is because I found it accessible. It represents a scene, a time of day, a quality of light and color that resonates with experiences I have had and environments I have seen – essentially a naive perspective to bring to a work that looks like art. I am, like most others who look at this painting, aware that it is to be considered as a work of art, since it conforms to some of the most basic conventions which we all know. Even without formal training in "how to look" at painting, we are members of a culture in which easel painting is considered a medium of artistic expression. We can, therefore, recognize in *Pink Sky* some of the attributes of a work of art.

It is, after all, hanging on a wall in a museum of art. It is an oil painting on canvas. Its dimensions, 39¾ x 32 inches, place it within the conventional size of an artwork in this medium. The date when it was painted, 1909, tells us it has survived, has been valued, and now is being preserved beyond the death of the man who painted it. The museum's documentation of this work includes the information that it was purchased for $15,000 and that its insured value now is many times that figure. It was a gift from the Owen and Leone Elliott Trust, which purchased it from the Willard Gallery in New York. *Pink Sky* forms part of the collection the Elliotts donated to the museum, a collection that provided the basis for adding significant space for the storage and display of works of art at The University of Iowa.

The painter is a man recognized as an artist, which lends further credence to the claim that we consider this example of his work as art. Feininger first exhibited a painting in 1910 and remained active in that medium, with regular exhibitions, until his death in 1956.[3] In 1960, as important works on Feininger began to be published, his history and stature as an artist was secured: "By the time the First World War ended in 1918, he was recognized as one of Germany's great painters. A big comprehensive show in 1917 was a turning point, and many shows followed thereafter."[4] A reviewer in 1917 had made the same point somewhat more modestly: "Among artists he is well-known."[5]

The form, the medium, the economic value, how the painting was acquired, how it has been displayed and circulated, and the status of the man who painted it, all define *Pink Sky* as a work of art. Yet, judging from the critics' articles and reviews, *Pink Sky* is not seen as an important painting. Although it has a respectable history of exhibitions, this painting has not usually been singled out for closer attention. Nor has it been awarded a prominent place in the context of Feininger's work. It is apparently a familiar painting to those who know his range and is now recognized as one that falls early in his career as a painter, but it is given no particular significance among the oil paintings that he did. A review at the time the Elliott Collection came to the University of Iowa Museum of Art commented that "the Feininger" was "outstanding"–but the wrong painting was reproduced with the title *Pink Sky,* confusing the reader about which work was considered so remarkable.[6]

*Pink Sky*'s place in the larger art world thus remains sketchy. It is not included in enough catalogues and exhibitions to locate its place in the environment of twentieth-century art. Perhaps its significance is confined primarily to the domain of Feininger's body of work. Certainly we can locate it there, and examine *Pink Sky* in the context of Feininger's changing worlds, to learn how each period or direction in his work illuminates the position of this painting. Recovering this context for *Pink Sky* may clarify the reasons for its "minor" status in Feininger's *oeuvre.*

Feininger was thirty-eight years old, living in Zehlendorf-Mitte on the outskirts of Berlin, when he painted *Pink Sky.* He had moved there in 1908 from Paris, where he had spent two years beginning to paint while working as an illustrator for various magazines. His main support had come from a contract with the *Chicago Tribune* to draw two comic strips each week for the newspaper. James Keeley, the *Tribune*'s editor, had been in Europe seeking new talent to rejuvenate the Sunday comics pages and offered Feininger a job in Chicago.[7] After some negotiation, they agreed that Feininger could send him the pictures each week and remain in Paris. Beginning in mid-1906, Feininger's two strips, "Wee Willie Winkie's World" and "The Kinder-Kids," ran on the *Tribune*'s comics pages each week. [*Fig. 1*] Before his contract ended, he had produced fifty-one pages of comics for the newspaper.[8]

Feininger had dreamed and worked for nearly ten years for an opportunity to return to the United States; becoming a skilled illustrator was the means to do that, he had hoped. Yet when the chance came, it

Figure 1.
LYONEL FEININGER.
"The Kin-der-Kids," 29 April 1906.
*The Chicago Sunday Tribune.*
23⅜ x 17⅜ in. (59.5 x 45.3 cm.).
Museum of Modern Art, New York.
*Gift of the artist.*

was too late, for he was beginning his shift toward painting and had carved out this time in Paris to gain training and experience.

It is not surprising that Keeley had approached Feininger with this offer in his search for a popular and well-known magazine illustrator. Since 1893, Feininger had been making drawings for magazines, first in Berlin, then for American magazines, and most recently for *Le Té-moin* in Paris. Feininger was now working across three cultures, and with considerable financial and critical success.

The strong tradition of magazine illustration was at its peak in Germany during the decade before World War I. The publication of political and social satire ranged from gentle humorous commentary to biting criticism, usually in cartoons and clever caricatures. The center of this publishing activity was Munich, and its focus was on the life and expression of the city's Schwabing district, where leftist politics, cabaret culture, art, and theatre met and mingled. *Simplicissimus* had sprung up in this environment in 1896, and in 1908 had a circulation of 86,000. For especially controversial issues, its circulation doubled. *Jugend* had a similar political orientation, and was slightly smaller, shaping its content around the Jugendstil or Art Nouveau design movement. The *Münchner Fliegende Blätter* was another popular weekly. Berlin had its own popular illustrated magazines, including *Lustige Blätter,* the *Berliner Illustrirte Zeitung,* and *Narrenschiff.* The well-known *Ulk* was the weekly magazine supplement to Berlin's largest and occasionally leftist newspaper, the *Berliner Tageblatt. Der*

*Wahre Jacob,* the socialist magazine aimed at the working class, had a still larger circulation.[9]

In the days before the halftone process had become practical for the reproduction of photographs, good satirical illustration was the cornerstone of these magazines and was also their greatest expense. They maintained their quality and status by hiring the best illustrators, and it was not unusual for individuals who later became recognized as artists to draw for these magazines.

There were parallels in the United States and France. The "Ashcan School" of American realists included many who had been newspaper artists. The Cubist painters Jacques Villon, Louis Marcoussis, and the Spaniard Juan Gris were among those who drew for the Paris magazines. The cartoons they published often provided material for their paintings, too. And there seemed to be no negative appellation for those who published their work in the popular press. In more general terms, it has been said that "the aspect of the caricaturist has much in common with that of the modern anti-classical artist. It can be assumed that caricature is one of the historical prerequisites of modern art."[10]

Certainly this was the case for Feininger. His early work for *Ulk* brought him to the attention of other Berlin magazines, and some of his illustrations were appearing in many of them. He was also sending work to America, where he hoped to establish a reputation that would allow him to return "home." In 1897, he was given a handsome salary and became a staff member at *Ulk.*[11] In the meantime, he continued to publish in *Harper's Young People* and *Judge* in the United States. By 1901, Feininger was recognized as *the* outstanding cartoonist in Berlin.[12]

We can trace Feininger's rise as an illustrator through his work as it appeared in the magazines, and also through his correspondence. In regular letters to his former Berlin schoolmate, Alfred Vance Churchill, and his boyhood friend, H. Francis Kortheuer, he told of the magazines and illustrators he admired, where he was succeeding in publishing his work, and his attempts to blend German and American styles of drawing. He contrasted his work with that of the romantic illustration of fairy tales:

> You know that although there are in Germany some splendid fairy-tale illustrators: Hermann Vogel, Richter, etc., yet none of them had paid much [attention] to anything more than the decorative and glamorous part of fairy- or wonder Tale depiction. . . . I get on a distinctly different, very individual,

un-traditional mission, such as is after all *the only thing to do* where the country for which I work and always mean to work (America) is itself in these matters so little traditional.[13]

Feininger had been doing caricatures as a means of learning drawing for several years, and his letters contain the names of Wilhelm Busch, originator of the *Max and Moritz* children's classic;[14] "Zim," the American Eugene Zimmerman, whose work he knew from *Judge;* Adolf Oberländer, whom he considered the most interesting of the *Fliegende Blätter*'s illustrators; and several other Americans, including Howard Pyle, E. A. Abbey, and A. B. Frost, whom he considered "the King of American illustrators of humorous subjects."[15]

He wrote little about the political satire that dominated the German magazines. He was more interested in comparing drawing styles and a range of humor. Certainly, as the offspring of a family of "48 refugees" to the United States, he was a liberal, but his work and his letters show little interest in external or internal politics. "I don't think it can possibly make much difference what I am, as I know as good as nothing about politics, and do not vote either, though I hope to become a staunch American citizen before long."[16]

His work for *Ulk* changed this, as his caricatures more frequently portrayed political figures and he began to make satirical points through his drawings alone. Witty gadgets and complicated contraptions navigated their way through many of the *Ulk* cartoons, directing their power against the police, being manned by a lumbering state bureaucracy, or portraying the folly of the Kaiser's plan to build a large naval fleet.[17] With *Ulk* as his base, and more frequent contact with writers and editors having sharper political views, Feininger's satirical drawings became more pointed on specific political events and issues.

The Biedermeier revival in Germany in the 1890s is evident in the satirical magazines, and Feininger carried aspects of the style from his illustrations into his early paintings. Biedermeier represented a romantic attachment to the pre-industrial age, emerging first in the artistic centers of Munich and Berlin. Tastes in clothing, furniture design, and decoration harked back to lines and textures not found in machine-made goods. Even in the magazines known for their progressive politics, such as *Jugend* and *Simplicissimus,* the illustrators adopted the costumes and gestures associated with "Grandfather Time." The stovepipe hat and the long frock coat became symbols of Biedermeier and could be seen often in the streets, in fanciful combination with the popular plaid sports clothes of contemporary

Anglo-American fashion. Elements of the style were mixed with floral decorative borders and other elaborations of Jugendstil design in some of the illustrated magazines. Romantic landscapes and seascapes became important themes for some of the painters during this period, and even more striking in its nostalgia for the past was the revival of mystical color schemes and meditative moods, drawn from styles of a hundred years or so earlier.

At this time there was a curious mixture of romanticization of the past and pessimism about the future, combined to create a modern popular style. Feininger drew on these forms in the clothing and gestures of the figures he sketched, probably reflecting the ways people appeared to him in the streets. Long, angular men, sporting stovepipe hats, loud plaid waistcoats, and oversized frock coats strode through his illustrations. The oddly mechanized contraptions that appear frequently in Feininger's cartoons also carry the flavor of the Biedermeier revival: propelled by elaborate gears or puffs of steam, these one-of-a-kind machines are at once examples of modern ingenuity and reminders of a simpler past.

The Biedermeier revival reached its peak in Germany in 1906, with an exhibition of German art of 1775 to 1875 in Berlin's Royal National Gallery. Feininger may not have seen this exhibit—this was just about the time he was moving to Paris. Yet the figures in his early paintings still carry the style: tall long-legged men and their short round companions often wear brightly colored ascots under their big black coats, and many wear crooked high stovepipe hats, *the* symbol of Biedermeier.[18]

Feininger was not interested in an extreme characterization in these human figures and consistently tried to inject whimsical humor into his drawings. In part, these were efforts to appeal to American audiences, for he often still considered the United States as his goal for his life and work. Of one set of drawings he had sent off to the United States, he wrote, "My drawings for *Harper's* are 'slightly' caricatured but in a way which, I flatter myself, does not cause repulsion, but only adds to the vividness of the characterization." He did not want his figures to appear "deformed."[19] The pure humor and fantasy in his work was also often at odds with the political content of the German magazines. The fantastic gadgets and whimsical conveyances he incorporated into many drawings expressed his own sense of humor while also giving his work particularly American themes. This fusion of German and American styles was described by Emil Preetorius in 1954 for a German exhibition that included Feininger's drawings:

These cartoons possessed a ghostly quality full of contrasts. They were old-fashioned and romantic, yet at the same time ultra-modern and technological. Great sensitivity was used with an acid sharpness in a peculiar and impressive manner.[20]

Throughout his fluctuating fascination with German and American illustration, Feininger was attempting to introduce "a very personal whimsical and fantastic cartoon style" into his work.[21]

It is clear that magazine work provided necessary income and kept Feininger in Berlin, despite whatever his other hopes may have been about moving, or returning to America. In light of these practical constraints, it is interesting that he did not seem to chafe under the demands of the work as he was doing it. Only later, when his career as a painter was under way, did he comment on the drudgery and a fear of losing his position that overshadowed his creative impulses. At the time, he seemed to take for granted that he could explore new directions and develop a style without either violating himself or his obligations to an employer. Or perhaps his American pragmatism prevented him from questioning the necessity of routine employment as a means of earning a living.

As his work was beginning to make its way into magazines, Feininger thrilled at reaching so many people through his drawings. The rewards of a hefty salary were not mentioned specifically in his letters. In 1896 he wrote to Churchill, "I am continually experiencing the gratification of knowing myself to be gradually becoming a popular artist, who is sure of finding both appreciation and gratitude for his endeavors! And it is after all a sweet sensation to know that one is in touch with so great a portion of humanity."[22] Creating a popular audience was possible only through the magazines.

As the contract with the *Tribune* came to an end, Feininger turned to *Le Témoin,* a short-lived publication edited by the brilliant designer Paul Iribe in 1906. The drawings Feininger created for this unusual magazine [*Fig. 2*] were the first he had done from his own ideas, not an editor's. Stimulated by his contact with other artists, notably Richard Götz, Feininger was becoming more daring in his caricatures and was continually making "notes," sketches of the scenes in the streets, cafés, and markets of Paris. These sketches, based on close observation of people, were the basis for many of his illustrations for *Le Témoin* and, later, his oil paintings. Several bear a striking resemblance to *Pink Sky*. Occasionally the drawings portray specific events: the double-page *L'Exode* depicts the expulsion of the Jesuits, whom Feininger had known well. More often, Feininger supplied the drawing,

Figure 2.
LYONEL FEININGER.
*L'Exactitude*, 1907.
Drawing for *Le Témoin*.
Location unknown.

and Iribe simply titled it, adding the critical perspective for which *Le Témoin* was known. In *La Doute*, the title Iribe gave Feininger's sketch of two workmen, the caption "Premier mai? Premier avril?" confirms the skepticism the artist may have attributed to his subjects when sketching them. The strong movement implied by the huge figures in *L'Exactitude* is given a similar twist by Iribe's addition of the words "Où allons-nous? Je ne sais rien. Alors pressons." Yet, because Feininger's work for *Le Témoin* was based exclusively on his own visual conceptions, the magazine became "the liberating step from pictorial journalism to independent picture-making."[23]

After his return from Paris, when Feininger's work for the magazines had come to an end, his paintings kept many qualities of his illustrations. The bright, flat planes of color that are so striking in his paintings can be traced to the experimentation in color lithography the newspapers and magazines allowed. Color reproduction was encouraged, indeed it was *the* reason for some publications, notably the Sunday comics supplement, and publishers allowed the illustrators great freedom in their use of color. The unusual combinations, the avoidance of the expected primary colors, and their application to the page in large flat blocks of intensity, all evident in *Pink Sky*, grew out of the confidence Feininger had gained in magazine illustration. Much later, reflecting on how his work had emerged from caricature and poster design, he wrote, "Simple, large color planes layed [sic] together on the painting surface is the aim; not a photographically diversified modulation of color, clear forms, which carry the space element and the subject in all simplicity and directness."[24]

The "silhouetted objects" which these simple planes of color implied often carried a striking and spontaneous sense of movement. The postures of his figures, the angles of their limbs to their bodies, the ways they hunch down into their shoulders as they stride through the streets in his paintings would be familiar to anyone seeing Feininger's cartoons. The sketching he began in the Berlin streets in 1891 continued through this period of his work. In her introduction to the comprehensive catalogue of Feininger's graphic work, Leone Prasse notes, "One becomes increasingly aware how the discipline of his earlier years from 1893 to 1907 as cartoonist and illustrator served him as an excellent training ground for accurate reporting and for drawing, especially that of the human figure in every conceivable posture."[25] His illustrations also show how he played with scale and perspective to enhance the visual effects. The relative size of his figures lends humor and whimsy to his compositions. Aunty Jim-Jam and Cousin Gussy, two conspirators in the comic "Kin-der-Kids," stand side by side, her long spare form accentuated by her sidekick's small round one. Feininger wrote in a letter in 1906 that he was learning that "the slightest difference in relative proportions creates enormous differences with regards to the resulting monumentality of and intensity of the composition."[26] He often inverted the expected rules of perspective and placed figures in steep angles, as if the whole scene were reflecting back from a fun-house mirror.

Undoubtedly, this playful portrayal of color, movement, and perspective gives Feininger's early oil painting much of its quality of fantasy and wit. This sense of humor did not end with his work for the illustrated press and his gentle wit found outlets in various forms throughout his life.

Through the demands of producing consistent work for the magazines, Feininger also gained discipline. Drawing from the life in the streets each day, he learned to render with quick spontaneity the outlines of a human figure, giving a characteristic thread through his work. At the time, he enjoyed the challenge and the opportunity to reach a broad public, a reward he would put aside when he turned his energies to oil painting.

Later, he denigrated aspects of his life as an illustrator—too much of it had been done under the pressure of others' demands. He saw himself during those fifteen years of work as "merely a drudge at political

cartoons for the bare necessities of sustenance for my family and self."
When he saw roots of his later work in those drawings, he saw the
magazine environment no longer as an opportunity to develop those
traits, but rather as a barrier that had threatened to squelch his
abilities as an artist: "I was invariably rated and threatened with loss of
position for the very traits which make an artist of original power."[27]
Thirty years later, his opinion had not greatly altered: "I was but a caricaturist, and my intentions regarding oil painting were vague. My
only outlet seemed to be the poster."[28] These recollections form a
definite contrast to his earlier views of the gratification and rewards
of being a "popular artist."

This later view of himself also contradicts the reputation his work
enjoyed in 1901. Hermann noted that Feininger "creates political
drawings of monumental effect in strong contrasts. . . . He possesses
an extraordinary gift for drawing, an extraordinary perception of
form."[29] The hundreds of cartoons he had drawn between 1897 and
1907 for the Berlin newspapers alone clearly established him as an
outstanding illustrator. In 1904, as a member of the Association of
German Illustrators, he was included in a major exhibition, the *Grosse
Berliner Kunstaustellung,* and shared the top place for largest number
of works exhibited. He was, in other words, securely established as a
leader in the art world of that time. His work attracted critical ac-
claim, was exhibited and published in the most prestigious of the
popular magazines. A key to the perception of Feininger as an artist
lay in the status of the illustrated magazines at the turn of the century.
Their quality and reputation, and their competition for the best illustration, distinguishes them from later manifestations of the picture
press. "Picture journalism," although a form of mass communication,
then carried many attributes of the status of art.


In 1908, Feininger's status changed, as he went from being a "well-
known illustrator, to an unknown painter."[30] Although thirty-seven
years old, he considered himself a "young" artist, launching into, for
him, a new medium. Yet, within five years he had established himself
at the center of European art movements, and his earlier reputation
as an illustrator was fading. *Pink Sky* was one of the works from this
important transitional period in his life as an artist.

From 1909 to 1912 he was exhibiting paintings with the Berlin Seces-
sion, a group linked with German Impressionism. Then, in May 1911,
he returned to Paris for two weeks where six of his paintings were on

exhibit at the Salon des Artistes Indépendants. At least as important was his first encounter with the Cubists, for he saw similarities between their work and his own compositions. That brief visit to Paris has been called "his initiation into the world of advanced art."[31] When he returned to Germany, he then established contact with his contemporaries there and "was increasingly a force in progressive art movements."[32] He was invited to join the Brücke group of German Expressionist painters, and exhibited at the first German Autumn Salon of 1913, a radical challenge to the established tastes in art. Work of the Blauer Reiter group, which included Wassily Kandinsky, and that of Paul Klee formed an influential part of this exhibit, and Feininger became closely associated with the group. Der Sturm was another radical group, and Feininger's first one-man exhibition, in 1917, was in the Sturm gallery. These associations and exhibitions established him the center of leading trends in German fine art.

He met Walter Gropius in 1918, and when Gropius founded the Bauhaus school in Weimar, he invited Feininger to join them as Form Master in the Graphics Workshop. From this position, Feininger continued painting, strengthened his friendships with other painters and artists, and became a spokesperson and influential speaker on matters of art and education. In 1925, the school was forced to close by the government in Weimar. Feininger moved with the school to Dessau, where he withdrew from teaching to the position of artist-in-residence, and continued to paint. In the meantime, the group Blaue Vier was formed from the "survivors" of Blauer Reiter; its members, Kandinsky, Klee, Jawlensky, and Feininger, exhibited their work together until 1934.

This increased involvement in the German art world virtually severed Feininger's ties with America. No longer was he submitting work to the illustrated press, and he was not yet recognized as an American artist. In 1929, the same year he was asked to do a one-man show at the National Gallery in Berlin, the Museum of Modern Art in New York was criticized for including Feininger in its exhibition *Paintings by Nineteen Living Americans* on grounds that he was not an American artist. His reputation in Germany in the meantime continued to become more established. In honor of his sixtieth birthday in 1931, one-man shows opened at the National Gallery in Berlin, in Essen, Hanover, and Leipzig.

In 1933, when the political situation in Germany forced the Bauhaus to close, Feininger returned to Berlin. His last major prewar "exhibition" was in 1937, as a prominent representative of what the Nazis labeled "Degenerate Art." The government confiscated 378 of his works in its sweep of German art.[33] That same year, Feininger moved back to America and took up permanent residence in New York.

Feininger was not immediately accepted into the world of American fine art. Socially, he had continued to feel like an American, and he still looked like one, with his long gait, thin frame, clean-shaven face, and the plaid shirts he often wore. But he hardly recognized the New York of his boyhood in the city around him, and felt the conflicting emotions of an alien, with ties to two countries headed toward another war against each other. Nor was he widely known as an artist in the United States, and several years passed before his work began appearing regularly in gallery and museum exhibitions. When his paintings did come into public view, the emphasis was clearly on the work in oil he had done as an established artist in Germany: there were few references to his earlier career as an artist and illustrator, or to the drawings from the press which had provided the basis of his later work. He continued to be viewed as an artist who "belongs to German art movements of 1909–1937,"[34] and when he was recognized in the United States, it was for the work he had done between those years.

Feininger was apparently introduced to the American art world through galleries, notably the Willard and Buchholz galleries in New York, which had many exhibitions of his paintings between 1941 and 1954. For Feininger, a high point of his return to the United States was winning the acquisitions prize for his painting *Gelmeroda XIII* at the Metropolitan Museum *Arts for Victory* exhibition in 1942.[35] But the smaller galleries were more influential in the distribution and sale of his work. The cynical view of Feininger as "a dealer's pet," presented

*Figure 3.*
LYONEL FEININGER.
Carved figures, n.d.
Location unknown.

in a review in *Art Digest* in 1943, suggests that his American market was created by exhibitions in these two galleries.[36] Extract the cynicism, and the review contains a clear account of how Feininger was introduced into the fold of American art. Through repeated showings of his work, the galleries attracted the attention of others. Museums around the country learned of his work in this way and began acquiring it for their collections. Recall that *Pink Sky* was purchased from the Willard Gallery by the Elliotts for their collection.

Many who saw this painting must have been surprised at its deviation from the later work that was more familiar to them. One reviewer, after seeing only black and white reproductions of *Pink Sky*, was disappointed at the color in the original.[37] In a 1956 Feininger show at the Willard, *Pink Sky* was the earliest work exhibited, distinctly different from all the other paintings. The reviewer for *Arts Magazine* devoted half of his short article to this painting that he considered "a curiosity, but an attractive one," in which the figures are far more differentiated from the buildings than in Feininger's later work. He described *Pink Sky* as "verging on the illustrative," with the negative connotation that "illustration" carried in the art world, and suggested it may be an "early eccentricity, when the Feininger, spare and dry, that the public came to know and admire is arranged about a gallery."[38]

Nearly three years after his death, when this show at the Willard was reviewed, Feininger's place in the American art world was defined primarily by his later work, much of it from the last twenty years when he lived in the United States and was being seen on gallery and museum walls. His background as an illustrator, the history that could account for *Pink Sky*, was no longer accessible.

The wit, color, and movement which characterize this painting were never entirely absent from Feininger's work, however. He often carved toys for his children, rough and angular little figures in proportions like his "Kin-der-Kids" cartoon characters or the people in *Pink Sky*. [*Figs. 3, 4*] In 1913 and 1914, he was involved in designing fanciful trains for mass production as children's toys (or for delighted adults, he said). In 1915, he made the Christmas ornaments for the family's tree in Zehlendorf. The boats in the harbors and the buildings along the streets of his small-scale "City at the Edge of the World" also show elements of his work as an illustrator. [*Fig. 5*] Even the church in *Gelmeroda*, the Metropolitan Museum's first Feininger acquisition, has its counterpart in the toy city.[39] The shapes, colors, and even the themes we see in *Pink Sky* run through many of these small-scale projects. The

Figure 4.
Lyonel Feininger.
Toy figures and village, n.d.
Location unknown.

"spare and dry" qualities of Feininger's later public work did not preclude expressions of fantasy and whimsy in other forms.

Feininger himself placed great value on these works which were not likely to be admitted to the social circle of the art world. He worked hard at this "other" art and anticipated with great pleasure how it would be received. He continued to draw on the early characters of his cartoons in the sketches he did for himself, which were included in his own definitions of his "work." As he wrote in a letter in 1953, describing his hours at the drawing board: "All the long evenings I have been creating demons, pixies, 'Mysterious Petes,' and lantern-jowled professors to pass the hours before one can call it decently 'a day' and creep into bed at ten o'clock."[40]

The continuities between these efforts, his work as an illustrator, and the work which followed may be further obscured by the fate of the illustrated press. After World War I, the German illustrated magazines never regained their circulation or their status as purveyors of art and politics. The postwar inflation, a bitter fact of life in Germany, destroyed production budgets and their readers' buying power. After 1918 the circulation of *Simplicissimus,* for example, which had been 86,000 before the war, never again rose to 30,000.[41] There was increased competition from new illustrated magazines, and journalism

*Figure 5.*
LYONEL FEININGER.
*In der Stadt am Ende der Welt*
(The City at the End of the
    World), 12 July 1912.
Ink.
12½ x 9½ in. (32.0 x 24.6 cm.).
Museum of Modern Art,
    New York.
*Gift of Mrs. Julia Feininger.*

between the wars was distinguished by the rise of photojournalism, which undoubtedly ate into the position of magazines based on older forms of illustration. These practical problems also undermined their appeal for the established illustrators, and the magazines' formula failed to attract new talent. The war and turmoil that followed, finally, had destroyed the traditional structure of authority that the magazines poked fun at. The changed mood of the country could not be captured in the humorous critical styles of the magazines.[42]

The popular magazines of the 1920s were of quite a different form and for the most part had stopped hiring illustrators as their artists. The status of these modern magazines had shifted, and they were less likely to be considered to contain "art." This newer definition and their role in society may have reflected back on the earlier illustrated magazines: once the new magazine forms became dominant, it would be pretentious or inappropriate for "journalism" from any age or era to be treated as "art." Such a definition, or, more accurately, redefinition, could prevent the contents of the illustrated press from being seen as relevant to "art," no matter what the form or content of the magazine.

We can now summarize the social history of *Pink Sky* to the time of Feininger's death in 1956. It was painted at a turning point in the artist's career, when his work for the magazines had ended. The continuities between Feininger's magazine work and this painting clearly established its "success" as an extension of the critical standards he had achieved in the art world of magazine illustration. His turn to painting eventually established Feininger at the center of several major movements in European art. Yet the style he developed with these new directions, occurring as it did in a different artistic context, began to obscure his earliest oil paintings, including *Pink Sky*. Several factors further excluded *Pink Sky* from consideration as a major artwork: the redefinition of illustrated magazines away from their content as "art" toward the domain of popular journalism; the absence of Feininger's toys and other humorous or playful works from consideration as part of his "art"; and the emphasis in American galleries and exhibitions on his later work, to the near exclusion of his 1908–11 paintings. All of these factors created or accentuated distinctions between *Pink Sky* and later oil paintings by Feininger. Each of these tendencies clarified the boundaries of the art world to which Feininger belonged, along lines that placed *Pink Sky* at the fringe of his work. Although treated as art, because from the time it was created it conformed to many of art's conventions, it was also subject to conventions which evolved to define what art is *not*. These other conventions ("art is not journalism"; "art is not toys or small wood carvings"; "serious art is the work of a mature artist") prevented the painting from being seen in 1960 as equal to the quality of other Feininger work.

This environment changed again, however, in the decade following Feininger's death, in ways that once again made *Pink Sky* accessible in terms of his other work made before and after 1909. The challenges to hierarchy and authority during the 1960s did not bypass the fine arts, and one effect of this shift in emphasis was renewed interest in popular expressive forms as art. This was an encouraging atmosphere for a reconsideration of Feininger's illustrations for the popular magazines. Two major biographies were published, and both Hess and Scheyer devoted much attention to Feininger's newspaper and magazine art.[43] These books were widely and warmly reviewed in the art press, in articles which now gave full consideration to Feininger's early career. A comprehensive catalogue of Feininger's graphic works demonstrated the close relationship many of his drawings, etchings, and woodcuts had to both his later paintings and his pictures for the press.[44] In 1964, the Willard Gallery held the first major exhibition in the United States of Feininger's drawings.[45]

This attention to the work was accompanied by a broader consideration of Feininger as an artist by again elevating his illustration to that status. Introducing his graphic work, Sherman Lee legitimized it, in part by referring to an earlier context where art and politics were explicitly integrated: he points out that the groups Blauer Reiter and Die Brücke recognized book illustration and broadsheet as important media of mass communication and folk art.[46] Alfred Werner, in *Arts Magazine,* recalled that by 1901 Feininger had been recognized as a "more than an ordinary maker of cartoons."[47] Mahonri Sharp Young commented on the value of cartoons because of their broad influence: "Here is a truly popular art, not a Pop Art for bored collectors in the latest of takeover bids; here is an art that fascinates tens of millions of people. . . ."[48] Feininger was seen, according to the fashion of the 1960s, as popular, populist, and a good artist. These attributes were no longer seen as inconsistent, so they allowed a unified framework to be constructed that admitted different segments of his work.

This is not to say that *Pink Sky* has now become a "major" Feininger. However, it is no longer seen as an eccentricity or an aberrant example of Feininger's work. The painting can now be understood and analyzed as a link between Feininger the illustrator and Feininger the painter. Once the boundaries defining his life as an artist had been moved back to the 1890s, art critics, reviewers, and his biographers could see, as if for the first time, the "seamless continuity" of Feininger's work.[49]

The enlarged framework gives greater access to more facets of Feininger, the individual and the artist. This is to be commended, but it should not obscure the point here: this reconstruction of Feininger's work remains a construction. Despite its relative newness, its accuracy, its accountability to more aspects of Feininger, it is still based on a selection of facts, materials, and language, woven together to make sense within a specific historical period. *Pink Sky* has not changed the world, but it is difficult to point to any works of art that have a singular and powerful effect on the course of human events. Rather, they work in response and relation to those events. Works viewed as art are always occurring, changing, gaining or losing impact and influence in relation to the dynamic worlds to which they belong, some of which constitute art.

## NOTES

1 Hanno Hardt and Karin B. Ohrn, "The Eyes of the Proletariat: The Worker-Photography Movement in Weimar Germany," *Studies in Visual Communication* 7, no. 3 (Summer 1981),

46–57; Karin E. Becker, "Forming a Profession: Ethical Implications of Photojournalistic Practice on German Picture Magazines, 1926–33," *Studies in Visual Communication* 11, no. 2 (Spring 1985), 44–60.

2   This framework draws extensively from Howard S. Becker, *Art Worlds* (Berkeley: University of California Press, 1982).

3   Hans Hess, *Lyonel Feininger* (New York: Harry N. Abrams, 1960), 51; chronologies of Feininger's life can be found in June L. Ness, ed., *Lyonel Feininger* (New York: Praeger Publishers, 1974), 20–23, and in Hess, 303–7.

4   Cleve Gray, review of Hans Hess, *Lyonel Feininger,* in *Art in America,* 1960, 79.

5   Charlotte Teller, "Feininger–Fantasist," *The International Studio* 63, no. 249 (November 1917), xxx.

6   *Apollo* 89 (June 1969), 475–76.

7   Hess, 29.

8   Martin Sonnabend, "Die 'Kin-der-Kids' von Lyonel Feininger," in Ulrich Luckhardt, *Lyonel Feininger: Karikaturen, Comic strips, Illustrationen* (Hamburg: Museum für Kunst und Gewerbe, 1981), 18.

9   Ann Taylor Allen, *Satire and Society in Wilhelmine Germany* (Lexington: University of Kentucky Press, 1984), 3–4.

10   Eberhard Ruhmer, *Lyonel Feininger* (Munich, 1961), 10, as cited in Ernst Scheyer, *Lyonel Feininger: Caricature and Fantasy* (Detroit: Wayne State University Press, 1964), 67.

11   Scheyer, 67.

12   Georg Hermann [Borchardt], *Die deutsche Karikatur im 19. Jahrhundert* (Bielefeld and Leipzig: Verlag von Velhagen & Klasing, 1901), 127, as cited in Ness, 17; see also Scheyer, 85.

13   Feininger to Alfred Vance Churchill, 22 June 1894; as cited in Scheyer, 62–63.

14   Ulrich Luckhardt, "Ein bekannter Maler – ein vergessener Karikaturist," in Luckhardt, 10.

15   Feininger to H. Francis Kortheuer, 10 March 1894, as cited in Scheyer, 64.

16   Feininger to Kortheuer, 6 December 1894, as cited in Scheyer, 69.

17   "Deutschmeer, D-e-u-t-schmeer, ü-ü-ber Alles!" Pen cartoon for *Ulk,* 1896, reproduced in Scheyer, 76.

18   Scheyer, 95–96.

19   Feininger to Kortheuer, 2 April 1894, as cited in Scheyer, 66.

20   Preface to the catalogue of Feininger exhibition in Munich, October 1954, organized by the Bayerische Akademie der Schönen Kunst, as cited in Scheyer, 72.

21   Scheyer, 63.

22   Feininger to Churchill, 36 [sic] April 1896, as cited in Hess, 22.

23   Hess, 37.

24   As cited in T. Lux Feininger, *Lyonel Feininger – City at the Edge of the World* (New York and London: Frederick A. Praeger, 1965), 35.

25 Leone E. Prasse, *Lyonel Feininger: A Definitive Catalogue of His Graphic Work* (Cleveland: Cleveland Museum of Art, 1972), 30.

26 Feininger to Julia Feininger, 1906, as cited in Scheyer, 123.

27 Feininger to Churchill, 13 March 1913, as cited in Scheyer, 166, 169-170.

28 As cited in T. L. Feininger, 35.

29 Hermann, *Die deutsche Karikatur,* as cited in Alfred Werner, review of Hans Hess, *Lyonel Feininger,* in *Arts Magazine* 36 (December 1961), 70.

30 Luckhardt, 9.

31 Scheyer, 132.

32 Ibid.

33 Alfred Werner, "Lyonel Feininger, Between Precision and Dream," *Art and Artists* 10 (December 1975), 26.

34 "Lyonel Feininger at the Modern," *Art in America* 51 (Winter 1963), 95.

35 T. L. Feininger, 109–10.

36 "Feininger Twice," *Art Digest* 17 (1 February 1943), 14.

37 "Feininger, Kuhn, Kuniyoski, Marin, Nordfeldt," *Art News* 55 (April 1956), 79.

38 "Lyonel Feininger," *Arts* 33 (December 1958), 36.

39 T. L. Feininger discusses the relationship between these works and his father's paintings throughout his book, *City at the Edge of the World.*

40 As cited in T. L. Feininger, 78.

41 Allen, 208–9.

42 Ibid.

43 Hess's book was published in 1960; Scheyer's was published in 1964.

44 Prasse, 1972.

45 Reviewed in *Arts Magazine* 38 (1964), 68.

46 Sherman E. Lee, foreword to Prasse, 9.

47 Werner, review of Hess, *Arts Magazine,* 70.

48 Mahonri Sharp Young, review of Ernst Scheyer, "Lyonel Feininger – Caricature and Fantasy," *Apollo* 83 (January 1966), 77.

49 Cf. Luckhardt, 9.

# SHIFTING TRADITIONS FOR A MOVING PICTURE
Feininger's *Pink Sky*

DUDLEY ANDREW

I

Here is a painting to enjoy and to understand, to enjoy because one *can* understand. Lyonel Feininger may have put off his first viewers in his paintings, but he caters to us. There is always a subject, a painterly subject (buildings, a train; in the case before us, a street scene). The technique announces itself in the extended figures, the orchestrated coloring. Best of all, there is purpose. One assists at a spectacle that has the force of reality (did he photograph the scene first, then arrange it for oil and canvas?), and at the same time one is privy to its interpretation. Even if we blush when asked what it means or, more acceptably, what it expresses, we feel we should be capable of saying something. For surely *Pink Sky* has, if not a point, at least a point of view. How shall we learn to adopt it?

A brush with art history has taught us to "place" this painting. A French street scene, 1909, done by a German-American proto-cubo-expressionist: this work marks a comfortable moment for us at the museum. We are relieved to note that it comes just before the explosion of Cubism, Futurism, and high Expressionism. On its way to abstraction, it is still, in 1909, responsible to its subject, still hopes to reveal something of the observed world. The artist likewise stands between two traditions. German and American, he has obviously imbibed a continental sophistication to temper the New World directness visible in both his technique and in the frontal presentation of his subject.

*Pink Sky* is one of fourteen Feininger paintings known to come from

Dudley Andrew is the Chairman of the Program in Comparative Literature and the Head of Film Studies in the Department of Communication Studies.

this year; all but two of these depict street scenes. It bakes a recipe of ingredients that includes not only certain obvious cartoon elements, but Fauvist colors, Biedermeier motifs, Jugendstil figures, and the search for irridescence associated with Delaunay and Franz Marc. *Pink Sky*, in brief, is easy to place if one makes the effort. The Biedermeier revival, for example, notable here in the tall, old-fashioned hats, peaked in an exposition of 1906, the year Feininger left Germany. Kandinsky's paintings of the time are equally touched by it. While Feininger can't be called a neo-romantic, he couldn't help but feel the influence of romanticism that coincided with a major retrospective exhibit of Caspar David Friedrich. No doubt Feininger was drawn to Biedermeier and Friedrich in the way he was drawn to Aubrey Beardsley: the liquid graphic possibilities fascinated him far more than their nostalgic romanticism. He could adopt whatever techniques and motifs were congenial to his more modern impulse. That impulse grew the next year when he met Delaunay and the Fauves. Franz Marc he had known for several years and felt moderately close to.

To an art historian, then, this is an eminently predictable, or at least reasonable, painting. Its accomplishment, and it is definitely his most complete version of this theme, permitted him to go on the next year to the more violent *Emeute* and finally to his own version of Cubist architectural composition by World War I. From this perspective Lyonel Feininger is less a vivid source for new trends in art than he is a name for a crossroads where many of the tendencies of our century meet and have their effect. This may reassure us, since Feininger evidently lived out this heteroglossia easily, even naturally, and since his painting synthesizes its elements so smoothly. Modern art, we amateurs can be relieved, does not need to be so arbitrary, difficult, and contradictory after all. Someone in 1909 inhabited its impulses with pleasure and ease, lived under the reassurance of a soft pink sky. It matters little that his name was Feininger.

Perhaps that name does matter to the amateur who may be reassured by this official "placement" of the painting but who is hardly satisfied to let things rest there. All of us, I imagine, are tempted to tumble down the hole of biography to get to the bottom of this or any work of art. Genius interests us more than does paint on canvas, genius layering that paint, shaping it. Here we have an American genius with whom we ought certainly to share something: an attitude, at least, perhaps a common history, an origin. How has Feininger become the man to paint *Pink Sky?*

But this passage quickly narrows. In the first place the painting is hardly personal or intimate in the manner of a tortured dream by Munch or a landscape by Van Gogh. And even were it personal, the life it might point to was, we quickly learn, far too modest to reveal anything striking about this striking piece of art. Feininger painted to perfect his art, not to express his life, which, it seems, was utterly enclosed within that art. The few biographical treatises we do have are ludicrous when they struggle to plant behind his work a network of psychological roots. Here is a sample:

> In the farmhouse in Sharon he met simple pious folk and "saw the Bible for the first time." In his own words, he remained "ever since fundamentally religious." The countryside offered divine protection and the companionship of plain, God-fearing people, while the big city often frightened the boy frequently left there by his parents to fend for himself. A painting of 1916, *The Deserted Child,* is unique in Feininger's work. It shows a boy abandoned and desolately huddled on the ground while several tall figures, their backs turned to him, walk off in different directions. It certainly has biographical significance. In moments of loneliness "he imagined faces lurking in the moving shadows" under the elevated and was haunted by "ghost-like apparitions and forms not of this world."[1]

He did more than once refer to the ghosts he lived with, and he drew ghosts frequently in his early years. Yet despite his explicit fascination with the term "fantasy," in Feininger fantasy seems tame enough. Feininger's fantastic subjects are always general, seldom nightmarish. They don't rise out of his art or seep out of his unconscious so much as underlie that art. We might say that a strong dose of fantasy was required for his early style with its interplay of graphics and narrative. The year before *Pink Sky,* he illustrated an edition of Norwegian folktales with sixteen full-page graphics, eight in color.[2] The tales helped organize his visual ideas. His was a socially mediated, quotidian fantasy, like that of Marc Chagall, a structural part of a working method. And his psyche, then, must be seen as another tool ready to serve art, not a sacred goal needing to be served by or to it.


II


Beyond biography, then, just why does this painting strike us as an appropriate representation, appropriate not directly to our times but to our sense of history? While it was not displayed in 1909, while Feininger's oils went unnoticed by the public who adored his cartoons, aren't we right to hold this painting up as expressing a social sensibility? Matisse, in a famous anecdote,[3] was so stunned by a companion painting (*The Green Bridge*) that he refused to hang his own inferior effort beside it. What startled Matisse about this style, making his painting less than appropriate? What did he recognize in it? In short, what is its place and significance in what might be called "the social history of vision"?

Although the very title of *Pink Sky* invites us to start with color, let's begin with the careering figures who live in its ambience. This painting depicts urban life. Let's face it as it faces us. These are funny folk. Their variety spreads out our interest, de-psychologizing the painting altogether if the cartoon motifs hadn't already done so. While the three large men who dominate the lower center are in a great hurry, to their sides and behind them are people in easy attitudes (one leans against a tree, another saunters along with a cane, while a third looks in her purse). This unconscious crowd is suffused in the beneficence of a pink sky at the end of day. Whether we take this as a precious visual moment or a portent signaling the end of the world, these figures don't mark it at all.

The isolated preoccupation of each character amuses us who are lifted enough above them to enjoy the ballet they comprise as a group. While the dominant flow is a funnel to the bottom of the canvas (an hourglass shape marked out by the street that constricts itself particularly around the tall man, squeezing him through at great speed), some characters resist this movement. The stranger (doubtless German) with the knapsack actually climbs back up the street, evidently staring in shop windows out of curiosity.

No one else is curious about anything. Rather they go through the motions proper to them. The five figures at the bottom, for instance, could form a military rank, but for their varied costumes and, more important, for the lack of synchronization in their steps. We note the stride of the two gentlemen whose arms are linked. They march together, to be sure, and quickly. Obviously outstripping the dwarfish loner on the left, they will momentarily overtake the curious woman in yellow who minces past the sinister, stationary fellow closest to us. This is a snapshot, or better, a single frame from a motion picture that watched the street fill up earlier in the day and will shortly watch it quiet down.

The fat man smiles. His partner comfortably holds a cigarette. Their amiable sociability contrasts with the lonelier looks of the others whose faces we can make out. Psychology is beside the point, for this is the human species in its ordinary behavior. Only the figure on the bottom right invites us to think with him. Is this Feininger, conjuring up the street scene behind him in repoussoir? Two years earlier he had appeared on the front page of the *Chicago Tribune* holding nine of his cartoon characters as tiny puppets dangling from strings. Standing around the corner from this street scene, Feininger here has let his puppets go. And they go predictably enough.

One can hardly help trying to urge this very ordinariness into taking on a more dramatic tone. Should we let ourselves imagine that all these characters form an interlocking intrigue? Or might we uncover some plot exploding in their midst? The fat woman crossing the street, for instance—has she overheard some secret exchanged between the strollers? She heads to pass the word to the spy who waits at the tree. Meanwhile the odd fellow with the knapsack, a counterspy, watches where the old woman has just exited.

The sinister figure staring at us from the bottom, the one we have imagined as Feininger himself, might invite such a paranoid reading, but the picture responds poorly to it. This may be a cartoon, like the "Wee Willie Winkie" strips Feininger had just finished for the *Chicago Tribune,* but the plot tying the characters together has been subtracted here. Aimless, these characters disperse themselves, unaware of this instant privileged by its representation.

With neither psychology nor narrative motivation leading it, the picture is directed powerfully by the architecture of the street, which advances from the backdrop to play a dominating role. These massive cliffs of buildings govern the flow of the figures in the valley below, disciplining their Brownian movement. The gentle curve of the street softens this control so that the figures are nudged and tumble gently down the path, unlike, for example, the rigid route Edvard Munch ordained for his young girl on the bridge in *Der Schrei,* or for his traumatized crowd in *Evening on Karl Johan Strasse* [*Fig. 1*], unlike Kirchner's *Die Strasse* with its stark Berlin lines. Trees and chimneys modulate the verticality of these flat edifices, while horizontally to the left a tributary cuts open the building mass; on the right a tree behind a wall lets us imagine the little square of a garden or schoolyard carved out from this brick and mortar world.

Another painter might have insisted on the contrast between the concrete harshness and the moving flesh that it surrounds. But Feininger's people are small ambulating blocks, hardened already in their solid colors, while his buildings, partly humanized, bend gently out of perspective. They don't mean to protect or oversee the life lived out in their midst; rather they seem to go about their own life independently, to have done so in fact for years. Clothed colorfully, they sport chimney top hats. Like the figures beneath, they reveal nothing of their inner life, presenting themselves boldly to no one, to us. Feininger discusses buildings anthropomorphically in his letters, mentioning, for example, "the quaint hold houses [of Brussels], three and four centuries old, some of them with their huge chimneys and quaint gables." In another place he finds himself taken by "the adorable custom of first painting the houses with chalky colors and leaving them to mellow down in delicious tints by wind and rain, none of your elegant grey streets as in our dear but sadly modern Berlin."[4]

A description of the painting written during World War II claims it to be a "Dr. Caligari" view of the "City at the End of the World."[5] [*Fig. 2*] Surely German Expressionist cinema did draw on paintings such as this one for the compositional flavor of its street genre, but Feininger's disposition is really quite other. Despite the winding streets, the prominent lampposts, and the distinct characters in their romantic Biedermeier garb, *Pink Sky* stands before us without mystery. The decor doesn't echo the paranoia of the characters. Indeed, there is no paranoia; no psychology at all. Most extraordinary – there are no shadows! If we are to think of this street scene in relation to the cinema, it would be the cinema of René Clair: *Le Million, Sous les Toits de Paris,* or *Le Quatorze Juillet.* Even in its gangster genres, French cinema left the streets to the people, as in this painting; whereas German street corners are places where, as in *The Blue Angel* and even in its rarer comedies, characters look over their shoulders or shy away from the inevitable shadows. [*Figs. 3, 4, 5, 6a, 6b, 7*]

This is the gayest of pictures. What tension there is springs from the layering of the cartoon characters like a transparency atop a more conventional study of architectural forms. The figures differ hardly at all from those Feininger sketched weekly for the *Chicago Tribune* up to 1907. Hans Hess points out the daring transposition of the inked "Kin-der-Kids" world into serious oils.[6] Toulouse-Lautrec might be cited as a precedent. Indeed the entire Art Nouveau tendency in design supported Feininger's interest in motion, costume, and caricature. He clearly draws on facets of the "Jugendstil" wing of Art Nouveau, although he never succumbed to its erotic decadence, its languid lines and flimsy support. Perhaps the directness he had needed to master in cartoon drawing saved him from both the sentimentality and the excessive sensuality of Art Nouveau.

With this in mind we might isolate the three characters in mid-plane just to the left of the tall running man. The elegant woman with the dark stocking so tantalizingly exposed could come from Toulouse-Lautrec or countless posters after him. Behind her saunters a Guy de Maupassant gentleman, chest out in the flush of class pride. The young man leaning against the tree bears the diffidence of the modern attitude. While all the others find their self-assurance in oblivious motion, he projects the undulating directionlessness of the Jugendstil sensibility.

To layer such figures on a more solid, traditional cityscape was the trick. Feininger's interest in architecture was lifelong. For most of us he is the skyscraper artist, the New Yorker who succeeded in imagining the great buildings that went up in his forty-year absence from the city of his birth. But his interest in architecture stems not just from New York massiveness; it began, he tells us, during his yearlong stay in Brussels. There, under the influence of the Jesuits which he was not ashamed to acknowledge, his love for Bach blended into a passion for the interlocking monumentalism of the Gothic style.[7] The Gothic style intrigued him, not for the heavy romanticism it conjured up in the nineteenth century, but for its organic design. Again his interest was in tune with the era. Robert Delaunay, whom he saw frequently in 1908, was just commencing his studies of the church of St. Severin. Along with Franz Marc and many others he was transforming architectural concerns into the first emanations of Cubism. Feininger, we know, would soon join them. Suddenly he found that his sincere and lifelong attraction to the architecture of the past meshed with the most up-to-date impulse in the transformation of graphic space.

The buildings in *Pink Sky* are by no means Gothic, but they bear their age as a testimony to their success. They have survived. On the street below, time is a river of people and carts passing, whereas for these buildings time falls in raindrops over centuries. You can see it on their stained façades. Feininger gives these buildings a solidity rare in modernism, even a three-dimensionality. It is this that contrasts so brazenly with the flat human figures. And this contrast in turn invites the most trenchant interpretation of the painting overall: that the view some feet above a human view (perhaps from a first-floor balcony or window) literally is condescending to modern life. The obsessive, self-absorbed movement of each isolated person is timed to the metronome of their watches and appointment books. They are full of self-importance, though their thin lives are visibly disappearing to leave the street to its own more methodical time, measured out naturally in seasons and days, in sunrises and, as here, in sunsets. Such was the view of one of Feininger's earliest critics. Writing casually in 1917 not about *Pink Sky* but about *Green Sky and Yellow Houses,* Charlotte Teller aptly put her finger on it:

> It was the houses. They looked so human. They had a sense of humour. But they were not at all dependent upon humanity laughing with them. There was humanity in the streets, quite a great deal of it coming and going. . . . They were just the sort of serious, self-important, long-legged pin-headed creatures to live in grinning houses, . . . not at all aware of their absurdity.[8]

It is true that Feininger did anchor certain of his street scenes with explicit satiric titles or phrases; the 1908 cover design for *Le Témoin* bears the caption, "Where are we going? I don't know but let's hurry." What caption should orient our painting? Surely it would mock these stupid figures whose sense of themselves inflates them like balloons. One biographer claims that "Feininger longed for the charm of a vanished pre-industrial age," and that his fairy tale topics are turned toward an earlier, purer era, so that even his numerous etchings of locomotives show "an antipathy to the age of speed."[9] The little catalogue put out by the Museum of Modern Art in its first recognition of Feininger asserted that after 1907 he aimed at a single theme, "How the individual responds to forces beyond the individual."[10]

Is his disdain so apparent as that? To my mind, the figures in our painting seem too varied, too balanced, to make a strong statement of any sort; the painter rather observes whimsically from above, so that even the ridiculous can become a fact of existence, a fact precisely for art. After all in literature, as E. M. Forster pointed out, "flat characters" have often served the richest novels.[11] Look at Dickens or Balzac. The trick is to keep them frontal and keep them moving. Their interrelation and vividness can then recover the energy of life. Feininger's refusal of psychological depth throws him back to the great social novels of the nineteenth century but perhaps prefigures post-psychological narratives in our own day, the novels let's say of Peter Handke or Thomas Pynchon, the films of Tati, as we shall see, but also of Scola ("Le Bal"), Fellini ("E la Nave va"), and others.

III

We haven't avoided biography in trying to account not just for the suitability of *Pink Sky,* but for its specific contribution to our social history of vision. Insofar as this work marks a resting zone in the struggle for a new paradigm, biography helps dramatize the tension that makes it vibrate in its allotted place. The specific tension I refer to is that between popular and elite art. Now we don't need to settle on Feininger's personal attitude toward modern man to realize that a painting such as this one contributes to a populist strain of art in our century. A political liberal, Feininger nevertheless frequently expressed disgust for the values of the bourgeoisie. He played to them in his political cartoons, yet escaped them for solitary summers on the Baltic where he felt most at home. He was perfectly placed to help effect that permeability between the formerly hermetic spheres of popular and elite art that may have been the most important cultural event of the turn of the century. An enthusiast of Bach who played chamber music all his life, who grew up in fact under the aura of the great music his parents played in concert halls throughout the world, Feininger was by 1900 perhaps the world's most famous cartoonist, his designs seen weekly by millions of Germans, Americans, and French.

In 1907, under the heady influence of Montparnasse (Delaunay, the Fauves), he sought to upgrade his ambitions by designing caricatures for *Le Témoin,* an upscale monthly edited in those crucial years by Paul Iribe. Here he was encouraged to explore the painterly reaches of his cartoon aesthetic and, with every issue, moved closer to what we see in *Pink Sky.* The experience was evidently exhilarating, for he had always complained that his German editors and public rejected his most personal fantasies, preferring obvious political designs. In one issue he draped his tall, seductive, jaded "L'Impatiente" against a sinister background of high old Parisian houses with their characteristic chimneys. Iribe rejoiced, and Feininger decided in a trice to renounce his sheerly commercial work and to devote himself completely to aesthetic research, to painting and engraving. He was a thirty-five-year-old apprentice, but an apprentice with an immense technical control gained in the daily grind of commissioned journalism. Feininger might have described his decision in more spiritual terms, and it is true that his caricatures dating from 1907 tempted one critic to compare him to Emile Nolde and Oscar Kokoschka,[12] as if caricature, particularly when intensely colored, was a modern way to the mystical. Why not? Critics would soon say the same for Georges Rouault.

The decision to abandon cartooning definitively for oil painting was genuinely heroic, a blow for the religion of art over the lure of commerce and facile popularity. Did Feininger hope to win over his large

Top to bottom from left: *Figure 1.*
EDVARD MUNCH. *Evening on Karl
Johan Strasse*, 1892. Oil on canvas.
*Rasmus Meyers Collection*, Bergen,
Norway. *Figure 2.* ROBERT WIENE,
director. *The Cabinet of Dr. Caligari*,
1919. *Figure 3.* RENÉ CLAIR, director.
*Sous les Toits de Paris*, 1930. *Figure 4.*
RENÉ CLAIR, director. *Le Silence Est
d'Or*, 1947. Second column: *Figure 5.*
VICTOR TRIVAS, director. *Dans les
Rues*, 1933. *Figures 6a, b:* JOSEF VON
STERNBERG, director. *Blue Angel*,
1929–30.

Top to bottom from left: *Figure 7.* BRUNO RAHN, director. *Dirnentragödie* (La Tragedie de la Rue), 1927. *Figure 8.* EMILE COHL, Animator-director for Léon Gaumont. *Fantasmagorie,* 1908. *Figures 9a, b.* PIERRE PRÉVERT, director. *L'Affaire Est dans le Sac,* 1932. *Figures 10a, b.* JACQUES TATI, director. *Playtime,* 1968. *Figure 11.* GEORGES MÉLIÈS, director. *Le Raid Paris-Monte Carlo en Deux Heures* (The Adventurous Automobile Trip), 1905.

following to serious painting? Did his fellow artists at Montparnasse expect from this conversion a windfall of popular enthusiasm for their own recondite experiments? This certainly never took place. Indeed, Feininger's reputation only gradually reemerged, and from the top down, from stray remarks tossed off by the likes of Matisse to descriptions of the Bauhaus where, although the first artist hired by Walter Gropius, he would always be mentioned behind the more illustrious members like Paul Klee.

Evidently this fall to relative obscurity presented Feininger no grave problem. If we can believe the interviews, he was, from first to last, interested only in tinkering with design to explore visual structures as they might promote fantasy. His idea to project his cartoon figures into a traditional architectural oil painting was less a stroke of genius than a step that needed to be taken in the history of modernist design. And it was a step marching in tune with modernism everywhere. He was, as we have put it already, one of the sites of a general cultural transformation that altered forever the relation of the high and low arts. Obviously there were other, more notable sites. If the art world was ready to accept a cartoonist like Feininger stepping up to their ranks, it was only because a number of important artists were simultaneously prepared to step down, to alter their art by taking seriously, for example, the silliness of the movies and other popular diversions. Feininger's appeal is, then, only the opposite side of the coin from Erik Satie's or Apollinaire's, men who at the same moment took account of the cinema and gladly fashioned their work under its influence.

While the first decades of this century mark an extraordinary attention paid to popular art, those arts themselves hardly participated in their proper upgrading. Without a hint of self-consciousness, the cinema remained at this time a fascinating but crude curiosity, amusement, and device, and no one in the business took it seriously as an art. Apollinaire might descend to incorporate cinematic elements in his verse, but neither Méliès, nor Zecca, nor Feuillade would imagine themselves contributing to painting or even to drama. They felt themselves firmly settled in the terrain of wax museums, music halls, and optical toys.

This peculiar situation rests on a double chronology in which the cinema, progressing happily in its own naive manner, became an unconscious partner in the heady development of fine art (Futurism, Cubism, and Dada just around the corner). To take our case, Feininger's heroic ascent from cartooning toward elite art in 1908 coincides but does not converge with the birth of the cinematic cartoon in that same year. For it was precisely in 1908 that another extraordinary caricaturist, Emile Cohl, a Parisian of nearly Feininger's reputation, would also abandon newspapers and journals for a more serious endeavor, this time for the movies. Both men were eager to research the graphic representation of motion, but in utterly different modes. The animated cartoons that Cohl truly invented as a form at this time served an utterly different social function from Feininger's motion-charged street scenes. Cohl's squiggles, which he modified from his journalistic line drawings and quick sketches, were immediately accessible to a broad public and became the first style of film animation.[13] [*Fig. 8*] Cohl in fact inherited the Daumier tradition of political satire from his own master André Gill. By the 1890s he was, like Feininger, working in many print forms, then expanding out to design toys and gadgets. As a Parisian, and a nearly destitute one, it was inevitable that he should encounter the cinema which in the first decade of this century was a booming new industry. Cohl was glad to have a real income at last, and very glad to experiment with the cinema. While his drawing, like Feininger's, had been noticed by critics, he was never interested in climbing the sacred mountain of art. Because of temperament, and because his quick-sketch style could so readily be modified for animating figures on celluloid, Cohl was the first known artist to have clearly influenced the direction of film history.

This is not to say that Feininger's graphics had no effect on cinema. With him the effect was delayed. As a rule the cinema lags a few decades behind developments coming from the higher arts. His elegant play with flat human figures can be seen as a source for cinematic animation only in the late 1930s in the tradition of deluxe design produced in the romantic fairy tales of Paul Grimault. Peter Max inherited this style in the sixties, and feature cartoons like *The Yellow Submarine* have become dominant in animation today.

The cinema was far more ready to adopt Feininger's subject and tone rather than his graphic style, for satire is an important intersection of the popular and the elevated. Clearly other caricaturists would need to be mentioned here (George Grosz, for one) but Feininger's less strident attitude permitted him to range widely, seeking comic and graphic effects that are closed to anyone striving to make the strongest possible point as quickly as possible. Satire can be employed in a truly aesthetic research into the possibility of graphic forms, for instance in lightening the tone of an otherwise heavy architectural study. Satire gives to our street scene a mock seriousness that depends both on our sense of mockery and of seriousness.

In its tenor and ambition *Pink Sky* relates to a cinema of graphic satire. This was not a contemporaneous cinema, for in 1909 cinema could only be a popular toy, but it does relate to a cinema coming a few decades later. The tradition of French cinematic satire, beginning with Jacques Feyder's 1923 *Crainquebille* and reaching a peak in the work of Jacques and Pierre Prévert's *L'Affaire Est dans le Sac* responds to the same interplay of disdain, wit, and distant human contemplation that emanates from *Pink Sky*. This tradition seems a far more likely descendant than *The Cabinet of Doctor Caligari* and the German street films which are too weighty, pretentious, and psychological. Prévert, we should not forget, worked continuously with Grimault, writing fairy tales for animation. In *L'Affaire Est dans le Sac,* he literally designed a street scene in Paris containing about the same number of character types as does Feininger's painting. Furthermore, none of these characters interests us psychologically whatsoever, but together they form a humorous pattern of absurd social behavior in a miniature city. [*Figs. 9a, 9b*]

Closer to our own day this same satiric impulse has produced the marvelous films of Jacques Tati. The misdesign of automoton characters in architectural space is the very subject of *Mon Oncle* (1957), a film which used satire to explore color and motion. Tati wears Feininger's mantle somewhat better than the anarchist Prévert, who prized spontaneity and lightness. Tati, on the other hand, is often linked to Robert Bresson, the deadly serious Dostoievskian director. Both men are obsessed by graphic design and precision of movement. Utterly independent, neither has compromised the slightest for a producer. Yet Tati remained a comic for all that, a wise, increasingly bitter observer of a mad urban culture. His last major effort, *Trafic,* is a caricature of the auto culture done with a concern for rhythm, sound, and color found only in the most cerebral avant-garde works. Here the characters, as in Feininger, seem dehumanized just to the extent that the environment, this time automobiles, takes on a wonderful anthropomorphism. The cars smile, extend their limbs in greetings, and become indistinguishable from their drivers. Tati, however, rejects easy sentiment. He would construct a perfect urban machine, proud of its perfection even if disdainful of its worth. His most ambitious work, the 1966 *Playtime,* turns a Paris street into a carousel, the cars, buses, and pedestrians unknowingly spinning around a carrefour to the music of a merry-go-round. [*Figs. 10a, 10b*] When they slow, someone inserts a coin in a parking meter, turns the handle, and starts the parade all over again. The architecture has changed, for Tati's street in Paris is situated near La Défense, is lined with oddly overhanging streetlights and flanked by immense mirror façades of buildings, but his fascination with the foibles of Parisians and tourists moving in unconscious patterns along the preformulated pathways of streets and buildings matches Feininger's concern. Both are comic artists playing with popular material. Both seek to achieve a precise representation of what might be termed the thoughtless ecology of urban life.

IV

Feininger himself might have worked in cinema had he been born half a century later, for *Pink Sky* is an index pointing to a rich cinematic future; its characters are at the point of falling out of a bygone Paris and into helter-skelter modernity. At the broad top of the hourglass design, however, amid the ancient buildings and the still more ancient sky, we are able to contemplate a past which this painting just as clearly signals. Feininger developed his art and his sensibility precisely between the dates 1880 and 1918 treated by Stephen Kern in a book fittingly titled *The Culture of Time and Space*.[14] In these relatively stable years preceding the First World War, Europe revolutionized its consciousness, perhaps making that war inevitable. Kern's fascinating collection of facts and anecdotes divides itself into chapters on the nature of time, the past, the present, the future, speed, the nature of space, of form, of distance, and of direction. He concludes with a discussion of the Great War and the simultaneous "Cubist War."

I would locate Feininger on center stage within this drama of changing paradigms. He is, to change the metaphor, part of a whole screen of figures on which a slower, more human world dissolves into the rush of modern experience. While no one would call it a watershed painting, *Pink Sky* embodies the shifting sensibility of the Belle Epoche in its most prominent aspects. Treating cartoon types seriously shows not merely a change in permissible subjects for oils, but alters the criterion of composed stateliness associated with the fine arts. Not only has the human figure become transient, a brief appearance on the public street, but that figure has lost its depth and consequently a good measure of our respect. Feininger makes us take interest in the interrelation of the people with the objects as though they were the moving parts of an urban machine.

We must remember that within a decade he would be chosen to direct the design wing of the architecture department of the Bauhaus, and that in his spare time he concocted crazy toys for children, remaining faithful to his first artistic impulses. Trains, boats, bikes, typewriters, and cameras were his passionate interests as a youth and he never gave them up.[15] I imagine his nonromantic attachment to Gothic architecture helped him view the ancient cathedrals as giant spiritual machines whose purpose is now lost. Even at the Bauhaus he was known to promulgate, against the published purpose of that institution, a functionless approach to design. Motion, balance, the appearance of rationality within the play of parts: this is what he sought.

The movies should have attracted him. Here was precisely the machine, half toy, half scientific instrument, ready to analyze the movement of horses, ready to satirize the gestures of contemporary society, ready to create a fantastic rush of people and objects through stop-action and under-cranking techniques. Emile Cohl's 1911 "Les Melons Baladeures" sends characters careering through Paris streets not unlike the one we are studying; mindlessly they leap over fences, race around corners, all pursuing a wayward "strolling watermelon." Fat men, thin men, women in full skirts. Feininger's characters need a melon to chase.

Obviously the motion pictures constitute a privileged emanation of the obsession with movement prevalent in this age. Kern constructs a collage of evidence:

> Scientific management, the motion studies of Muybridge and Marey, early cinematography, Cubism and Futurism reflect aspects of each other across the cultural spectrum like images in a house of mirrors. As the Cubists broke up and recreated bottles and guitars, Gilbreth broke down and reconstructed work processes. He made wire models of workers' movements from cyclegraphs similar to the wire-and-plaster models of birds in flight that Marey made from chronophotographs. Gilbreth's use of successive photographs to analyze motion derived from Muybridge's serial photographs of a galloping horse. Muybridge later used the technique to capture the grace of a woman stooping to pick up a basket; Gilbreth used the motion picture camera to make chronocyclegraphs; the term for a film's composition—"montage"—is the French word for the assembly of a product from component parts; around 1912 the Cubists began to experiment with "Cubist Cinema"; and the Futurists were inspired by its suggestion of new possibilities for a kinetic visual art. Marcel Duchamp observed that "the whole idea of movement, of

speed, was in the air," and acknowledged that his *Nude Descending a Staircase* was inspired by chronophotographs and motion pictures. The cinema reproduced the mechanization, jerkiness, and rush of modern times.[16]

Whether Feininger was out to satirize modern frenzy or to celebrate it makes little difference. This pre-Cubist painting partakes of the vision of its age. Kern ends his chapter on speed:

> Taylorism and Futurism, the new technology, the new music, and the cinema had set the world rushing. But beneath there ran countercurrents. As quickly as people responded to the new technology, the pace of their former lives seemed like slow motion. The tension between a speeding reality and a slower past generated sentimental elegies about the good old days before the rush. It was an age of speed but, like the cinema, not always uniformly accelerated. The pace was unpredictable, and the world, like the early audiences, was alternately overwhelmed and inspired, horrified and enchanted.[17]

*Pink Sky* displays a certain nostalgia in its Biedermeier costumes and charming buildings, even in the gentle curve of its streets. But it celebrates the modern day in its color and motion. Soon such streets would be straightened out for automobiles, and not everyone would rue that day. Marinetti after all had gleefully predicted "that someday the Danube would run in a straight line at 300 kilometers an hour."[18]

*Pink Sky* is not yet Cubist or Futurist, but it is headed in that direction. Feininger has evaporated all traces of atmosphere, so that the pink sky descends toward the pinkish street as one flat field pulled toward another related field. Yet we have a sky and a street for all that. Here lies the painting's most living tension: the great effort to throw the street out the back of the picture frame into real volume runs up against the equal effort to arrange colored patterns on a flat canvas surface. Such play of depth and surface is surely one of the principle games and joys the graphic arts promise the modern viewer, and its centrality to the birth of Cubism, Futurism, and Abstract Expressionism is a commonplace. But *Pink Sky* brings to this artistic issue a very fresh technique drawn from the repertoire of popular graphics. The human figures, great gobs of solid colors, seem movable, like the plastic colorforms children today move around on some perspective backdrop. Don't you want to peel off the little man on the left and put him right under the lamppost or bring the languid young man from the tree up to center stage? Perhaps we might even make the woman in white prance across the rooftops? This urge is set up by the separation each character enjoys from the backdrop, a separation brought about by the prominent outline each figure receives in his or her complementary color. Today such fringing with complementaries is routine, but in 1909 it must have made these figures leap off the canvas. In addition, it is obvious that, contrary to accepted practice, the figures were painted in first and the background then brought up to meet them. This gives to the people that thin, layered appearance, as though they really exist on transparent cells laid down atop a more traditional street scene.

The color play that these cartoon techniques provide moves the painting toward abstraction. Blocks of related colors (blues and purples, blues and greens, oranges and reds) are geometrically dispersed around the rectangle of the canvas. As in Matisse's paintings of the period, this sometimes makes us guess at the objects depicted. Is the man with the cane carrying a bluish newspaper under his left arm, or are we seeing through the space between arm and torso to the bluish building behind? As in Matisse we must ask here: does color define objects or blotches?

Feininger explicitly acknowledged his debt to the Fauves during this period, but as regards color, I believe he brought something to them as well, or at least he contributed to the rethinking of color that characterized the early years of the century. Once again we can see the contamination of fine art by popular culture, for Feininger's mastery of color derived from years of experience with color printing required by the various forms of advertising and journalism in the late nineteenth century. Limited in the number of colors he could employ, "Feininger was a master in the orchestral blending of his four favorite colors: olive, violet, blue-gray and rose."[19] He employed color not solely for its immediate visual pleasure but explicitly to modulate the sense of figural depth in his designs.

> Do not think exclusively of the key-stone [which gives the design in contour lines]. The whole [printing process] must be conducted like an orchestra. Only in this way can you achieve the magic integration of the hues and their values with the rich complementing function of shades, textures, and blots. Without this integration your work will always remain just a contour-drawing to which color has been added.[20]

In another letter, written just after he had finished our painting, he indicates his satisfaction with this aspect of his art: "By 1908 I experimented with colored outlines and contrasting surfaces. The new figure notes dated 1908 will show you these and likewise that I followed motion very closely. . . . [By] 1910 I had attained to greater rhythm, somewhat neglecting color, of which I felt perfectly sure."[21]

Feininger championed a brand of coloring that would become important to modern graphics and the animated film. In 1909 this popular color technique converged with experiments in oil painting that had begun at least with Gauguin. Gauguin, Matisse, and the serious art world began to take account of popular color methods on the heels of a general European infatuation with Japanese woodblock prints. While Feininger may not have been inspired by the ukiyo-e school, he shared with it a concern for achieving planar variation via large color blocks. Is it coincidental that these very different traditions both focus on satire and social representation? We mustn't forget that the woodblock print in Japan was the site of a competition between popular and refined art, as when the fancy surimono was prized by connoisseurs who dismissed ukiyo-e as vulgar. Feininger, in a completely different setting, reproduced that competition, and he did it in part under the trend-setting eye of Paul Iribe, who was a constant supporter of Japonism.[22] Some scholars have seen the drawings Feininger did for *Le Témoin* to be explicitly indebted to the ukiyo-e manner of handling figures and architecture on patterns of colored planes.[23] Because Japonism omits details, it conforms to Feininger's own predisposition for dramatic graphics. At this very moment he wrote that he wanted above all to play "with relative proportions to create enormous differences with regard to resulting monumentality and intensity in composition."[24] How well this describes the prints of Hokusai or even Utamaro. How well it describes *Pink Sky*.

Curiously, during this very decade another popular art was experimenting with color effects. In 1906 the Pathé Frères motion picture company, trying to wrest control of the cinema from George Méliès, perfected a color stencilling technique that they applied to deluxe versions of their movies, selling them for three times the black-and-white price. This process required the creation of figure cut-outs from a black-and-white version that, when laid over a second print and bathed in dye, would selectively color the appropriate objects on the screen. Multiple colors required multiple stencils. These brilliant little films share with *Pink Sky* the excitement over vivid figures moving swiftly on a stable screen. Before the stencil process was perfected, the central figure or object of a film might be hand colored, frame by frame. Méliès' "Paris to Monte Carlo," for example, shows a spectacularly red car riding over streets, mountains, and, to our amusement, shopkeepers. [*Fig. 11*] The manually applied red never stabilizes itself, rather pulsing around the screen. Did some viewers neglect the silly trumped-up story to concentrate on the pleasure of seeing a single color move at will around a screen? Did Delaunay or

Matisse go to the movies at this time? How seriously did they take the flood of cartoon books and journalistic caricature designs that could be seen everywhere in Paris? Evidently they did take Feininger seriously, at least once he started painting.

And what of *Pink Sky?* How much of an interest in pure picture space can we attribute to it? Even without considering the prototypes of Japanese prints, this "street" can easily become a "field" on which regular shapes of colors alternate in formal patterns. The hats clearly match the chimneys and the windows. Door frames repeat the stains on the walls. Colored modules everywhere bring the painting forward and prepare us for Mondrian twenty years down the road.

But we aren't at Mondrian yet, and Feininger had two years to go before acknowledging himself as a proto-Cubist. The pink street lamp dead center in the scene brings to this lovely thoroughfare the delicate shade of an eternal dusk. These funny characters who interest us as types are literally defined by the colors they proudly sport. The frail lady at the bottom has so touched up her face that its flesh tones are paper thin whereas our visitor with the knapsack sports a robust blue and purple. They have decked themselves out with harmonious colors. It is Feininger who outlines them with the complements and spreads them in patterns around the street. They are alive and moving, while at the same time they are bloodless social statistics, mere patterns of gestures and functions required in a city and in a painting.

Despite the tactile richness of oil on canvas, this to me is a motion picture, a lovely animation we project through the thin celluloid of its base. If Feininger helped the vanguard of European painting soon to lift itself into sheer abstractions, mightn't it have been because the movies, every movie, proved the point of *Pink Sky,* mechanically bringing to life the little characters of contemporary history as they go about their roles in a space that itself can bend? Feininger announces here the serious philosophical role to be played by popular art. But it is no longer a role he wants to play. Instead we will find him in his Baltic Sea retreat, where, far from urban life, he will dream up Cubist cityscapes. Feininger by 1912 has aimed to become a truly abstract painter, no longer needing to attend closely to his subjects. He can stop painting modern life, cease being concerned to render that curious mixture of oldness and modernity Paris possessed before the Great War. For why should he bother? After all, Paris and modern life were now available to him at the movies.

# NOTES

1 Ernst Scheyer, *Lyonel Feininger—Caricature and Fantasy* (Detroit: Wayne State University Press, 1964), 19.

2 Ulrich Luckhardt, *Lyonel Feininger: Karikaturen, Comic strips, Illustrationen, 1888–1915* (Hamburg: Museum für Kunst und Gewerbe, 1981), catalogue numbers 148–151 taken from *Norwegische Volksmarchen,* ed. P. Asbjornsen and Jörgen Moe (Berlin: Hans Bondy Verlag, 1908).

3 James W. Lane, "Feininger's Counterpoint in Paint: Lyonel out of Johann Sebastian," *Artnews* 40 (March 15–31, 1941), 39.

4 Feininger correspondence of October and November 1890, cited by Scheyer, 41, 43.

5 Lawrence Campbell in *Artnews* 55 (April 1956), 79, repeated this reference to *The Cabinet of Dr. Caligari* made in that same journal by James Lane on 15 March 1941, 39.

6 Hans Hess, *Lyonel Feininger* (New York: Abrams, 1961), 39–40.

7 Correspondence with Alfred Vance Churchill, 7 October 1890, reprinted in June L. Ness, ed., *Lyonel Feininger* (New York: Praeger, 1974), 176.

8 Charlotte Teller, "Feininger—Fantasist," *The International Studio* 63, no. 249 (November 1917), xxv.

9 Scheyer, 93.

10 Alois Schardt in *Lyonel Feininger and Marsden Hartley* (New York: Arno Press for the Museum of Modern Art, 1966), 15.

11 E. M. Forster, *Aspects of the Novel* (New York: Harcourt Brace, 1927), 67.

12 Eberhard Ruhmer, *Lyonel Feininger* (Munich, 1961), 13.

13 Donald C. Crafton, *Before Mickey* (Cambridge: MIT Press, 1982), 48-67. See also his doctoral thesis, "Emile Cohl and the Origin of the Animated Film," Yale University, 1977.

14 Stephen Kern, *The Culture of Time and Space, 1880–1918* (Cambridge: Harvard University Press, 1983).

15 Hess mentions Feininger's love of modern gadgets on p. 13.

16 Kern, 117.

17 Ibid., 130.

18 R. W. Flint, ed., *Marinetti, Selected Writings* (New York: Farrar, Straus & Giroux, 1971), 94–95.

19 Scheyer, 83.

20 Scheyer (p. 83) quotes Feininger indirectly through a German catalogue.

21 Feininger correspondence with Churchill, 13 March 1913, reprinted in Scheyer, 166–70.

22 Scheyer, 106.

23 Ibid., 123.

24 Feininger correspondence of 1906 in *Lyonel Feininger Exhibit* (Detroit: Detroit Institute of the Arts, 1941), 98.

*With gratitude to my colleague and viewing companion, Franklin Miller, for his discreet suggestions and his animated concern.*

# TRUCKIN' UNDER A PINK SKY, SEEING RED

GEOFFREY WAITE

## I. On Theme and Method

At a glance you sometimes see only a picture in blue or orange or pink before you, but on close inspection it turns out to be – very often without even the artist being fully aware of it – a blob of viscid, malodorous, asphyxiating gas of antiproletarian culture. Vigilance of the highest order is needed here.[1]

Lunacharsky

Whoever is acquainted with the prismatic origin of red will not think it paradoxical if we assert that this color – partly *actu,* partly *potentia* – includes all other colors.[2]

Goethe

 $T$ he occasion of this exhibition and volume of essays ought to be welcome: a collective, interdisciplinary approach from the peripheries of art history to the centripetal question "human rights/human wrongs: art and social change." So we want to be clear about the thematic and the methodological presuppositions underlying our project, especially if we would expose and then activate productively any substantial contradictions that might inform it.

Now, the cumulative historical record of the complex relation of art to progressive social change is by no means unambiguously strong. Indeed, art and, as important, ways of seeing it always have *tended* to serve the ideological interests of ruling classes. Generally true for all artistic media, and by no means always the "fault" of artists themselves, this complicity is particularly the case for the "high art" forms we are concerned with here, namely sculpture and oil painting.

Equally questionable, however, is the proposition that the "avant-

Geoffrey Waite is an Associate Professor in the Department of German and the Program in Comparative Literature.

garde"—represented to us by the American artists Arneson (for the 1980s), Pollock (for the 1940s), and Feininger (for the early twentieth century)—has been more committed to *substantial* social change than have been "traditional," "institutional," or even "mass cultural" kinds of artistic production, against which the cultural "vanguard" perennially reacts. Whatever its function in other societies or historical periods, art under advanced capitalism, especially when it is isolated by artists or viewers from other social and political practices, is at best a "pseudo-revolutionary irritant."[3] Art increasingly has become a displaced, fragmentary, co-opted, and surrogate resolution of those profoundly exploitative modes and relations of production that serve very precisely the basic imperative of capital, which is to produce, if need be at any social cost, the highest possible economic profit. And it is under capital that modern Western art has been created and viewed, including the objects that draw our interest here.

Recall Walter Benjamin's classically laconic thesis: "For the cultural heritage we survey has an origin that we cannot contemplate without horror: it owes its existence not merely to the effort of great geniuses who created it, but to the anonymous toil of their contemporaries. There is not a single artifact of culture that is not simultaneously an artifact of barbarism."[4] The surplus leisure time prerequisite to produce "fine art," and to otherwise try to develop the five human senses to their fullest potential, has been possible only because of horrific divisions: divisions of geographical region (town versus country; nation versus colony; First versus Second and Third World); divisions of gender and race (male versus female; white versus nonwhite); and, in the last instance, divisions of labor itself (mental versus menial), most typically articulated as social classes.

By the same token, however, not only are the producers of art implicated by Benjamin's argument, but also all of us consumers. "And just as no artifact is free of barbarism, so too the process of its reception, by means of which it has been passed on from one recipient to the next, is equally fettered."[5] We should be wary of the overly nihilistic tone of Benjamin's observations, a tone that cries out to be understood in the context of the catastrophic personal and historical moment in which he penned them, not long before his suicide in 1940 in flight from the agents of fascism. Survivors must never foreclose a priori the possibility of progressive artistic productions and reactivations, always in combination with other social practices. But Benjamin's darkly luminous thesis is one significant criterion against which all art and every vision of art must be judged. The leisure time needed to enjoy art is still the function of the divisions of labor that permitted its creation.

We are led by the uncompromising dialectic of production and consumption from thematic to methodological assumptions. The mandate of this symposium is to bring into fruitful intercourse different "humanist disciplines" outside of "traditional" art history and criticism. But all individual academic divisions of labor are effects, *collectively*, of economic divisions of labor that our academic disciplines must sooner sustain than ever call radically into question. If anything, then, Jürgen Habermas understates his persuasive case against the shrinkage of the rational public sphere since the Enlightenment into specialized, institutional discourses when he argues, for example, that "what accrues to culture through specialized treatment and reflection does not immediately and necessarily become the property of everyday praxis."[6] Communal vision is something worth fighting for. To the degree, however, that what is meant by the term "communal" is an aggregate assemblage of "individual" points of view (no matter how "liberal" or "pluralistically" these be expressed, deployed, or united), such superficial community can only serve to replicate a mode of vision blind to the divisive and extractive socioeconomic conditions under which even relatively nonalienated art has been created and enjoyed. This argument should not evoke mere moral indignation against the all-too-easy presumption that we know in advance what "human rights" or "human wrongs" are. There is nothing "wrong," on its own terms, with viewing art generally or "avant-garde" art in particular as having a *necessarily* emancipatory, humanistic impulsion. Nor is there anything "wrong" with assuming that *inter-* (as opposed to *extra-*) disciplinary vision is a necessary or even sufficient response to the human wrongs perpetrated in the long nightmare of history. It would be naive to expect middle-class artists or critics to cut their own (ideological) throats. The thematic and methodological presuppositions of our conference are *precisely* required if middle-class society is to maintain power hegemonically, that is to say, by means of "noncoercive coercion," by means of culture and not always naked force alone. So it would not be "wrong" but *correct* from the bourgeois perspective to view Arneson's *Minuteman* as a cry of protest against "man's inhumanity to man," while being resolutely oblivious to the fact that this imploded head represents a white male impaled on a Christian cross. It is similarly *correct* to be oblivious to the fact that violence committed in defense of socialism is not the same thing as violence perpetrated by imperialist aggression, and oblivious, finally, to the fact that neither Arneson's grotesquely sublime head nor any bourgeois vision of it can do much on its own to prevent someone from walking into the museum, seeing *Minuteman,* and exclaiming: "You see, *that's* how those bastards [whoever they may be] should be treated!" Art history (high and low, premodern, modern, and postmodern) is littered with such responses.[7] And for every paranoid, Cold War, McCarthyite hack who saw in "pinko" Abstract Expressionist paintings like Pollock's *Mural* "actually secret maps of strategic United States fortifications"—and he *did* see them[8]—there are today a dozen clear-headed, well-educated, and very clever CIA administrators and operatives who, against all liberal and not-so-liberal protests to the contrary, still see in American abstract art a quite effective weapon of cultural politics: proof positive to be held up like Medusa's severed head to artists and audiences in exploited, developing nations that the cutting edge of vision lies elsewhere than in "mere representation" or "socialist realism," let alone "Soviet propaganda" to the contrary.[9] But, again, this entire mode of perception and the coterminous refusal to see it *as* visual ideology are not "wrong." On the contrary, they are *exactly correct* for the American bourgeoisie, *more correct still* for transnational capital, as it seeks cultural legitimation while feeding on the carcasses of the workers of the world.

Thus we can have no bone to pick with the discipline of art history (for being, say, "a positivistic stance and a stiltified language intent on preserving its declared boundaries") that we should not have already with most middle-class art and vision. A work of art and its verbal representations, no matter what academic discipline produces them, may share common cause as signs. But signs are themselves contested sites, "arenas of class struggle."[10] We need to develop what John Berger has called "another way of seeing" signs, a way of seeing that sometimes makes appreciative use of other, bourgeois ways of seeing ("interdisciplinary" *or* "disciplinary"), *but* on behalf of a different collective constituency always already excluded from bourgeois modes of perception. We require *potential* and *actual* ways of seeing blobs of pink color *red.*

## II. Leopards in the Louvres

"There are antiquities, drawings, and paintings, all sorts of things. It is most instructive . . . perhaps you are not acquainted with it. Oh, it's something worth seeing, at any rate once. . . ." The severe barrenness of the staircase sobered them, and their feeling of awe was intensified by a haughty attendant in a red waistcoat and gold-braided uniform who was apparently waiting for them on the landing. So they entered the French Gallery respectfully, walking as quietly as they could. Then they went non-stop through the rooms one after the other, their eyes dazzled by all the gold frames, seeing the pictures going past—far too many of them to be taken in properly. To understand them they would have to spend an hour in front of each one. *Sacrédié*, what a lot of pictures, they went on forever! Must be worth a mint of money.[11]

Zola

For most people, the attempt to view and understand art always confronts guards, whether these be real or symbolic. As is the case in our society with "high culture" generally, not everyone has access, in all senses of the word, to an artifact like Lyonel Feininger's painting known as *Pink Sky (Street in Paris)* or *In a Village Near Paris*.[12] Lucy Lippard gives us insight into a first kind of barrier.

Once museums were free, at least. Now, though tax exempt, most have "discretionary admission" fees. Prominently displayed signs "suggest" that you pay at least $1.50 a head. The less comfortable the visitor is in bedraped and bepillared halls, the more likely s/he is to pay the demanded fee than to hand over the penny that is equally legitimate. The richer you are and the more at ease in your society, the less humiliating it is to "play poor." *A Black family in their Sunday best hesitates before the cashier at the Met, reluctantly turns back and leaves, despite the protestations of a concerned middle-class visitor who tries to convince them they can pay a dime.*[13]

I take Lippard's analytic anecdote to suggest that the transparent lucite box (always partially filled with paper currency) near the entrance of the University of Iowa Museum of Art, quite independent of the intention of the staff, necessarily is discriminatory in a society systemically grounded in racial, gender, and class discrimination and exploitation. This lucite box is potent as a *symbolic* obstacle, if not as an imagined reality. Even were a viewer, of whatever class, to pass by without paying tribute on the way into the museum, or rather on the way out, since it is most visible when walking in that direction (folks in the Athens of the Midwest are said to be politer than in the Big Apple), how would s/he be equipped to view the art on display? All of us are more or less "trained" to see though an optic determined by the commodification of aesthetic production and consumption, whether this means the impatient, value-consuming attention span weaned on TV and programmed to wander through museums exactly as it cruises shopping malls, *or* the patient, value-producing techniques of connoisseurship employed by the professional art critic and historian.[14] A commonly overheard snippet of conversation in museums begins with the question "If you could own anything here, what would it be?" But of course few of you could ever afford it, let alone in a social formation in which recession is properly defined as a recurrent condition wherein workers cannot buy back the commodities *they themselves* produce. As for the unemployed, they would be masochistic indeed to go to a museum only to see all those fetishized objects of leisure and surplus value that have risen as sea foam to the surface of civilization from the long undertow of expropriated human history, all those mysterious "perceptible yet imperceptible" commodities in which "a definite social relation between people assumes in their eyes the fantastic form of a relation between things."[15]

Museums and books are institutions overdetermined in their Apollonian power, as are all the institutions maintained by society to teach sight so as to preserve itself in blindness. The drunken, carnivalesque wedding-party hilariously depicted in Émile Zola's *L'Assommoir* broke into the Louvre and momentarily disrupted the massively hegemonic function that museums in the Second Empire had come to represent, ever since a century earlier the French Revolution had liberated art collections to public view. But the cities from which such Dionysiac revelers emerge, and to which eventually they and we must return, remain the same squalid sites of conflict and struggle. Because modernist and postmodernist minimalists are really closet naturalists, Franz Kafka was able to compress Zola's episode into a single, brilliant parable.

> Leopards break into the temple and drink to the dregs what is in the sacrificial pitchers; this is repeated over and over again; finally it can be calculated in advance, and it becomes a part of the ceremony.[16]

The self-serving belief entertained by humanists is that what is needed to combat the grubby institutionalization of art is, well, a humanist education. Thus armed, we catch our private, privatized glimpses of the transcendent, nonalienated reality of art through the glass darkly of the crass, commercialized art world. To see *Pink Sky (Street in Paris)* properly we seek out the most authoritative guide we can find. But upon opening Hans Hess's massive study *Lyonel Feininger* we are confronted with yet another guard. This time it is discursive, hence subtler, but no less real. The *first* sentence reads:

> Like all Americans, Lyonel Feininger was the child of a new country and of a European ancestry at the same time. . . .[17]

And so it goes. At least *some* Americans living under capitalism (in fact, for this and other reasons, *most* of humanity) are never in *any* sense allowed to "see" *Pink Sky* (*Street in Paris*)—one of three artifacts at this colloquium on human rights and human wrongs. [*Pl. 1*]

By means if need be of class betrayal, *some* of us are going to have to try to see with and for significant numbers of other viewers. Resisting co-option as best we can, we Leopards in the Louvres must stand in and intervene for excluded sight.


### III. LOOKING BACK TO 1908–09

The barricades at Villeneuve-Saint-Georges, near Paris, the shooting down of the strikers who built these barricades (on Thursday, July 30 [1908])—these events are renewed evidence of the sharpening of the class struggle in Europe. . . . When the workers were carrying out a wounded comrade past General Virvaire, who directed the operations against the strikers, there were shouts from the demonstrators: *"Saluez!"* And the general of the bourgeois republic saluted his wounded enemy.[18]

Lenin

Those years are the lively childhood of our era. . . .[19]

Shattuck

If you think of the times in which Feininger painted *Pink Sky* (*Street in Paris*) [*Fig. 1*] as part of *La Belle Epoque* or "the banquet years," and hence of a "charmed way of life now lost" (Shattuck, p. 6), you commit an obscenity against the heroic, if as yet rather inchoate, economic and political and social struggles of the working classes and their allies during the complex "interrevolutionary period" in Europe from 1905 to 1917. Lenin put it succinctly: the "immediate task" then was to "dig—even under the most difficult conditions—for ore, to extract iron, and to cast the steel of the Marxist world outlook and of the superstructures corresponding to this world outlook."[20] Our problem today still is to unify analyses of base and superstructure in an emancipatory way. Given the sheer complexity of Western capitalism, this struggle also entails, as a necessary but insufficient condition for emancipation, dialectically fusing socioeconomic interpretations with ways of seeing cultural artifacts. We require, along with ultimately more important activities, a way of seeing such hegemonic transactions whenever we look even at single works of art.

It is certainly possible to see Feininger's *Pink Sky* (*Street in Paris*) as hovering *between* art history and other history. This in any case was the artist's intention. The "street" aspect of the painting was "seen"

*Figure 1. Cedar Rapids Gazette, 8 April 1962. Photo feature by Jane Boller and L. W. Ward.*

(the term is, according to the anti-empirical, quasi-phenomenological theory at hand, only partially right) by Feininger during his intermittent stay in France, particularly in and around Paris from 1906 to late 1908. He then moved back to Germany, where, apparently on two Sundays in a new studio in a suburb of Berlin, he painted *Pink Sky* (*Street in Paris*), dated on the back of the canvas May 23 and June 6, 1909. From the point of view of his theory of painting, he always worked at a specific distance from a bracketed and reduced reality. Phenomenologically speaking, a work like *Pink Sky* (*Street in Paris*) is supposed to be seen as an eidectic image of already mediated apperception.

> I draw quite spontaneously and almost instantaneously whatever interests me; however, never with the intention of making pictures out of these drawings. No, first the irresistible longing for a particular composition must manifest itself in me and *then* sometimes, years later, there may be a painting which for me represents reality as I experienced it—while the "real reality," if

by chance I encounter the same situation again, in contrast to my picture, looks very dreary to me and contaminated with unsympathetic associations. . . . Paintings have to sing, must enrapture, and must not stop at portraying an episode.[21]

The seemingly obligatory scare quotes around "real reality" mark a very deep problem in art, epistemology, and politics. In Feininger's case, the inverted commas contaminate objective reality, even as they would inoculate against objective reality the purity of Feininger's aestheticizing intent and its concomitant desire to affect the viewer in necessarily nonspecific ways. This problematic has less to do with phenomenological or even hermeneutic "openness," however, than with the closure of political ideology. There is never any time like the present to resist being "enraptured" by art at the expense of the other "episodes" of life and struggle. The Parisian or other urban, suburban, and village "street scenes" that mattered back in 1908–09 did not look much like Feininger's even *before* he began his preliminary sketches, sitting at his window. If we want some concrete image of that "scene" we might do worse than imagine a space somewhere between two photographs by the great early photographer Eugène Atget, somewhere between the precisely focused empty cobblestoned streets and the more diffused image of the workers who actually built and maintained them. [*Figs. 2, 3*]

According to a historian of caricature, Feininger's contemporary Georg Hermann Borchardt, Feininger was "the principal Berlin

Figure 2. EUGENE ATGET. *Montmartre,* n.d. Photograph.

Figure 3.
EUGÈNE ATGET.
*Steelworkers*, n.d.
Photograph.

draftsman," a man who "creates political drawings of monumental effect." But, as Borchardt was swift to remark with undisguised satisfaction, Feininger did not "submit" his political cartoons to any one political "tendency."[22] Is it odd that political caricature "without tendency" could be said to have "monumental effect"? What *kind* of effect? The deepest effectivity of bourgeois political cartooning (from Feininger to Oliphant and Garry Trudeau) is to have no *specific* effect at all, to defuse effective *political* radicalism in advance, to obviate it before the fact under the cover of the surrogate "radicalities" of satire, irony, and other "rights of individuals." Perhaps *Pink Sky* (*Street in Paris*) can help us see this contraction and make use of it.

But to move toward that end we need to know more about the specific mnemonic image represented by the painting. Feininger had just begun making his first oil paintings in April 1907. The interesting technical problem he then faced was incorporating caricature and cartoon figures from the "sub-art" genre into the resistant "high art" medium of brush stroke and oil paint. These figures represent a kind of carnivalesque, Rabelaisian intrusion into a hegemonic sphere. While not unprecedented in oil painting, having for example a crucial modern forerunner in Courbet, this general type of intervention marks, on formal terms alone, an exciting moment in modern art.[23] Here an expatriate American artist attempts to push the great tradition of European oil painting forward by "canonizing a junior branch," as the Russian Formalists used to say, namely by "elevating" the allegedly lower, but more popular, form of the cartoon into history's most dominant two-dimensional medium.[24] Yes, *Pink Sky* (*Street in Paris*) is an important and unjustly ignored painting. It is additionally significant in the context of the conjuncture in art history to which it contributes, since it was made at exactly the same time as such seminal modernist works as Picasso's *Demoiselles d'Avignon,* Schönberg's *Second Quartet,* and Worringer's *Abstraction and Empathy.* It is obviously important for Feininger's own career, if for no other reason than that it was one of his earliest oils. The painting is no less significant, however, for its way of representing a specifically *bourgeois* way of seeing and being seen during the period of *trasformismo:* the desertion to the political right begun under pressure from socialism by liberals in the nineteenth century, and still with us today. "Talking left and acting right"[25] is the recurrent and symptomatic condition of the liberal middle-class spirit.

Feininger himself recalled the period when he painted *Pink Sky* (*Street in Paris*) in these terms:

> When I started back in 1907, my first paintings [*sic*] I was but a caricaturist and my intentions regarding oils were vague. . . . My ideal was to build up pictures formed of silhouetted objects. . . . I had seen shooting-gallery figures [*Schiessbudenfiguren*] of cut sheet iron, and painted in a simple array of more or less violent colors, with no modeling.[26]

Less than a year after General Virvaire, under orders from the "Radical" Clemenceau, was shooting down strikers at the barricades, workers vilified by the same bourgeois press for whom Feininger had worked, our American compatriot was still concerned primarily with the formal problem of recycling the shooting-gallery figures we see before our gaze in *Pink Sky* (*Street in Paris*).

Such is the wont of many artists, and it is important to remind ourselves that there is nothing *necessarily* "wrong" with it. The solution of purely technical problems is an absolutely crucial component of any art worth the name. The problem for us is that *if* we are to see "social content" in *Pink Sky* (*Street in Paris*), *then* we must see the painting against the backdrop of an historical period which, although virtually invisible in the work itself, nevertheless serves as what the French Marxist philosopher Louis Althusser might call the "determinate absence" of what *can* be seen on its symptomatic surface. As much as we must respect intentionality up to a point, we have to read the painting also as what Walter Benjamin might have called a "dialectical image," which is to say we have to read it *against* Feininger's explicit, aestheticizing intentions, forcefully *rereading* the figures within the *mise en scène* established by his city, suburban, or village street. Feininger's "shooting-gallery figures" are effects of a *combinatoire,* a larger matrix or cast of characters circulating through his drawings and paintings during this period of his work. The specific figures under the pink sky seem relatively free from overt political encoding. But they are formally (and for the painter politically) interchangeable with figures in similar, even identical "street scenes" that *do* appear to have manifest social content, including references to the degradation of women and depictions of political insurrection. We must, in effect, "see" other artifacts produced by Feininger around *Pink Sky (Street in Paris)* whenever we view it, much as Freud had suggested at the turn of the century (drawing an analogy with Galton's "composite family photographs") that we must view the most "static" and docile dream images as containing condensed, overdetermined, and supercharged protonarratives or (*pace* Feininger) "episodes."[27]

Thus this "street" is populated not only with its manifest figures but with latent uprisings of anarcho-syndicalists and other petty-bourgeois "revisionists from the Left" from the pen-and-ink drawing *Emeute,* 1909 [*Fig. 4*], soon to be translated into oil; or, alternatively, the "same" street contains carnival celebrants as in *Carnival in Arcueil,* 1910; or staid bankers, as in *Fin de séance,* 1909; or workers on their way to or from jobs, as in *Green Bridge,* 1909; or unemployed day laborers, as in *Arbeitslose,* 1910.[28] It is the "same" street in *Pink Sky (Street in Paris)* that will be rearticulated, usually with the human figures evacuated from it, over and over again throughout the later development, from as early as 1912 to the end of his life, of the style Feininger called "prism-ism."[29]

Whatever else you may think of a relatively benign, upper bourgeois aesthete like Feininger, sitting at his window and looking down on the urban "nature" he so mistrusted and even despised, you have to admit that he was true to his intentions. When it came time to convert his "intuitive" sketches into oil, it was at least a *powerfully effective* closed grammar or economy that would generate the individual figures populating pictures like *Pink Sky (Street in Paris)*. It is as if some obscure repetition compulsion always just barely warded off disaster (Painter's Block? Death Itself?) by endlessly reworking the same set of images, even down to seemingly peripheral details, and by allowing only a displaced visual mood of catastrophe to seep through in the form of skewed perspectives, garish cartoon colors, angled stage-set buildings, and displaced persons. The street lamps under this cold, pink sky are not to be confused with the gaslights first introduced into the arcades of nineteenth-century Paris. For Feininger they existed first only in his pen and watercolor illustration for Bret Harte's "A

Ship of '49," as early as 1890, or in the street traversed by the excited citizens in *Alarm! "Bereit sein ist alles!"* of 1903, an image that found reincarnation as late as 1942.[30] Although she is no mere detail, the woman painted full-length with a child in the middle ground of *Pink Sky (Street in Paris)* appeared at least two years earlier in one of Feininger's fashion caricatures and she will reappear as late as 1922, in

*Figure 4.* LYONEL FEININGER. *Emeute,* 1909. Ink. Location unknown.

*Lady in Mauve.*[31] She *may* even be visible in Feininger's depiction of the theme of infanticide, one of the very rare attempts made by Feininger (not to say art history *tout court*) to problematize sexist modes of representation (see *The Manhole,* 1908[32]). In *Pink Sky (Street in Paris)* a central male figure–part of a double self-portrait of Feininger himself–is likewise a displaced image from anterior cartoons and paintings.

Such transcendentally self-referential intertextuality is in itself hardly unusual in cultural history. But the point to be made, again, is that *if* we are asked to look at this painting *on the condition or premise* that we see it in terms of the notion that art "is" an instrument of progressive social change, *then* we have to produce a vision that is not just based on some theme somehow already "in" the painting. We must be prepared to ground our vision in the larger social context in which we view and Feininger painted it, and this includes the necessity of seeing his own collateral works of the same period. Although it lies somewhat outside the scope of this paper, we also would have to consider the works of other contemporary artists, such as Ernst Ludwig Kirchner. The certain apocalyptic tone of Feininger's painting corresponds to, and to some extent may even predate, similar manifestations in other media. So, for instance, the "Expressionist" *Bürgerschreck* lyrics of Georg Heym will follow Feininger's *Pink Sky (Street in Paris)* by a couple of years. Robert Wiene's hugely influential "pseudo-Gothic" movie *Dr. Caligari's Cabinet,* which so reminded the great film historian Siegfried Kracauer of Feininger's early paintings, was not released by Decla until 1919–1920. All artistic media, including Feininger's early cartoons and paintings, helped set a mood of nihilism and apocalypse that became self-fulfilling prophecies: first in the period culminating in the war hysteria of 1914, and then in the antidemocratic cultural despair of Weimar. Nor has this mood vanished today.

Sociological and intertextual interpretation has little to do, however, with any academic "discipline" or "interdiscipline," since it cuts across them all. Such rudimentary and preliminary interpretative moves simply are required, if we are to get any sense of what Feininger's formalistic vision (which seems intentionally and systematically indifferent to historical or social or political specificity) might have to do with our topic of human rights. But the problem at hand is only partially artistic or methodological, and profoundly ideological. While we have no power or desire to legislate what Feininger or anyone else "should" paint, we must be vigilant indeed about modes of vision blind to the full ideological and political implications of artifacts and visual acts. Bourgeois critics for their part are precisely *not* free (whether they should be or not is another question) to see anything they want. Their vision is circumscribed by the interests of their class. Part of our task is to call attention to this specific horizon of freedom. Lenin was right: "This absolute freedom is a bourgeois or an anarchist phrase (since, as a world outlook, anarchism is bourgeois philosophy turned inside out). One cannot live in society and be free from society."[33]

We are continually confronted by the claims of this "absolute freedom." It is demanded by Feininger's anarchistic vision of interchangeable shooting-gallery figures *and* demanded by critics who, in their rush to find relationships between "art and social change" where they simply did and do not exist, will inevitably cut loose *Pink Sky* (*Street in Paris*) from its social and ideological determinations, whether these be on a painting in 1908–09 or on its viewers in 1985–86. Communists salued General Virvaire, but they are not duped by him.


IV. From *Flâneur* to Trucker, and Beyond

The *flâneur* becomes deeply involved with the crowd, only to relegate it to oblivion with a single glance of contempt.[34]

Benjamin

−"Where're we going?"
−"I haven't a clue."
−"Okay, let's hurry!"[35]

Characters in a Feininger cartoon

Keep on truckin' . . . truckin' on down the line.
Old blues line, Blind Boy Fuller and Bull City Red, among others

You're walking. And you don't always realize it,
but you're always falling.
With each step, you fall forward slightly.
And then catch yourself from falling.
Over and over you're falling
and then catching yourself
from falling.
And this is how you can be
walking and falling
at the same time.

Laurie Anderson, *"Big Science,"* 1982

What, then, *is* to be seen in *Pink Sky* (*Street in Paris*)? Many things, undoubtedly, in addition to the traces of a painter's intent in 1909, traces of the rest of his *oeuvre,* and thus traces of otherwise occluded historical referents. At least three forms of "subject" are here at work. First, we see a street scene in a dual relation: to nature, namely denuded trees in a cold season at twilight, and to various human types. This dual relation constitutes the "viewed subject." Second, we see a certain way of painting or showing this scene: the "viewing subject." And we see a way of constructing viewers, the "subjects of vision," who are, however momentarily, "subjected" to look only at what they are shown.[36] At the same time, we have already begun to see that *all* these subjectivities are inscribed by more or less conscious, more or less contradictory, ideological positions. Not exempted is the charge of this conference to see political content in an apolitical intention, to see a message of change in a scene populated by ostensibly interchangeable subjects.

There is a time-honored way of handling such contradictions, and it requires the category of "isolation" or "alienation." Now, you can't tell from the mere *mention* of these terms how someone is going to *use* them. They can conceal class exploitation, or they can reveal it. But we can pretty well predict how "isolation" or "alienation" will be employed by bourgeois critics, and it ultimately will reveal less about artifacts than about these viewers' prejudices and interests. Kept suitably vague (never plunging to the root of economic divisions of labor), alienation can always be "cured," so the broken record goes, by more good will on earth, better education, nicer guys as elected officials, more interdisciplinary ways of seeing. . . . So in 1977 there was an exhibition at the Indiana University Art Museum, *German and Austrian Expressionism, 1900–1920. Pink Sky (Street in Paris)* was, for its early date among other reasons, a prominent star in the show. The catalogue went on (p. 117):

> *Pink Sky* is one of a minority of paintings by Feininger which include people; they are shown as types or characters, rather than as individuals. It has been suggested that a social comment is intended, that the pedestrians rush on purposelessly and seem uneasy in their roles. Although sixteen [note this!] people are present, they are isolated, without interaction. The painting is also about motion, as each figure moves at its respective pace in the limited space.

There seem to be some "mistakes" here. Certainly Feininger's *early* paintings more often contain figures than not; and for some reason *one* of them in this painting has been left uncounted, raising the question: Which one? Nevertheless, this description is useful, since it captures in a nutshell the "common sense" perception of *Pink Sky* (*Street in Paris*) as formal and thematic artifact. An art critic writing in World War II had already given us a similar retrospective interpretation of Feininger's early career as a painter:

> From 1907 to 1912 [Feininger] concentrated all his efforts on the one theme: how the individual responds to forces beyond the individual. He shows how modern man tries to transcend the isolation into which his own overstressed individuality has betrayed him.[37]

Less dependent on tautological psychologizing, Hans Hess describes *Pink Sky* (*Street in Paris*) in terms of its form as "essentially a study in space and speed."[38] By relating the tone of Feininger's early painting to the fantastic works of James Ensor, Hess also seems to suggest that it signifies "a new awareness of the many forms a *persona* can take; it was an enlargement of life beyond the bourgeois establishment. It was a protest against the belief that man is no more than a member of society."[39] This interpretation, too, is crucially muddled to the extent that such *criticism* (Hess's own as well as Feininger's) of bourgeois vision is already an essential *component* of bourgeois vision. "Man," according to this visual ideology, can find "his" true identity only outside society. *That* is what art is for. That's why art has significant exchange value as a "transcendent" inflation hedge. That's also why art can have so much use value as a neatly trimmed hedgerow to block from view the disquieting sights on the other side of the tracks of capital. But how does the formal "speed" of Feininger's painting *Pink Sky* (*Street in Paris*) relate to the semantic "alienation" experienced by bourgeois critics whenever they view it?

First take a short step further back in time. Mid to late nineteenth-century Parisian *flânerie,* as exemplified in art by Charles Baudelaire and as analyzed by Walter Benjamin, was a mode of trackless perambulation and aimless but always stylish movement. It was also a specific way of seeing so as to be seen. *Flânerie* was thus a formally composite gaze, a kind of ceaselessly articulated shot-reverse-shot, as well as an epistemologically perverse culmination (at the threshold of the postmodern, late capitalist condition) of the fundamental aesthetic imperative of Enlightenment: *disinterested interest.* The nineteenth-century *flâneur,* Benjamin mused, once meandered through the commercial arcades of Haussmann's Paris with a turtle on leash, allowing it to prescribe the tempo of his gait.[40] As Benjamin also argued, the *flâneur* had something in his living motion of the internally contradictory form of the commodity. Both were *apparently* self-composed and self-produced "personalities," circulating on their own volition without ulterior aim. For his part, the *flâneur* was a pseudo-artisanal point of atavistic resistance, of relatively (if only briefly) nonalienated labor, cut adrift in the industrial age of Second Empire France. He was a glamorous subjectivity negotiating his way through a spiritless bourgeois collectivity, trying gamely but ineffectually to hold out against forces conceivable always only as "abstract." *Flânerie* was a way of motion and vision designed to perceive imaginary compensations for the dreary workaday reality of capital.[41] The entire bourgeois view of artifacts is not radically different.

*Flânerie* also represents another kind of visual motion, a way of seeing women according to a perversely embedded chauvinist antimony: either women are mothers, or they are whore/angels. "Helen of Troy under every skirt," as Mephisto was pleased to inform Faust.[42] According to Benjamin's no less sardonic formula, "the only sexual communion of the *flâneur* is with a whore. . . . Such an image is the whore: saleswoman and wares in one."[43] This vision, too, is an irreducible part of the bourgeois, male view of women and of art. Traces of this gendered imaginary are discernible in *Pink Sky (Street in Paris)*. The only aura-like, lightly colored figures in the painting are women. Look at the faceless woman with a child, ambivalently hiking up her long, pale dress (out of middle-class fastidiousness or sexual provocation?). Look at the young woman sharper "in focus" in the immediate foreground that extends into the viewer's space—her eyes seem to seek out "our" gaze. But now reflect on the *male* gaze as the objectifying, reifying look of the Other.[44]

Crucial questions of gender coding aside, with *Pink Sky (Street in Paris)* in 1908–09 we are, for other social and historical reasons, a step past nineteenth-century *flânerie*. The *flâneur* was a still rather distant predecessor of our own postmodern "mall rats." His was a stage of perception before electronic media advertising would drastically constrict the human attention span to a minimal, even subliminal point zero. *Pink Sky (Street in Paris)* represents a moment of transition between *flânerie* and the cultural speed of our own time, a step further on down the capitalist line. The symptomatic "motion" of Feininger's painting is no longer that of *flânerie,* but something uncannily closer to home.

According to a critic widely thought to be an authority on such matters, "it has been said of men like Degas and Lautrec that they lived before it became necessary for the artist to be part of the absurdity he described."[45] Whoever said (or dreamed) this knew little about Baudelaire, not to mention many courageous artists in history, nor did he (most likely it was a he) reflect very hard about what the category "absurdity" really boils down to after the existential dross evaporates. But this remark brings us nearer to one problem in Feininger's street, namely the question of just *who* is moving along under this pink sky. For one thing, Feininger himself, not entirely unlike Benjamin's *flâneur,* mixes ambiguously in with the crowd, although necessarily moving now with greater velocity.

*Pink Sky* (*Street in Paris*) can be seen to contain one self-portrait of the artist and even, by a process analogous in two-dimensional art to the early animated French cartoon (or medieval European depictions of the Stations of the Cross, if you prefer), possibly *two* self-portraits, or rather a *dual* one. Feininger's theory of painting entailed the desire "to formulate a *perspective of objects,* quite new, quite my own; I would like to place myself into the picture and there observe the landscape, the objects that are painted."[46] He was one of many artists who have wanted to be absorbed into his own theatricality.[47] He, too, would simultaneously see and be seen, would self-consciously see himself seeing and being seen, would have us see ourselves as himself. The picture frame of *Pink Sky* (*Street in Paris*) thus reasserts the ancient desire of two-dimensional painting (and the newer desire of cinema) to become at once window frame and mirror frame. The *mise en scène* becomes a *mise en abîme,* and vice versa. Gazing into this Mirror of (Bourgeois) Princes, we are alerted to a desire to "frame" us by means of art.

Feininger has been described as "a tall, angular, and boyishly jerky man" and it has been said that his figures "move and act as if animated not only by the spirit but by the body of their maker."[48] The operative notion here presumably would encourage us to see the single male figure walking toward us in his long coat and top hat from the approximate center of *Pink Sky* (*Street in Paris*) as a dark version of Feininger's first self-portrait in oils, *The White Man,* 1907. [*Fig. 5*] He is equally the double of the puppeteer self-portrait for the *Chicago Sunday Times* [*Fig. 1, p. 31*] of 1906, who can manipulate his own creations. In *Pink Sky* (*Street in Paris*), however, the strings leading from the extended fingers either have disappeared or have become invisible functions of the post-*flâneur*'s imaginary (self-) control. Feininger, the argument would continue, also appears in the painting with his face "in focus," now in the form of the repoussoir locking the viewer's gaze in and out of the lower right-hand corner of *Pink Sky* (*Street in Paris*). It is as if "Feininger" has moved up in the meantime, while we were daydream-

Figure 5.
LYONEL FEININGER.
The White Man, 1907.
Oil on canvas.
Estate of the artist.

ing elsewhere. "Feininger" has slipped through the faceless or grotesque crowd *into* signatory "individuality."

The heterogeneous "camera angle" of *Pink Sky* (*Street in Paris*) also
strives to locate the viewer as subject of vision in dual or duplicitous
ways. "We" are looking *down* on the street, as from a window, for example, "to look down on" the young woman in the foreground. Yet at
the same time we see the bottom part of the frame of the street lamp
(the larger one that ambivalently reflects or casts pink light) and a
sharply angled view of the human figures (drastically foreshortened to
the point that they seem almost headless and brainless). So we are also
looking *up* the dizzyingly precipitous street as if from a point
somehow on it. Multiple perspective, even to this point of vertiginous
but relatively horizontal *Verstiegenheit,* is not as such a novelty in art
history. In this modern form it serves, for example, as a desecrating
parody of the vertically elevating, soaringly transcendent visual teleol-
ogy of, say, Masaccio's fresco *The Trinity with the Virgin and St. John.*
[*Fig. 6*] Then, in the Quattrocento, we were thought to translate in
the mind's eye our empirical, bodily selves gradually upwards toward
eventual face-to-face eye contact with God Himself.[49] But this contact
was of course impossible to realize *hic et nunc,* especially not in an era
of history when, not incidentally, a woman's alleged transgression in
Eden was held up as the source of the necessity of menial labor and of

Figure 6.
MASACCIO.
*The Trinity with the
Virgin and St. John,* 1425.
Fresco.
Santa Maria Novella,
Florence.

the social divisions dependent on it. Now, in 1908–09 or 1985–86, we are circulating in more "jerky" and concretely secular modes and relations of production and therefore in the more humanistic visual perspectives ultimately derived from them.

If camera angle in the cinema is "the strongest means of characterization" and, hence, "not reproduction but genuine production,"[50] then this is no less true for the manipulation of point of view desired by the window/mirror frame of Feininger's *Pink Sky (Street in Paris).* Feininger and we are supposed both to watch the crowd and be watched by it, both be part of the crowd and distant from it. It is through exactly this optic that we would-be augurs in the temple of fine art are asked to contemplate the human wrongs of our supposedly forever alienated human condition.

But the middle class has views of crowds, ways of moving in them, and so of relating individuals to each other, which need not be our own, nor certainly that of any authentic communal vision. The 1981 Nobel Prize for Literature was paid to a man who thought that "there is nothing that man fears more than the touch of the unknown. . . . It is only in a crowd that man can become free of this fear of being touched."[51] But what if this "man" is just that, *a man, a male bourgeois?* And we know from historians that real crowds are rarely, if ever, the faceless, mindless, irresponsible mob they *must* appear to be to the class that fears nothing more than the driving motivation of gender or class struggle behind the "rural panic" and "Terror" during the French Revolution, behind the spirit and reality of the Paris Commune of 1871 ("rumor" had it that the Louvre had been burned!), behind the collective actions of women in Barcelona from 1910 to 1918, or behind the storming of the Winter Palace in 1917.[52] *Pink Sky* (*Street in Paris*), through its positing of a multiple point of view and through its self-portraiture of the viewing subject, is nothing if it is not *also* a function of this fundamental aspect of bourgeois visual ideology – this gut fear of crowds, this regurgitating attempt to purge the fear of the gender and class Other aesthetically, whenever it cannot be purged by other means.

This way of seeing or "interpellating" subjectivities has much to do with space, the flickering, heterogeneous space of indeterminate perspective, but also, as even the critics already cited have maintained, with time, motion, speed. According to the "traditional" art historian who has looked most carefully at Feininger's *oeuvre*, the painter's predominantly male figures "stride" with what is called "an inner speed, hitherto unknown in drawing."[53] This may be, but then the bourgeois vision immediately reacts to this imagined speed in order to slow down, contain, and arrest it by converting it into formalist terms as, for instance, a problematic of Futurism. But Feininger's post-*flâneur* figures do not just "stride." Call it truckin', truckin' under a pink sky.

Now, truckin' is a way of standing still, while seemingly moving fast. "–'Where're we going?' – 'I haven't a clue.' – 'OK, let's hurry!' " Virtually all earlier figures in the long history of caricature, including Wilhelm Busch's characters and the Katzenjammer Kids, from whom Feininger's figures learned much, were always going in specific directions, usually with intentional vengeance. But truckin' is the way of going nowhere fast, or rather nowhere fast in style. It, too, is a dominant way of bourgeois art and bourgeois art history. As is inevitably the case with modern art and modern vision when they feel "isolated" and "alienated" from other social practices (most notably from active membership in progressive parties), truckin' is a mode of aimless locomotion in an age of advanced technology. It is in its primary form an amalgam of mechanical and human movement. The *flâneur* was walked by his turtle in the arcades to see and be seen. The trucker must move quicker to negotiate the sordid scandals of more advanced stages of increasingly devolving capital. Critics have often intimated that Feininger's formative experience as a youth growing up in New York City was determined by two supposedly contradictory experiences: the "aristocratic aloofness" of Feininger's class heritage and upbringing, which never left him; and the equally deep impact made on him by "the severer life" of the city.[54] Beyond these typically partial insights lies the sheer mechanical power in the belly of the beast of capital, seemingly so independent of mere human will, and always threatening to intrude suddenly into the sequestered world of art. Under these objective and psychological constraints, the trucker can only try to move with individual style, and perhaps, if s/he has the leisure time to do so, paint or view with individual style. But s/he is always ultimately powerless qua individual.

During the course of his analysis of what early Soviet cinema had rejected and had assimilated from bourgeois modes of perception, Sergei Eisenstein came to recall his visit to the financial district of New York City. He placed his finger near the pulse of truckin' when he juxtaposed the "maelstrom" of the stock market to the traffic on the streets outside.

> As you make your merely minute progress amidst a tightly packed glacier of other humans, sitting in similarly high-powered and imperceptibly moving machines, you have plenty of time to ponder the duality behind the dynamic face of America, and the profound interdependence of this duality in everybody and everything American.[55]

The actual speed of Wall Street ticker tape contrasts dialectically with the unusable speed of American cars, and so reveals the value of such commodities to be primarily in exchange, not use. The ticker tape, the cars, and the drivers all seem to move somewhere, seem to be indices of progress, seem to bring a better life for the subjects of capital. And while you can take the American boy out of this capital, you can't likely take American capital out of the boy. So the pedestrians truckin' under the pink sky of the French street in our expatriate Feininger's German painting *replace* automobiles. These reified beings in *Pink Sky* (*Street in Paris*) negotiate their imaginary space either grotesquely or in style, but in either case with passing little emancipatory impulse.

Feininger had brought his figures, including his own self-portrait, into his oil painting from his "political" cartoons. Eventually these figures were to be almost wholly absorbed by the "higher" genre, elided by an increasingly abstract "prism-ism." But we catch up with these truckers later on down the line, "back in the USA," in the cartoon medium from which they had struggled in 1908–09 to free themselves. They resurfaced in Robert Crumb's work for *Zap* and other comic books, as part of Crumb's attempt in the late 1960s and early 1970s to capture the underground conscience of America. [*Fig.* 7] Today, as

*Figure 7.* ROBERT CRUMB. "Keep on Truckin' . . . ," from *Love to Ten—An Anthology of Robert Crumb in Zap Comics.* (Edinburgh: Reallusion, n.d.), n.p.

part of the postmodern cultural pastiche of the 1980s, they necessarily reappear—again in comic books but now also on mudflaps and bumper stickers distributed by the deeply troubled U. S. automobile and truck industries to real truckers ("Keep on Truckin'!"), most of whom have as soon heard of L. Feininger as of R. Crumb. Crumb's original figures always moved precariously close to the edge of sexism, racism, and sado-masochism—when they were not more or less willingly leaping into these abysses. They truck'd through and past the one uniquely political moment in recent American history with their profoundly apolitical message of proto-postmodern despair. The subsequent trajectory of this specific cultural motion has tended toward an increasingly familiar ideological position from which you can't tell whether *criticism* of despair is not itself the ultimate form *of* despair: Capitalism, communism, individuals, collectivities . . . , as Archie Bunker and Paul de Man and Jacques Derrida and Laurie Anderson and all the other Talking Heads say: What's the difference? [*Fig. 8*]

And so it has come to pass that a visual ideology always already *potentially* contained within Feininger's gentle, upper-middle-class vision has become *actual*. The possibility for bourgeois art, *or anything else bourgeois,* to become related to social change in progressive ways has evaporated in the "viscid, malodorous, asphyxiating gas of anti-proletarian culture." It has degenerated into the middle-class/professional-managerial class fantasies of a baby-boom culture trapped in the ceaseless walking-while-falling "dialectic of colonization and privatization."[56] It has become impacted in the mire of liberal humanist confusions and self-legitimations with regard to the actual sources of human wrongs and human rights.

When he wasn't strutting about in the late 1960s reveling in sexism and touting the infantile disorders of the "Street Fightin' Man," Mick Jagger (Crumb's rough equivalent in rock music), wanted "every red door painted black." Can we still see red? Not, certainly, if we see as connoisseur-*flâneurs* or "counter-"cultural truckers or postmodern yuppies. Not, that is, if we remain middle-class individuals *alone*.


## V. Seeing Red

I spend one or two hours daily in making notes of all sorts of passers-by on the street from our windows. . . . It is of greatest value to me. . . . I don't think it can possibly make much difference what I am, as I know as good as nothing

*Figure 8.* ROBERT CRUMB. "The Workaday World Must Go On . . . ," from *Plunge into the Depths of Despair* (Berkeley: Last Gasp, 1983), n.p.

about politics, and I do not vote either, though I hope to become a staunch
American citizen before long.[57]

Feininger

This woman whom I see coming toward me, this man who is passing by in the
street, this beggar whom I hear calling before my window, all are for me objects—of that there is no doubt.[58]

Sartre

I am a partisan, I live, I feel pulsating already in the virile consciousness of
those on my side the activity of the future city that my side is building. And in
it the social chain does not weigh on the few. In it what happens is not due to
chance or fate, but to the intelligent work of citizens. No one in it sits by the
window looking, while the few shed their blood in sacrifice. . . . I live, I am a
partisan. This is why I hate those who do not take sides, I hate those who are
indifferent.[59]

Gramsci

At least *one* figure in that staunch American citizen Lyonel Feininger's window-sized *Pink Sky* (*Street in Paris*) is turned momentarily
away from the dominant perspective insisted upon by the multiple
subject of this framed artifact. Most notably he is the seventeenth,
*parergonal* figure passed over by critics who can only count to sixteen
(not to say 1916): the proletarian with the rucksack and cap looking
toward his and our right. *He* stands in for *us*, glancing as he does away
from the mutually imbricated, narcissistic, shot-reverse-shot system
of bourgeois vision. He decentralizes this vision and its visual field so
as to undermine the centralization which the "existential" middle-
class viewing subject, as perceiver, simultaneously effects.[60] We can't
see what he sees, this one significant countervailing force of vision in
the picture. Does he look through a house window or into a shop?
Into a doorway at a snarling dog, or a friend? We are not supposed to
know and perhaps not even to ask. Maybe he is reading some sort of
propaganda on a poster, even a leftist one. Whatever he is doing, this
seemingly marginal figure and these seemingly marginal possibilities
are just what is at stake in this now dialectical image of *Pink Sky* (*Street
in Paris*) and in our symposium. Feininger did not show us the man's
face, even though he stands in that part of the "depth of field" in the
painting where faces are relatively distinct and personalized.

Communists *know* what the man looks like. His is not the face of a
single individual. Or rather his is, and at the same time is more. But
we have to look for it after the year 1917, as in a photograph taken by
Viktor Bulla of workers of the Putilov tractor factory at a meeting for

the reelections of the Petrograd Soviet in the terribly difficult year of 1920, when every available force of Western capital was marshalled against the first great working-class revolution. [*Fig. 9*] Here each person's face, man and woman, within the extraordinary depth of field is in focus (although, as some blurred faces attest, no one has been compelled to remain at attention). Each person stands, and is to be seen, as an *individual*; and as a self-conscious, *particular* member of his and her class; and, in however preliminary a form, as a class-conscious part of *universal* humanity.[61] The slogans written by the workers testify to concerns that are painfully modest and audaciously powerful. Dialectically, these slogans are local and international:

> To repair an engine is to get to the root of poverty and thus defeat capitalism once and for all.
>
> Long live the feast of the universal armies of workers!

Truckin' or otherwise moving through our museums and catalogues past the work of Arneson, Pollock, and Feininger, we learn to see *this* red.

*Figure 9.* VIKTOR BULLA. *Workers of the Putilov Factory at a Meeting for the Reelections of the Petrograd Soviet,* 27 June 1920. Photograph.

# NOTES

1  A. V. Lunacharsky, "Lenin on Culture" [1930], in the Supplement to V. I. Lenin, *On Culture and Cultural Revolution* (Moscow: Progress Publishers, 1970), 260. Translation slightly modified; see *Pravda*, 21 January 1930.

2  Johann Wolfgang von Goethe, *Theory of Colours* [1808], trans. Charles Lock Eastlake (London: John Murray, 1840), 313–14. Translation slightly modified; see Goethe, *Zur Farbenlehre*, in *Goethes Werke, Hamburger Ausgabe in 14 Bänden*, vol. 13, ed. Dorothea Kuhn and Rike Wankmüller (Hamburg: Christian Wegner Verlag, 1955), 499.

3  Yuri Barabash, *Aesthetics and Poetics* (Moscow: Progress Publishers, 1977), 71–72. My essay will proceed in agreement with the argument of another leading Soviet scholar. "Broad generalized concepts like 'mass' culture and its pseudo-antagonist 'elitist' culture, which are used by capitalist propaganda, bear an immense ideological load and embrace key areas of bourgeois cultural life. At the same time (and this is very important), they stand in direct relation not just to the 'shopwindow' of bourgeois cultural life (which in itself reveals much) but also to its 'inner sanctum'—to its underlying philosophical and theoretical conceptions." See Alexander Kukarkin, *The Passing Age: The Ideology and Culture of the Late Bourgeois Epoch*, trans. Keith Hammond (Moscow: Progress Publishers, 1979), 82.

4  Walter Benjamin, "Theses on the Philosophy of History" [1940], in his *Illuminations*, ed. Hannah Arendt, trans. Harry Zohn (New York: Schocken Books, 1969), 256. Translation slightly modified; see "Über den Begriff der Geschichte," in his *Gesammelte Schriften*, ed. Rolf Tiedemann and Hermann Schweppenhäuser (Frankfurt am Main: Suhrkamp Verlag, 1980), vol. 1, no. 2, 696.

5  Benjamin, *Illuminations*, 256–57; *Gesammelte Schriften*, vol. 1, no. 2, 696–97.

6  Jürgen Habermas, "Modernity–An Incomplete Project" [1980], reprinted in *The Anti-Aesthetic: Essays on Postmodern Culture*, ed. Hal Foster (Port Townsend, Washington: Bay Press, 1983), 9.

7  Two examples will have to suffice, although such forceful "misreadings" could be illustrated equally well by taking, say, the reception of Picasso's *Guernica* (1937), or the heresy trial of Paolo Veronese in 1533, or the response during the German Peasant Wars of 1525–26 of authorities to Tilman Riemenschneider's altars, not to mention to the artist himself. Not long ago, a Peruvian Indian artist by the name of Quintanilla stopped painting explicitly political works. One of the wealthiest landowners near Lima had purchased one of Quintanilla's huge canvases depicting a mounted landowner whipping a group of terrified peasants. After paying the artist, the buyer said, without a trace of irony, "Now there's a painting that shows how Indians should be treated!" (Cited in Gerald Gassiot-Talabot, "Is Confrontation Possible?" in *Art and Confrontation: The Arts in an Age of Change*, trans. Nigel Foxell [Greenwich, Connecticut: New York Graphic Society, 1968], 95.) Similarly, there may have been little one could do in the 1920s to prevent an Australian artist, art critic, and fascist, Blamire Young, from demanding that Goya's representations of inhumanity be placed in every classroom in his country so that little children would be "steeled" for the "inspired and magnificent brutality" necessary to "reinvigorate" an "enervated world." See Young, *"Los Proverbios," Examined and Now for the First Time Explained* (London: Jonathan Cape, 1923), Dedication. But it was possible then and necessary today to prevent fascists from *existing* in the first place, and so from *having* such a vision or from realizing it.

8  William Hauptman, "The Suppression of Art in the McCarthy Decade," *Artforum* (October 1973), 50.

9  See Eva Cockroft, "Abstract Expressionism: Weapon of the Cold War," *Artforum* (June 1974), 39–41.

10  V. N. Vološinov, *Marxism and the Philosophy of Language*, trans. Ladislav Matejka and I. R. Titunik (New York and London: Seminar Press, 1973), 23.

11  Émile Zola, *L'Assommoir* [1877], trans. Leonard Tancock (Harmondsworth: Penguin, 1970), 86, 88–89. Translation slightly modified; see Zola, *L'Assommoir*, in his *Oeuvres complètes*, ed. Henri Mitterand (Paris: Cercle du livre précieux, 1967), vol. 3, 655, 658.

12  There is some mild controversy over the title of the work in question and it is not known what title (if any) Feininger himself had in mind (even though the stretcher is precisely dated "Sund[ay]. May 23 [19]09 Sund[ay]. June 6 [19]09"). In spite of the facts that the earliest known American reference to the painting (by Charlotte Teller in *The International Studio* 63: 249 [Nov. 1917], xxv–xxx) calls it *In a Village Near Paris* and that Teller herself had visited Feininger's studio, I do not yet regard this title as authoritative. It does not appear in the body of Teller's essay, which does not discuss the painting explicitly, but only in the form of an unsubstantiated caption. We would need to research more fully the German art journals and other sources in which Feininger's early exhibitions were mentioned. In any case, many of Feininger's other early works depict similar street scenes that are explicitly Parisian. The designation "village near Paris" could easily signify Montmartre – to my mind the likely "source" of the image, although we must remember that Feininger rarely painted "from nature," not even always during the period of his earliest oils. In any case, the question is ultimately moot for my purposes: the sky is pink and I will refer to the painting according to its "popular" title.

13  Lucy Lippard, "This Is Art?: The Alienation of the Avant-Garde from the Audience" [1977], in her *Get the Message?: A Decade of Art for Social Change* (New York: E. P. Dutton, 1984), 77.

14  See the historian Carlo Ginzburg's important discussion of the social and ideological determinations on the techniques of connoisseurship developed by Giovanni Morelli: "Clues: Roots of a Scientific Paradigm," *Theory and Society* 7 (1979), 273–88.

15  Karl Marx, *Capital: A Critique of Political Economy* [1867], ed. Frederick Engels, trans. Samuel Moore and Edward Aveling (New York: International Publishers, 1977), vol. 1, 72. Translation slightly modified; see Marx, *Das Kapital: Kritik der politischen Ökonomie* (Berlin, German Democratic Republic: Dietz Verlag, 1947), vol. 1, 86.

16  Franz Kafka, "Leopards in the Temple," trans. Ernst Kaiser and Eithne Wilkins, in Kafka, *Parables and Paradoxes, in German and English* (New York: Schocken Books, 1975), 93.

17  Hans Hess, *Lyonel Feininger* (New York: Harry N. Abrams, no date [1960/1961]), 1. Hereafter cited as Hess, *LF*, with appropriate page numbers.

18  V. I. Lenin, "Inflammable Material in World Politics" [1908], in his *Collected Works* (Moscow: Progress Publishers, 1973), vol. 15, 185. Hereafter cited as *CW* with appropriate volume and page numbers.

19  Roger Shattuck, *The Banquet Years: The Origins of the Avant-Garde in France, 1885 to World War I*, rev. ed. (New York: Vintage Books, 1968), 3.

20  Lenin, "Heroes of 'Reservation' " [1910], in his *CW*, vol. 16, 373. For a relevant overview of this period of European history, see *The International Working-Class Movement: Problems of History and Theory*, ed. B. N. Ponomarev, trans. Vladimir Yeryomin, 7 vols. (Moscow: Progress Publishers, 1983–), esp. vol. 3, 212–50, 275–97, 298–306, 316–26, 347–54. The currently much-discussed topic of the relationship between the "cultural" and the "political" avant-

garde (I am thinking of the work of Western Marxist theorists such as Peter Bürger, among others) ought to be inextricably linked to this kind of *economic and social history.* "It is true that at first the representatives of bohemia (the then *avant-garde*) demonstratively declared their indifference to politics. However, had revolutionary ideas not been in the air bohemia would not have been in a position to create its conception of the 'bourgeois' and to define its nonconformist attitude toward this conception. Without the inspiring support of revolutionary political thinking bohemians would simply have had no basis for asserting their role as opponents of existing social standards: especially inasmuch as considerable courage was required for this, since the rejection by the *avant-garde* of bourgeois standards simultaneously implied rejection of the capitalist market, which had taken the place of aristocratic patronage for writers and artists. At first glance this would seem to have meant ostracism and death from starvation in a garret. But only at first glance: the *avant-garde* phenomenon remained a part of bourgeois society because it needed its money. Its 'split' from society was characterized by confrontation not only with the bourgeois but also with the revolutionary scientific outlook on the world." See Kukarkin, *The Passing Age*, 96–97.

21  Feininger to Alfred Kubin, 21 January 1913. Cited by June L. Ness in her Introduction to *Lyonel Feininger*, ed. Ness (New York and Washington: Praeger Publishers, 1974), 15–16.

22  Georg Hermann [pseud. for Georg Hermann Borchardt], *Die deutsche Karikatur im 19. Jahrhundert* (Bielefeld and Leipzig: Verlag von Velhagen & Klasing, 1901; Sammlung illustrierter Monographien, vol. 2), 127. Borchardt goes on to chide Feininger for his "Yankee-ism, snobbism, and burlesque exaggeration."

23  Compare T. J. Clark's discussion of Courbet's *Burial at Ornans* (1849–1850). "The critics did not object to the exploitation of popular art; on the contrary, it was already accepted as a source of imagery and inspiration, as the way to revive the exhausted forms of 'high art.' But to adopt the procedures and even the values of popular art—that was profoundly subversive. Instead of exploiting popular art to revive official culture and titillate its special, isolated audience, Courbet did the exact opposite. He exploited high art—its techniques, its size, and something of its sophistication—in order to revive popular art. His painting was addressed not to the connoisseur, but to a different, hidden public; it stayed close to the pictorial forms and types of comedy which were basic to popular tradition; it transformed its sources, but only in order to enforce their supremacy; not, certainly, to excuse their shortcomings. He made an art which claimed, by its scale and its proud title of 'History Painting,' a kind of hegemony over the culture of the dominant classes. Needless to say this was a utopian claim. His art, like any other, would in the end be assimilated. But for the moment, for a few years, the attempt troubled the public it excluded." Clark, *Image of the People: Gustave Courbet and the 1848 Revolution* (London: Thames and Hudson, 1973), 139–40. I leave over to the reader the task of judging Feininger's painting in this theoretical and historical context. For what it is worth, my own view is that Feininger's entire enterprise—as it developed from his earliest paintings on—must be seen in terms of the collapse of the attempt he made in the first decade of the twentieth century to create a counter-hegemonic (formal) intervention into the medium of oil painting. His concerns were ultimately too exclusively formalistic to achieve any real breakthrough in this regard. The *success* of *Pink Sky* (*Street in Paris*) resides in the fact that it already so early and so precisely shows the contradictory tensions of this eventual and symptomatic *failure.*

24  This partial (because internal) notion of the progress or process of art history as a dialectical movement by means of which "higher" and "lower" forms and media interact is extrapolated from Viktor Skholvsky's "law of literary history" and Mikhail Bakhtin's theory of literary "carnivalization." For a succinct and critical discussion of both topics, see Tony Bennett, *Formalism and Marxism* (London and New York: Methuen, 1979).

25  See Norman Stone, *Europe Transformed, 1878–1919* (Cambridge, Massachusetts: Harvard University Press, 1984), 45. On France, see 271–303; on Germany, 159–97.

26  Feininger to his son Lux, 2 July 1946. Cited in Hess, *LF*, 42–43.

27  See Sigmund Freud, *Die Traumdeutung* [1899/1900] (Frankfurt am Main: S. Fischer Verlag, 1977), 246–47 (Part 6, Chapter A, Section 3).

28  For illustrations of all these works, see Hess, *LF*, 45, 175 (two versions of *Emeute*); 253 (*Carnival*); 252 (*Fin de séance*); 252 (*Green Bridge*); and 46 (*Arbeitslose*).

29  For illustrations of similar streets in later paintings, see Hess, *LF*, 25–300. Feininger himself explicitly rejected the term "Cubism" as applicable to his work, coining the appropriate neologism "prism-ism" for it, although apparently only once using this designation. See his letter to Alfred Vance Churchill, 13 March 1913. Cited in Hess, *LF*, 56. Hess's general (and, as far as it goes, accurate) thesis with regard to Feininger's early *style* of painting is that the artist was attempting to achieve a kind of synthesis of Cubism and Futurism. "The interpenetration of events is a Futurist discovery, the revelation of simultaneous view is a Cubist discovery, and the *summary presentation of the sequence of events* is Feininger's contribution. All three have in common the inclusion of the time sequence in the pictorial event." Hess, *LF*, 53; emphases added.

30  For an illustration of an early version of the lamp, see the splendid catalogue by Ulrich Luckhardt, *Lyonel Feininger: Karikaturen, Comic strips, Illustrationen* (Hamburg: Museum für Kunst und Gewerbe, 1981), Fig. 47. For *Alarm*, see Hess *LF*, 289.

31  For these illustrations, see Hess, *LF*, 36, 95, respectively.

32  For an illustration of this important and disturbing painting, see Hess, *LF*, 49. I am currently working on an interpretation of it according to the criteria suggested in this essay.

33  Lenin, "Party Organization and Party Literature" [1905], in his *CW*, vol. 10, 48.

34  Benjamin, "On Some Motifs in Baudelaire" [1939], in his *Charles Baudelaire: A Lyric Poet in the Era of High Capitalism*, trans. Harry Zohn (London: NLB, 1973), 128. Translation slightly modified; see Benjamin, "Über einige Motive bei Baudelaire," in his *Illuminationen: Ausgewählte Schriften*, ed. Siegfried Unseld (Frankfurt am Main: Suhrkamp Verlag, 1980), 204.

35  "'Où allons-nous?' 'Je n'en sais rien.' 'Alors pressons.'" This is the caption to *Exactitude*, 1907. See Hess, *LF*, 37, 38.

36  I have adopted these three categories of subjectivity, here applied to a two-dimensional object, from the semiotic system of Émile Benveniste, *Problems in General Linguistics*, trans. Mary Elisabeth Meek (Coral Gables: University of Miami Press, 1971). For an introductory application of Benveniste's discourse analysis to literary and cinematic texts, see Kaja Silverman, *The Subject of Semiotics* (New York and Oxford: Oxford University Press, 1983), esp. 43–53, 194–201. For a more critical analysis, see Collin MacCabe, "On Discourse" [1976/1978], in his *Tracking the Signifier, Theoretical Essays: Film, Linguistics, Literature* (Minneapolis: University of Minnesota Press, 1985), 82–112, esp. 83–92.

37  Alois J. Schardt, "Lyonel Feininger," in the exhibition catalogue *Lyonel Feininger–Marsden Hartley*, ed. Dorothy C. Miller and Hudson D. Walker (New York: The Museum of Modern Art, 1944), 15.

38  Hess, *LF*, 47.

39  Hess, *LF*, 48.

40 Benjamin, "The Paris of the Second Empire in Baudelaire" [1938], in his *Charles Baudelaire*, 54; "Das Paris des Second Empire bei Baudelaire," in his *Gesammelte Schriften*, vol. 1, no. 2, 556–57.

41 Benjamin, *Charles Baudelaire*, 35–66; *Gesammelte Schriften*, vol. 1, no. 2, 537–69.

42 Goethe, *Faust* ("Hexenküche," 1. 2604), in *Goethes Werke, Hamburger Ausgabe in 14 Bänden*, vol. 3, ed. Erich Trunz (Hamburg: Christian Wegner Verlag, 1963), 84.

43 Benjamin, "Paris–The Capital of the Nineteenth Century" [1935], in *Charles Baudelaire*, 171. Translation slightly modified; see Benjamin, "Paris, die Hauptstadt des XIX. Jahrhunderts," in his *Illuminationen*, 179–80.

44 See Simone de Beauvoir, *The Second Sex* [1949], trans. H. M. Parshley (New York: Vintage Books, 1974), 259–60. I am indebted to Genevieve Lloyd's remarkable discussion of de Beauvoir's extension of Hegel's master-slave dialectic to describe gender relations. See "Masters, Slaves and Others," reprinted in *Radical Philosophy Reader*, ed. Roy Edgley and Richard Osborne (London: Verso, 1985), 291–309. Compare further Catharine A. MacKinnon's significant, if I think ultimately overstated, gloss on de Beauvoir's thesis of male representation: *"Power to create the world from one's point of view is power in its male form.* The male epistemological stance, which corresponds to the world it creates, is objectivity: the ostensibly noninvolved stance, the view from a distance and from no particular perspective, apparently transparent to its reality. It does not comprehend its own perspectivity, does not recognize what it sees as subject like itself, or that the way it apprehends its world is a form of its subjugation and presupposes it. The objectively knowable is object. Woman through male eyes is sex object, that by which man knows himself at once as man and as subject." See MacKinnon, "Feminism, Marxism, Method, and the State: An Agenda for Theory," in *Feminist Theory: A Critique of Ideology*, ed. Nannerl O. Keohane, Michelle Z. Rosaldo, and Barbara C. Gelphi (Chicago and London: University of Chicago Press, 1982), 23–24.

45 Shattuck, *The Banquet Years*, 27.

46 Feininger, in his autobiographical essay for *Les Tendances nouvelles*. Cited by Hess, *LF*, 55.

47 I take the terms "theatricality" and "absorption" from Michael Fried, *Absorption and Theatricality: Painting and Beholder in the Age of Diderot* (Berkeley, Los Angeles, London: University of California Press, 1980).

48 Hess, *LF*, 31. Hess's book lacks a theoretical model for grasping the implications of Feininger's insertion of himself into his paintings. This deficiency leads to a very instructive contradiction. On the one hand, Hess argues for a hermetically sealed quality of Feininger's work: "It is as if [Feininger] . . . had created a world of fantasy to be inhabited by himself. He has no intention of taking us into this world and we remain the spectators: there is no entry into it. It is so personal that it defies any attempt to take part in the game." Hess, *LF*, 31. On the other hand, when later discussing the same problem of self-representation in another painting, Hess claims that "the painter forces one to take his own view and makes the traditional comfortable role of the spectator impossible." Hess, *LF*, 47. Now, it is not fortuitous that throughout his study Hess pays lip service to the term "dialectics." He even makes a rather shamefaced "allusion" to Marx's thesis that "mankind always sets itself only such tasks as it can solve" (most explicitly stated in the 1859 Preface to *A Contribution to the Critique of Political Economy*). Hess's version is that "art, like society, only sets itself the problems that it can solve at any given state of development." Hess, *LF*, 53. If Hess's vision is incapable of solving the hermeneutic problems *it* sets itself, this is not in spite of, but just *because* of the fact that his book on Feininger remains the authoritative *bourgeois* treatment of the subject–for the contradiction that art and artists are solipsistically isolated and yet somehow socially accessible is a constitutive feature of middle-class aesthetic judgment.

49  Compare this interpretation of Masaccio's fresco with John White, *The Birth of Pictorial Space* [1957] (London: Faber & Faber, 1977), 138–40, and 196–97. Further see Michael Baxandall, *Painting and Experience in Fifteenth Century Italy* (Oxford: Oxford University Press, 1972), 118–28, and Norman Bryson, *Vision and Painting: The Logic of the Gaze* (New Haven and London: Yale University Press, 1983), 107–110.

50  Béla Balázs, *Theory of the Film: Character and Growth of a New Art*, trans. Edith Bone (London: Dennis Dobson, 1952), 47.

51  Elias Canetti, *Crowds and Power* [1960], trans. Carol Stewart (New York: Farrar, Straus & Giroux, 1973), 15–16. Canetti's attempt to construct historical and national prototypes of crowds is exceedingly subjective, rapidly degenerating into impressionistic stereotypes. See, on France, 173–74 and, on Germany, 179–83.

52  I am thinking in particular of Georges Lefebvre, *The Great Fear of 1789: Rural Panic in Revolutionary France* [1970], trans. Joan White (New York: Pantheon Books, 1973), and the work of George Rudé, esp. *Ideology and Popular Protest* (New York: Pantheon Books, 1980). Also Temma Kaplan, "Female Consciousness and Collective Action: The Case of Barcelona, 1910–1918," reprinted in *Feminist Theory: A Critique of Ideology*, 55–76.

53  Hess, *LF*, 37.

54  Compare, for instance, Hess, *LF*, 1–2; Schardt, "Lyonel Feininger," 7–8; and Ernst Scheyer, *Lyonel Feininger: Caricature and Fantasy* (Detroit: Wayne State University Press, 1964), 5–6. It would be futile of course to seek a single literary "source" for such deeply ingrained consensus views.

55  Sergei Eisenstein, "Dickens, Griffith, and the Film Today" [1944], in his *Film Form: Essays in Film Theory*, ed. and trans. Jay Leyda (San Diego, New York, London: Harcourt Brace Jovanovich, 1977), 196.

56  See Fred Pfeil, "Makin' Flippy-Floppy: Postmodernism and the Baby-Boom PMC," *The Year Left: An American Socialist Yearbook*, 1 (1985), 278. This interesting essay linking postmodern cultural politics to the PMC (the professional-managerial "class" of the baby-boom generation) is a rather uneven response to Fredric Jameson's important article "Postmodernism, or the Cultural Logic of Late Capitalism," *New Left Review*, 146 (July/August 1984), 53–92.

57  I have combined two early letters. See Feininger to H. Francis Kortheuer, 6 December 1894, cited by Scheyer, *Lyonel Feininger*, 69; and Feininger to Alfred Vance Churchill, 24 June 1893, cited by Hess, *LF*, 11. We have no evidence that Feininger's position in this regard ever substantially changed, even during the years when he was doing political cartoons or, certainly, thereafter.

58  Jean-Paul Sartre, *Being and Nothingness: A Phenomenological Essay on Ontology* [1943], trans. Hazel E. Barnes (New York: Washington Square Press, 1966), 340.

59  Antonio Gramsci, "Indifferents" [1917], in *History, Philosophy and Culture in the Young Gramsci*, ed. Pedro Calvacanti and Paul Piccone, trans. Pierluigi Molajoni, et al. (Saint Louis: Telos Press, 1975), 65–66.

60  This sentence is written in critical response to Sartre's existentialist analysis of the "Look of the Other." The "Look" arguably informs (if in unacknowledged ways) the theory and practice of bourgeois vision. Compare Sartre, *Being and Nothingness*, 340–400, specifically p. 343.

61  The crucial categories "individuality," "particularity," and "universality," used here to analyze a two-dimensional object, are bowdlerized from the Hegelian "Doctrine of Notions." Compare *Hegel's Science of Logic*, trans. A. V. Miller (London: George Allen & Unwin, 1969),

600–22, and *Hegel's Logic: Being Part One of the "Encyclopedia of the Philosophical Sciences"* *(1830)*, trans. William Wallace, rev. ed. (Oxford: At the Clarendon Press, 1975), 226–30. The specifically historical-materialist inflection on my application of these categories has its immediate source in Lenin's reading (in 1914–1915) of Hegel. See Lenin, "Philosophical Notebooks," in his *CW*, vol. 38, esp. 85–243, 317–20, 354–63.

# JACKSON POLLOCK

American, 1912-1956

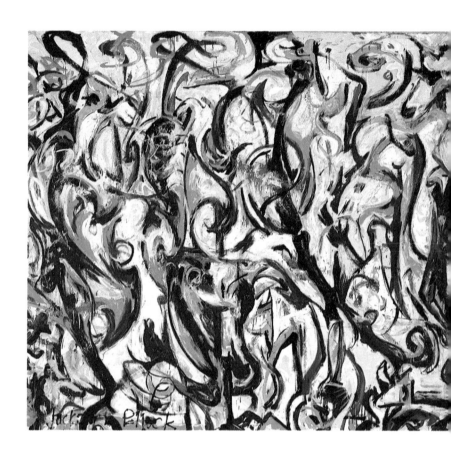

Plate 2

*Mural*, 1943
Oil on canvas
19 ft. 10 in. x 8 ft. 1¼ in.
(604.9 x 247.3 cm.)
University of Iowa Museum of Art
*Gift of Peggy Guggenheim*

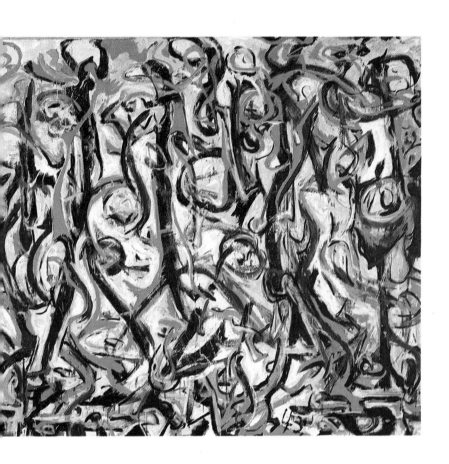

# POLLOCK'S *MURAL*

RUDOLF E. KUENZLI

Jackson Pollock's *Mural* is by far the most prominently displayed art-work at the Museum of Art of The University of Iowa. Measuring eight by twenty feet, it takes up an entire wall of the centrally located Sculpture Court. Its monumental size, its colors, and its rhythmical lines impose themselves on any visitor to the museum. Pollock spe-cialized in large-scale works, and this is his largest painting. Since my first visits to the museum, this painting has fascinated me and has left me with more questions than answers. Its stubborn resistance to my attempts at conceptualizing its meaning has prompted me to read what seems to be an endless number of studies on Pollock. I have found analyses of even the most insignificant drawings in Pollock's notebooks, but to my astonishment only a few brief and rather ob-scure references to *Mural*.[1] None of the Pollock scholars seems to have seen this work. Its size has made it impossible for the museum to lend it to every major Pollock exhibition. Ironically, Pollock's largest work has remained obscure because of its size and because of its geo-graphic location. Were it permanently exhibited in the Museum of Modern Art in New York, critics would soon recognize *Mural* as one of Pollock's most important works. How did this painting ever come to The University of Iowa – and at a time when the university had no art museum?

## *Mural's* LIFE

Peggy Guggenheim, who lived in Europe between 1920 and 1941, re-turned to New York with a group of French Surrealists shortly after

Rudolf E. Kuenzli is a Professor in the Department of English and the Program in Comparative Literature.

the Nazis' occupation of Paris. Her house at 155 East Sixty-first Street became a meeting place for the European Surrealists and young American artists. André Breton and his wife, Marcel Duchamp, Yves Tanguy, Kay Sage, Nicolas Calas, Gordon Onslow-Ford, Kurt Seligmann, Stanley William Hayter, Max Ernst, and Matta gathered there with Alfred Barr, James Johnson Sweeney, Leo Castelli, Julian Levy, and Pierre Matisse, who represented the museum and gallery world, and with the young American artists Robert Motherwell, William Baziotes, David and Suzy Hare, Arshile Gorky, and Jackson Pollock. The opportunities for young American painters to meet established European painters in New York during World War II were not unlike those available during the First World War, when Duchamp, Picabia, and many other European painters and collectors lived there in exile. In October 1942, Guggenheim opened her gallery, Art of This Century, with an exhibition of Surrealists. From May 18 to June 26, 1943, she organized a *Spring Salon for Young Artists,* at which Pollock exhibited his painting *Stenographic Figure,* which, according to one critic, "made the jury starry-eyed."[2] Acting on the advice of Matta and Howard Putzel, her secretary, Guggenheim gave Pollock a one-year contract, which allowed him to return to full-time painting. At the same time, Guggenheim made definite arrangements for a one-man show of Pollock's work and also commissioned a large mural for the entrance hall of her home. Pollock was ecstatic, since his employment with the WPA Federal Art Project had been terminated in January of that year. He wrote to his brother Charles on July 19, 1943:

> Things really broke with the showing of that painting [*Stenographic Figure*]. I had a pretty good mention in the *Nation*—I have a year's contract with [Art of This Century] and a large painting to do for Peggy Guggenheim's house, 8' 11½" x 19' 9". With no strings as to what or how I painted it.
>
> I am going to paint it in oil, on canvas. They are giving me a show Nov. 16, and I want to have the painting finished for the show. I've had to tear out the portion between the front and middle room to get the damned thing up. I have it stretched now. It looks pretty big, but exciting as hell.[3]

From the time of his first contract with Peggy Guggenheim until the closing of the gallery in 1947, Pollock was the central artist at Art of This Century. Guggenheim gave him four one-man shows. The first took place in November 1943, but *Mural* was not finished. In her book *Confessions of an Art Addict,* Guggenheim describes the birth of *Mural:*

I commissioned Pollock to paint a mural for my entrance hall, twenty-three feet wide and six feet high. Marcel Duchamp said he should put it on a canvas, otherwise it would have to be abandoned when I left the apartment. This was a splendid idea, and—for the University of Iowa—a most fortunate one, as I gave it to them when I left America. It now hangs there in the students' dining hall.

Pollock obtained a big canvas and tore down a wall in his apartment in order to make room to hang it up. He sat in front of it, completely uninspired for days, getting more and more depressed. He then sent his wife away to the country, hoping to feel more free, and that when alone he might get a fresh idea. Lee came back and found him still sitting brooding, no progress made and nothing even attempted. Then suddenly he got up and in a few hours painted a masterpiece.

The mural was more abstract than Pollock's previous work. It consisted of a continuous band of abstract figures in a rhythmic dance painted in blue and white and yellow. . . .

We had great trouble in installing this enormous mural, which was bigger than the wall it was destined for. Pollock tried to do it himself, but not succeeding, he became quite hysterical and went up to my flat and began drinking from all the bottles I had purposely hidden, knowing his great weakness. He not only telephoned me at the gallery every few minutes to come home at once and help place the painting, but he got so drunk that he undressed and walked quite naked into a party that Jean Connolly, who was living with me, was giving in the sitting room. Finally, Marcel Duchamp and a workman came to the rescue and placed the mural. It looked very fine, but I am sure it needed much bigger space, which it has today in Iowa.[4]

*Mural* was exhibited for the first time during Pollock's second one-man show, March 19 to April 14, 1945. This enormous work was not brought to the gallery, but visitors were "invited to view a Mural . . . from 3 to 6, at 155 East 61st Street, 1st Floor." [Fig. 1] Judging from the four reviewers of the exhibit (Howard Devree, Clement Greenberg, Parker Tyler, and Manny Farber), only Manny Farber seems to have made the special trip and seen *Mural,* which he judged as "an almost incredible success. It is violent in its expression, endlessly fascinating in detail, without superficiality, and so well ordered that it composes the wall in a quiet, contained, buoyant way. Pollock's aim in painting seems to be to express feeling that ranges from pleasant enthusiasm through wildness to explosiveness. . . . The style is very personal and, unlike that of many painters of this period, the individuality is in the way the medium is used rather than in the peculiarities of subject matter."[5]

Although Pollock dated *Mural* as having been done in 1943, he could well have painted it in 1944, since we know for sure only that it was finished by the time of his second one-man exhibition in March

*Figure 1.*
Peggy Guggenheim and
Jackson Pollock in front of
*Mural,* 1946.

1945. For his fourth and last one-man show at Art of This Century (January 14 to February 1, 1947), *Mural* was again shown, but this time it was moved into the gallery and exhibited in the lobby. A photograph shows Pollock standing in front of the painting at Art of This Century. In early 1947, *Mural* was still undated and unsigned.[6] He probably soon afterward dated and signed it for the exhibition *Large Scale Modern Painting* at the Museum of Modern Art in April of that year.

In summer 1947, before Peggy Guggenheim departed for Europe, she gave *Mural* on loan to the Yale University Art Gallery, which exhibited it for a while, but then put it in storage in 1948. When Guggenheim became aware that *Mural* was no longer on display at Yale, she wrote from Venice on October 3, 1948, to Lester Longman, then chairman of the art department at The University of Iowa, and offered *Mural* to the university. The personal acquaintance between Guggenheim and Longman, who had often visited her gallery and had seen *Mural* at her house, accounted for Guggenheim's decision to give *Mural* and other paintings to The University of Iowa. On November 11, Guggenheim wrote a second time and again offered the large painting, which Longman accepted in his letter of November 29, 1948. His response to the offer had been delayed, because he had to canvass faculty opinions. He also had to find a place to exhibit the monumental work, since the university did not have an art museum at that time. But *Mural* did not actually arrive in Iowa City until October 1951. Yale was certainly anxious to ship it. They rolled the painting around a big drum and crated it. The delay was caused by Longman's difficulties in getting the one hundred dollars needed to pay for packing, shipping, and insurance. When the painting finally arrived, it was first hung in the mural studio, which was in the Art Building.[7] In 1952, it was moved to the north lobby of the then recently opened University Library and hung high up on the west wall, out of reach of any would-be Pollocks.[8] When the present Museum of Art was opened in 1969, *Mural* became the focal point of the permanent collection. Guggenheim's claim that *Mural* was hung in the students' dining hall, which probably worried her and her readers, and certainly horrified Pollock scholars, was quite mistaken.

It is well known that Guggenheim attempted in the early sixties to get back many of the Pollock paintings. She felt a special attachment to *Mural,* which Pollock had painted for her. In 1961, she wanted the large painting back and offered in exchange Braque's *Still Life* (1926). In 1969, she stated in an interview:

> The Pollocks I gave away, because I had a contract with him and I had too many. I never would have had space for them all. But there was one particularly that I regretted having given away: a mural that he painted for me specially. I tried to get it back again. I offered them a Braque instead, and they replied, "We prefer American art." Very nice of them really. Rather touching.[9]

In its thirty-five years at The University of Iowa, *Mural* has led a very sedentary life. In 1973, it was restored by Louis Pomerantz, who also re-stretched the painting, which had been improperly stretched by Pollock. The restorer thereby uncovered two inches of canvas on the bottom right that had previously been around the edge of the stretcher and had therefore not been painted upon by Pollock. Because of its size and condition, *Mural* has been lent to only three exhibitions: one in 1962 at the Dallas Museum of Contemporary Art, another in 1967 of Pollock's work at the Museum of Modern Art and the Los Angeles County Museum, and, in 1982, a Pollock exhibition at the Centre Georges Pompidou in Paris. One indicator of the increasing importance of this painting is the changing value for which it has been insured. In 1951, when *Mural* first arrived here, it was insured for

$500. In 1967, the insurance value was $150,000, and in 1982 well over $1,000,000.

## POLLOCK AND AUTOMATISM

In late 1943, when Pollock prepared himself to paint *Mural*, he answered the question "Do you find it important that many famous modern European artists are living in this country?" with the following statement:

> Yes, I accept the fact that the important painting of the last hundred years was done in France. American painters have generally missed the point of modern painting from beginning to end. . . . Thus the fact that good European moderns are now here is very important, for they bring with them an understanding of the problems of modern painting. I am particularly impressed with their concept of the source of art being the unconscious. This idea interests me more than these specific painters do. . . .[10]

Pollock had little regard for an isolated American art. He was very interested in the French Surrealists' notion of the unconscious as a source of art, which had preoccupied him at least since 1939, when he entered psychoanalysis with Jungian analysts who used his art as a therapeutic aid. From about 1938 on, Pollock had been searching for a grammar, a language, in which he could express his unconscious. In summer 1940, he wrote to his brother Charles: "I haven't much to say about my work and things – only that I have been going through violent changes the past couple of years. God knows what will come out of it all – it's pretty negative stuff so far. . . . I haven't been up to any of those competitions. Will try when my work clears up a little more."[11] In those two years Pollock probably attempted to free himself from the representational style of his teacher Thomas Hart Benton. His art "cleared up" in the early forties, when he appropriated Picasso's style of the thirties. He was especially obsessed by the power and energy of *Guernica*. A large number of his drawings of that period contain iconographic elements of that work, and his oil paintings of the early forties indicate the strong impact of Picasso. Lee Krasner, Pollock's wife, recalled Pollock's sense of fierce rivalry with Picasso: "'God damn it,' he once shouted about some Picasso illustration, 'that guy missed nothing.'"[12] Or, "Damn that Picasso. Just when I think I've gotten somewhere I discover that bastard got there first."[13]

The significance of the European Surrealists' presence in New York for Pollock lay in their pointing out a language other than that of Picasso, a language that would enable him to overcome Picasso and allow him to express his unconscious more directly. As a result of the suggestions of the Surrealists, Pollock became interested in automatic painting. In his First Surrealist Manifesto of 1924, Breton defined Surrealism as "psychic automatism in its pure state, by which one proposes to express – verbally, by means of the written word, or in any other manner – the actual functioning of thought. Dictated by thought, in the absence of any control exercised by reason, exempt from any aesthetic or moral concern."[14] Although Breton suppressed the notion of automatism in his Second Manifesto (1930), he asserted its key role in his important essay "Genesis of Surrealism in the Plastic Arts," which was first published in English in Peggy Guggenheim's *Art of This Century* (1942) and was therefore known to the young American artists:

> I maintain that automatism in writing and drawing . . . is the only mode of expression which gives entire satisfaction to both eye and ear by achieving a rhythmic unity, as recognisable in drawing or in an automatic text as in a melody or a bird's nest. . . . The surrealism in a work is in direct proportion to the efforts the artist has made to embrace the whole psycho-physical field, of which consciousness is only a small fraction. In these *unfathomable* depths there prevails, according to Freud, a total absence of contradiction, a release from the emotional fetters caused by repression, a lack of temporality and the substitution of external reality by psychic reality obedient to the pleasure principle and no other.[15]

The above-quoted passage, read in isolation, explains very well Pollock's notion of automatism, which informed his creation of *Mural*. But if we read Breton's whole essay, we realize that in spite of Breton's advocacy of automatism, he seems to have thought of it only as a means to arrive at unusual figuration. The lines produced through automatic drawing were to reveal, at some point, recognizable shapes. Breton was adamantly opposed to abstract art, which he condemned as being inhuman. Even in the essay for Peggy Guggenheim's *Art of This Century,* he still favored the illusionistic paintings of Magritte, Tanguy, Brauner, Carrington, and Ernst.[16] Breton's impact on Pollock might have been limited to Pollock's reading the passage quoted above. Since Breton refused to learn English during his four-year stay in New York, he had very little direct interaction with the young American artists.

The catalyst for American painters was Matta, who in 1934 had left Chile and had joined the Surrealists in Paris in 1937. In 1939, at the age of twenty-eight, he came to New York, where he sought contact with young American painters. Fully aware of the limitations of Surrealist painting, Matta attempted to form a new group with young Americans, in order to revitalize Surrealist art through pure automatism. Through this group's projects in experimental automatism he attempted to challenge Breton's and the other Surrealists' preference for figuration and representations of dream images. Matta began meeting with this loosely formed group of Americans on Saturdays in his studio during the fall and winter of 1942, and of these sessions he recalled: "These artists I started meeting—[Busa], Pollock, Kamrowski, Baziotes, Motherwell—were full of vitality. But in some funny way they were painting from color reproductions instead of painting about themselves."[17] The young Americans, who were not at all interested in illusionistic Surrealist paintings, accepted Matta because he shared their dismissal of Salvador Dali and other Surrealist painters as illustrators of dreams, and because he showed them experiments in spontaneous improvisation. Previously, in Paris, Matta had explored chance creations by pouring paintings (coulages) with Gordon Onslow-Ford and Wolfgang Paalen. They recognized that abstract automatism was *the* largely unexplored direction in Surrealist painting.[18]

Robert Motherwell had already met Matta in 1941 and had spent that summer with him in Mexico. "In three months of that summer of 1941," Motherwell stated, "Matta gave me a ten-year education in Surrealism."[19] It was primarily Motherwell who, after his schooling in automatism, met with the group's members and explained to them Matta's ideas of abstract automatism. Of his first meeting with Pollock, Motherwell recalled: "I asked Baziotes who he thought to be the most talented of his friends. Baziotes thought probably Pollock. He gives the impression of being very tough and he didn't know how receptive he would be to the idea. I remember that Baziotes called up Pollock and we made a date to go and spend a whole afternoon with him. I talked, I guess, for four or five hours explaining the whole Surrealist thing in general and the theory of automatism in particular. . . . I showed Pollock how Klee and Masson made their things, etc. And Pollock, to my astonishment, listened intently; in fact, he invited me to come back another afternoon, which I did. This would be the winter of 1942."[20]

Group members also met in their studios and did their own experimentation. Gerome Kamrowski remembered one such meeting:

There is some concern where Pollock really developed his pouring or dripping form. From my experience . . . he was exposed to it from some surrealist
devices of automatic painting.
Baziotes did bring Pollock over to the place I was working at Sullivan Street
at that time. Baziotes was enthusiastically talking about the new freedoms
and techniques of painting and noticing the quart cans of lacquer asked if he
could use some to show Pollock how the paint could be spun around. He
asked for something to work on and a canvas that I had been pouring paint
on and was not going well was handy. Bill then began to throw and drip the
white paint on the canvas. He handed the palatte [sic] knife to Jackson and
Jackson, with his intense concentration, was flipping the paint with abandon.
Baziotes encouraged Jackson to continue and looked at me to see if I would
mind this use of my materials. There was a palatte [sic] nearby and soon several brushes were wielded by us to develop into a very free kind of activity.
Some one must have said "well let's see what it looks like" and while the
surface was not too heavily loaded we still kept the picture flat and stood up
and away from it to look at it.
Baziotes had obviously made his point. Jackson was puzzling the thing out
and was more or less relaxed about it so we just stopped.[21]

Pollock fully confirmed Kamrowski's notion that he discovered automatic painting in these "Surrealist" experiments. When John Bernard Myers, who worked for the Surrealist New York magazine View,
asked him if he had ever been influenced by the Surrealists, Pollock
answered, "Yes, in one way: their belief in 'automatism' or making a
picture without 'conscious' control of what would happen on the canvas before beginning one."[22]

Motherwell considered automatism as *the* needed principle in
American art at that time: "In this sense the theory of automatism was
the first modern theory of creating that was introduced into America
early enough to allow American artists to be equally adventurous or
even more adventurous than their European counterparts. It was this
that put America on the artistic map, so to speak, as authentically
contemporary."[23] And according to Peter Busa, Matta's insistence on
automatism completely changed their idea of painting, and encouraged them to use large canvases: "We always had this idea that we
were making pictures instead of the picture making us. The change in
our thinking stemmed from a sense of relief which resulted from a
feeling that we were breaking down the barriers between art and life.
This feeling freed our sense of scale."[24]

The young American painters around Matta were invited to exhibit
their work as early as the following year. Motherwell and Baziotes
participated in the only group exhibition of the Surrealists in New
York, *The First Papers of Surrealism,* which was organized by Breton

and Duchamp and took place from October 15 to November 17, 1942, at the headquarters of the Coordinating Council of the French Relief Societies. Pollock was invited by John Graham to participate with his painting *Birth* in the exhibition *American and French Paintings*, which was held at the McMillan Gallery from January 20 to February 6, 1943. Peggy Guggenheim asked Pollock, Motherwell, and Baziotes to take part in Art of This Century's *Exhibition of Collage* (April 16–May 15). One month later, when Pollock showed his *Stenographic Figure* at Guggenheim's *Spring Salon for Young Artists* (May 18–June 26, 1943), he had his breakthrough, which led to the contract with Peggy Guggenheim and the commission to paint *Mural*. In addition to promoting Pollock, Guggenheim gave one-man shows to Hans Hofmann, William Baziotes, Robert Motherwell, David Hare, and Mark Rothko.[25] With some justification, Peggy Guggenheim claimed that "Abstract Expressionism began in my Gallery. You couldn't explain it. It was like a sudden burst of flame."[26]

### THE IMPORTANCE OF *Mural*

During World War II New York became the international art capital because of the presence there of the French Surrealists and other artists. The young American painters suddenly found themselves in the center of artistic developments, which, according to Clement Greenberg, gave young American artists self-confidence and made them eager to compete with these established foreign artists:

> What turned out to be another advantage was this country's distance from the war and, as immediately important as anything else, the presence in it during the war years of European artists like Mondrian, Masson, Léger, Chagall, Ernst and Lipchitz along with a number of European critics, dealers, and collectors. Their proximity and attention gave the young abstract-expressionist painters self-confidence and a sense of being in the center of art. And in New York they could measure themselves against Europe with more benefits to themselves than they ever could have done as expatriates in Paris.[27]

The center for the Surrealists in New York was Peggy Guggenheim's home, according to an article in *Time* in 1942: "Today surrealism's headquarters is a dignified old mansion on Manhattan's fashionable East Side overlooking the East River. . . . The group's financial angel, who lives in the mansion and is married to Surrealist Ernst, is black-haired husky-voiced Peggy Guggenheim, niece of philanthropic Copper Tycoon Solomon Guggenheim. Peggy Guggenheim . . . practically supports the group by collecting its pictures. . . ."[28] Pollock's *Mural*, located in the entry hall of the Surrealists' "headquarters," can thus be seen as his competition with and challenge of French Surrealism.

While Pollock was still using Picasso's iconography in 1942 and 1943, he was at the same time experimenting with a new language that would allow him to "directly" express his unconscious. His *Stenographic Figure* (1942) [*Fig. 2*], which caught the attention of Peggy Guggenheim and the judges at *Spring Salon for Young Artists* in 1943, used shapes and composition that were derived from Picasso. But over this painting he scrawled a free "stenography" of the unconscious in the form of improvisational yellow, orange, and black lines as a kind of automatic over-writing. In his *Composition with Pouring* (1943) and *Untitled Abstraction* (1943) he superimposed upon these paintings free-flowing lines produced by dripping paint. *Guardians of the Secret* (1943) [*Fig. 3*] contains a painting within a painting. The two guardians in the style of Picasso on either side, and the dog at the bottom of the composition, protect the central panel, the unconscious, (re)presented by free, automatic lines.

This struggle between the inherited language (Picasso's iconography) and Pollock's new "direct language of the unconscious," which takes place in *Stenographic Figure* and *Guardians of the Secret*, is also present in *Mural*, but now the new, nonfigurative language dominates, and the figural and nonfigural elements are integrated within the overall rhythmic pattern of the work. *Mural* also radically differs from his other paintings of 1943 and 1944 by its sheer size.

Although Pollock had taken mural-painting classes from Thomas Hart Benton in 1931 and 1932, and in 1936 had worked in David Alfaro Siqueiros's workshop, he had never painted a mural prior to the one he did for Guggenheim. In the Federal Art Project, Pollock had joined the Easel Division and had therefore not been involved with mural painting. The many delays preceding the creation of *Mural* were probably due to the large dimensions of the canvas that he had to paint. In examining Pollock's layering of the colors in *Mural*, it becomes evident that he started by drawing in black paint the very evenly distributed life-size stick figures,[29] who seem to walk from right to left. In painting these figures first, he was able to divide the enormous canvas into a number of smaller areas. He then seems to have rapidly filled the spaces between the stick figures with white, and then with blue-green, pink, yellow, blue, and finally red brush strokes, working with one color all over before using the next one. These colors are quite evenly distributed throughout the painting, thus creating similarly colored rhythmic units in the areas between the

*Figure 2.* JACKSON POLLOCK. *Stenographic Figure,* 1942. Oil on canvas. 40 x 56 in. (101.7 x 142.4 cm.). Museum of Modern Art, New York. *Mr. and Mrs. Walter Bareiss Fund.*

stick figures. The strident black vertical lines thus form the macro-rhythm of this painting, and the improvisational lines of the other colors create rhythmic micro-units produced by curved, dynamic strokes. The automatic lines almost seem to submerge the stick figures into their rhythm. Pollock, who painted this twenty-foot-long canvas in a single session of frenzied activity, dissolved his own self into the improvisational rhythms of his colors and lines. Taken in this sense, the stick figures might be interpreted as representing human beings, whose selves are engulfed by the unconscious. *Mural* would thus present the Surrealists' central tenet, but Pollock's paintings would challenge their "illusionistic language" through his "direct" enactment of the unconscious.

The dynamic rhythm of the improvisational lines is arguably the dominant element in *Mural*. These rhythmic patterns might potentially provoke an experience in the viewer related to the experience of listening to music. Pollock was convinced that "[abstract art] should be enjoyed just as music is enjoyed."[30] His favorite music was jazz. Lee Krasner recalled that "he would get into grooves of listening

*Figure 3.* JACKSON POLLOCK. *Guardians of the Secret,* 1943. Oil on canvas. 48⅜ x 75⅜ in. (122.9 x 191.4 cm.). San Francisco Museum of Modern Art. *Albert M. Bender Collection, Albert M. Bender Bequest Fund Purchase.*

to his jazz records – not just for days – days and nights, day and night for three days running until you thought you would climb the roof! The house would *shake.* Jazz? He thought it was the only other really creative thing happening in this country. He had a passion for music."[31] Pollock probably experienced in the strong, dynamic rhythms and free improvisations of jazz a release from the self and a submersion into his unconscious. The improvisational, rhythmic lines in *Mural* might thus be considered as his new language, through which he attempted to produce a similar experience of the unconscious for the viewers of his painting. Motherwell clearly felt that Pollock's rhythmic improvisations were *the* vehicle through which he expressed his inner drives: "I think [Pollock] responded to rhythm more than anything else in art. Indeed, perhaps it is not too much to assert that his greatest works are marked by the intensity and violence of his rhythms, . . . and as in a Celtic dance, measured, despite its original primitive impulse."[32]

Gestural, physiological automatism[33] in the form of improvisational strokes became Pollock's vehicle to express the unconscious in *Mural,* with which he challenged the Surrealists. He was convinced that his spontaneous lines responded much more directly to unconscious drives, impulses, energies, and rhythms than did the Surrealists' detours via figuration and illustration of dream images.[34] Indeed, the word "direct" was one of Pollock's favorite expressions. In an interview with William Wright he stated: "Painting, I think, today – the more immediate, the more direct – the greater the possibilities of making a direct – of making a statement."[35] He hung these improvisational, rhythmical, seismographic markings of his unconscious in the entry hall of the Surrealists' "headquarters" in New York. The French Surrealists probably did not understand this more direct type of automatism; they probably regarded Pollock's *Mural* as the work of a wild, primitive, uncultivated, uninhibited American, a myth which the French have used since Pollock's first exhibition in Paris in 1952 to explain his works.[36]

In light of Pollock's artistic development, *Mural* is *the* pivotal work, since it marks the turning point from his earlier dependence on Picasso's and other artists' iconography to the development of his own physiological automatism, which he used fully in his well-known works with poured lines in the years from 1947 to 1950. The experience of painting this first large-scale painting also prompted him to move away from easel painting to the larger format of his future paintings. When he applied for a Guggenheim Fellowship in 1947, he stated:

> I intend to paint large movable pictures which will function between the easel and the mural. I have set a precedent in this genre in a large painting for Miss Peggy Guggenheim which was installed in her house and was later shown in the "Large Scale Paintings" show at the Museum of Modern Art. It is at present on loan at Yale University. I believe the easel picture to be a dying form, and the tendency of modern feeling is towards the wall picture or mural. I believe the time is not yet ripe for a *full* transition from easel to mural. The pictures I contemplate painting would constitute a halfway state, and an attempt to point out the direction of the future, without arriving there completely.[37]

*Mural* is, with the possible exception of an untitled work of 1937, his first all-over painting. It has no center, it has no beginning and no end.

Peggy Guggenheim correctly observed that "the mural was more abstract than Pollock's previous work." It is even more abstract than most of his paintings of 1944, 1945, and 1946, such as *Totem Lesson 1* (1945), *Equine Series* (1944), *The White Angel* (1946), and *The Child Proceeds* (1946). From the point of view of rhythmic patterns, it is most closely related to *Summertime: Number 9A* (1948), which also seems to contain suggestions of a series of black stick figures. A study of *Mural* thus raises questions in regard to the traditional periodization of Pollock's work.

## *Mural* as Critique of Culture

Traditionally mural paintings have been the most obvious form of public art. Murals generally have expressed collective values, be they historical, political, mythological, or religious ones. Pollock was very well acquainted with the traditional functions of murals. Besides taking classes in mural painting from Thomas Hart Benton at the Art Students League, he watched Diego Rivera paint murals on movable wall panels at the New Workers' School on West Fourteenth Street. Pollock also did action posing for Benton and José Clemente Orozco, who together painted murals at the New School for Social Research. In 1936, Pollock and his brother Sanford worked in David Alfaro Siqueiros's workshop, where he learned new techniques in mural painting, and where he helped build floats for Communist demonstrations. When he painted *Mural,* he was well aware that he broke radically with the conventions of mural painting. Although he painted it during World War II, he did not depict a historical scene or a political theme. He did not even choose a theme from mythology, which he used in *She-Wolf* and other paintings in 1943. The seemingly apolitical nature of *Mural* is even more surprising since his favorite paintings of Picasso were his two most overtly political ones, *Guernica* (1937) and *Girl with Cock* (1938). How could Pollock, who had very leftist political views, suddenly be so apolitical and embrace automatism in the middle of World War II? How can we see *Mural* as presenting a critique of, and not an escape from, war culture?

Pollock certainly rejected the political art of Benton, Siqueiros, Orozco, and Rivera in his *Mural* because, in Donald Kuspit's view, "he recognized that their ideological orientations, however heroic and grand, were nevertheless premised on the unquestioned conventional secular assumption of the ultimate banality—and therewith non-apocalyptic character of the world."[38] Traditional political painting, according to Pollock, was not radical enough. In *Mural* and his later all-over paintings he seems to present a primitive, preconscious state. In immersing himself in his unconscious, he believed he had found a primal layer that was below the layers of cultural and linguistic codes, below figuration, logic, and any kind of hierarchy and dualism. He must have been convinced that only through a collective re-creation of this primal state, which we can reach in our subconscious, could a society be created in which catastrophes such as the war would be impossible. Jazz and primitive art were, according to Pollock, already at work in reconnecting people with their unconscious. *Mural* and his later all-over paintings were his contribution to this revolutionary process. In the face of the insanity of the war, Pollock's paintings are thus his critique of the shallow rational world that makes such carnage possible, and they present a vision of a totally new order, which at the same time is the most ancient, most primal order. *Mural* could thus be read as presenting the revolutionary process in which the consciousness of people, presented by the stick figures, is being engulfed, erased by the unconscious.

Taken in this sense, *Mural* is very much public art that attempts to depict, as do traditional murals, collective values. Pollock's critique of war culture is not unlike that of the Zurich Dadaists during the First World War. According to Hans Arp, "while the thunder of the batteries rumbled in the distance . . . we searched for an elemental art that would, we thought, save mankind from the furious folly of these times. We aspired to a new order that might restore the balance between heaven and hell."[39] Like the Dadaists, Pollock made himself a primitive in *his* search for a new order. Through physiological automatism he believed that he could directly present deeper levels of primal rhythm. C. G. Jung's notions about the primitive might have attracted him, especially if we rewrite the following passage by substituting "painting" for "thinking": "The primitive does not paint consciously, but rhythmic patterns appear. The primitive cannot assert that he paints; it is rather that 'something paints in him.' The spontaneity of the act of painting does not lie, casually, in the conscious mind but in his unconscious. Moreover, he is incapable of any conscious effort of will; he must put himself into the 'mood of willing.'"[40] Pollock seems to confirm Jung's observations when he states: "The source of my painting is the unconscious. I approach painting the same way I approach drawing. That is direct—with no preliminary studies."[41]

In his attempt to bring about a new social order by connecting people's lives again with their unconscious, Pollock must have agreed with John Graham's conviction that "the purpose of art in *particular* is to reestablish a lost contact with the unconscious, . . . with the primordial racial past and to keep and develop this contact."[42] The ideal viewers of Pollock's *Mural* therefore experience the deeper levels of their own unconscious through the rhythmic patterns of the painting. The presentation of the unconscious on the canvas directly awakens the unconscious of the viewer, and thus the conceptual levels of apperception are bypassed. "The unconscious," Pollock stated, "is a very important side of modern art and I think the unconscious drives do mean a lot in looking at paintings."[43] Thus, Pollock refused to "explain" his paintings; he even warned critics that explanations would destroy the effect and purpose of his works. He also realized that the more descriptive titles of his abstract works were impeding the experience of the viewer, since these titles prompted thematic readings. He therefore abandoned these titles and replaced them with numbers.

Pollock's language of the unconscious, through which he attempted to revolutionize society, was new and unfamiliar. But Pollock did not expect difficulties in the communication process, since he thought that his paintings would directly awaken the unconscious in the viewer. The endless studies on Pollock and his work are a clear indication that his language was not understood. Clement Greenberg, his chief early promoter, saw only the formal innovations in Pollock's work. He saw in these paintings an experimentation so advanced that it put American avant-garde art ahead of Parisian art.[44] In their necessarily indeterminate nature, Pollock's works have suffered even worse appropriations. His paintings were hailed as representing American freedom; they were used by the CIA for propaganda purposes, as weapons against the Soviet Union during the Cold War.[45] In America, Pollock's improvisational rhythms were imitated by young artists who did not understand that these paintings were, according to Pollock, the direct presentation of the unconscious.

In part because of Pollock's gradual awareness that his automatism was misunderstood, that it therefore was unable to reconnect people with their unconscious, he began to paint again figuratively in 1951. In his letter to Alfonso Ossorio in 1951, Pollock announced his change from improvisational automatism to figurative painting, and he predicted the reactions of the art community to this change: "I think the non-objectivists will find them disturbing—and the kids who think it simple to splash a Pollock out."[46]

NOTES

1  The only previous discussion of *Mural* can be found in Stephen Foster, "Turning Points in Pollock's Early Imagery," *The University of Iowa Museum of Art Bulletin* (Spring 1976), 125–37.

2  Excerpts from Jean Connolly's review in *Nation* (29 May 1943) are quoted in Francis V. O'Connor, *Jackson Pollock* (New York: The Museum of Modern Art, 1967), 29.

3  See O'Connor, *Jackson Pollock*, 28.

4  Peggy Guggenheim, *Confessions of an Art Addict* (New York: Macmillan, 1960), 106.

5  Manny Farber's review appeared in *New Republic* (25 June 1945) and is quoted in O'Connor, *Jackson Pollock*, 37.

6  The photograph showing Pollock in front of the undated *Mural* in 1947 is reproduced in Francis V. O'Connor and Eugene Victor Thaw, *Jackson Pollock: A Catalogue Raisonné of Paintings, Drawings, and Other Works* (New Haven: Yale University Press, 1978), vol. 4, 231.

7  My interview with Lester Longman, 12 October 1985.

8  My interview with Ralph Ellsworth, then Head of the University Library, 14 October 1985. The archives of the library were searched for a photograph of *Mural* in the north lobby, but none was found.

9  Interview with Christopher Andreae, published in *The Christian Science Monitor* (4 February 1969), 14.

10  This questionnaire and Pollock's answers were published in the February issue of *Arts & Architecture* in 1944, reprinted in O'Connor, *Jackson Pollock*, 32–33.

11  See O'Connor, *Jackson Pollock*, 24–25.

12  Cited in B. H. Friedman, *Jackson Pollock: Energy Made Visible* (New York: McGraw-Hill, 1972), 183.

13  Conversation between William Rubin and Lee Krasner Pollock, April 1967, quoted in William Rubin, "Pollock as Jungian Illustrator: The Limits of Psychological Criticism," *Art in America* 67 (December 1979), 88. Henderson, his Jungian analyst in 1939 and 1940, who encouraged Pollock to produce symmetrical, mandala-like images, also recalled: "I encountered the strongest possible resistance at first. As a true son of Picasso, he felt bound to uphold the dogma of the contemporary art world of his time. . . . He fought me tooth and nail." (Quoted in Bernice Rose, *Jackson Pollock Works on Paper* [New York: New York University, 1967], 10.)

14  André Breton, *Manifestoes of Surrealism* (Ann Arbor: The University of Michigan Press, 1969), 26.

15  Peggy Guggenheim, ed., *Art of This Century: Objects, Drawings, Photographs, Paintings, Sculpture, Collages, 1910–1942* (New York: Art of This Century, 1942), quoted from André Breton, *What Is Surrealism? Selected Writings*, ed. Franklin Rosemont (New York: Monad Press, 1978), 224–25. Breton's essay was later included in his *Le Surréalisme et la peinture* (New York: Brentano's, 1945).

16  But Breton did reject in that essay the "ultra-retrograde technique," the academicism of Salvador Dali, whom he had championed in the early thirties. Breton's critique of Dali, however, seems to have been caused by Dali's sympathies with Franco's fascism and his leanings toward the Catholic church rather than by his style of painting.

17  Sidney Simon, "Concerning the Beginnings of the New York School: 1939–1943. An Interview with Peter Busa and Matta," *Art International* 11 (Summer 1967), 17.

18  See Gordon Onslow-Ford, "The Painter Looks within Himself," *London Bulletin* (June 1940), 30–31; Wolfgang Paalen, "The New Image," *Dyn* (April–May 1942), 9.

19 Sidney Simon, "Concerning the Beginnings of the New York School: 1939–1943. An Interview with Robert Motherwell," *Art International* 11 (Summer 1967), 21.

20 Ibid.

21 Kamrowski recalled this session in his letter to B. H. Friedman in 1972, quoted in Jeffrey Wechsler, "Surrealism's Automatic Painting Lesson," *Art News* 76 (April 1977), 45–46. Kamrowski still has this collaborative painting, which he described in his letter.

22 John Bernard Myers, "Surrealism and New York Painting 1940–1948: A Reminiscence," *Artforum* 15, no. 8 (April 1977), 56.

23 Simon, "An Interview with Robert Motherwell," 23.

24 Ibid., 19.

25 See Melvin Lader, "Peggy Guggenheim's Art of This Century: The Surrealist Milieu and the American Avant-Garde" (Ph.D. diss., University of Delaware, 1981).

26 Quoted in Harold Rosenberg, "Collector as Creator," *Saturday Review* 43 (12 November 1960), 30.

27 Clement Greenberg, "'American-Type' Painting," *Partisan Review* 22 (Spring 1955), 118.

28 "Surrealists in Exile," *Time* 39 (20 April 1942), 50.

29 Pollock used these stick figures in some of his drawings of 1943. They can also be found in his painting *Portrait of H. M.* (1945), which Peggy Guggenheim gave to The University of Iowa, and in the book jacket which he designed for Guggenheim's *Out of This Century* (1946).

30 See "The Artist Speaks, Part 6," *Art in America* (August–September 1965), 111.

31 Cleve Gray and Francine du Plessix, "Who Was Jackson Pollock?," *Art in America* 55 (March–April 1957), 51.

32 Quoted from Robert Motherwell's statement in "Jackson Pollock: An Artists' Symposium, Part I," *Art News* 66, no. 2 (April 1967), 65.

33 Nicolas Calas, in his book entitled *Confound the Wise* (1942), distinguishes three types of automatism, and defines physiological automatism as "the free movement of the arm and the hand." (Quoted by Robert Hobbs, in "Early Abstract Expressionism: A Concern with the Unknown Within," in Robert Hobbs and Gail Levin, *Abstract Expressionism: The Formative Years* [New York: Whitney Museum of American Art, 1978], 17.)

34 André Masson's automatism, which Pollock greatly admired, might be an exception. His automatic pencil drawings between 1924 and 1929, and paintings like *Interwoven Lovers* (1943), seem to be especially closely related to Pollock's notion of automatism. Clement Greenberg, who championed Pollock, wrote of Masson: "André Masson's presence on this side of the Atlantic during the War was of inestimable benefit to us. Unfulfilled though he is, and tragically so, he is still the most seminal of all painters, not excepting Miró, in the generation after Picasso's. He, more than anyone else, anticipated the new abstract painting, and I don't believe he has received enough credit for it." ("Contribution to a Symposium," in *Art and Culture* [Boston: Beacon Press, 1961], 126.) William Rubin examined the relationship between Masson and Pollock in "Notes on Masson and Pollock," *Arts Magazine* 34 (November 1959), 37–43. It seems, however, that even Masson, similarly to Ernst in his *frottages*, expected from his automatism the emergence of figuration. In an exchange between Masson and Matisse at Grasse, Masson stated: "I begin without an image or plan in mind, but just draw or paint rapidly according to my impulses. Gradually, in the marks I make, I see suggestions of figures or objects. I encourage these to emerge, trying to bring out their implications even as I now con-

sciously try to give order to the composition." (Quoted in William Rubin, *Dada and Surrealist Art* [New York: Abrams, 1968], 176–78.)

35  Interview with William Wright in summer 1950, quoted in O'Connor, *Jackson Pollock*, 81.

36  See the catalogue of the most recent Jackson Pollock exhibition at the Centre Georges Pompidou in Paris, *Jackson Pollock* (Paris: Centre Georges Pompidou, 1982).

37  O'Connor, *Jackson Pollock*, 39–40.

38  Donald Kuspit, "Abstract Expressionism: The Social Contract," *Arts Magazine* 54, no. 7 (March 1980), 119.

39  Hans Arp, "Dadaland," in his *On My Way* (New York: Wittenborn, Schultz, 1948), 39.

40  C. G. Jung, *Psyche and Symbol: A Selection from the Writings of C. G. Jung*, ed. Violet de Laszlo (Garden City, N.Y.: Doubleday, 1952), 116. Violet de Laszlo was Pollock's Jungian analyst from 1940 to 1942. The original text is: "The primitive does not think consciously, but that thoughts appear. The primitive cannot assert that he thinks; it is rather that 'something thinks in him.' The spontaneity of the act of thinking does not lie, casually, in the conscious mind but in his unconscious. Moreover, he is incapable of any conscious effort of will; he must put himself into the 'mood of willing.'"

41  See O'Connor, *Jackson Pollock*, 40.

42  *John Graham's System and Dialectics of Art*, ed. M. E. Allentuck (Baltimore: Johns Hopkins University Press, 1975), 95, quoted by Robert Hobbs in Hobbs and Levin, 13.

43  Interview with William Wright in summer 1950, quoted in O'Connor, *Jackson Pollock*, 79.

44  See Serge Guilbaut, *How New York Stole the Idea of Modern Art: Abstract Expressionism, Freedom, and the Cold War* (Chicago: University of Chicago Press, 1983). Guilbaut's study renders a good analysis of Clement Greenberg's role, but it shows very little understanding of Abstract Expressionism.

45  See Eva Cockroft, "Abstract Expressionism: Weapon of the Cold War," *Artforum* 12 (June 1974), 39–41; Max Kozloff, "American Painting during the Cold War," *Artforum* 13 (May 1973), 43–54.

46  O'Connor, *Jackson Pollock*, 59.

# HUMAN WRONGS:
## Jackson Pollock's *Mural*

ANTONIO R. DAMASIO, M.D.

### FIRST IMPRESSIONS/LATE IMPRESSIONS

I still remember my first reaction to *Mural:* It made me think of music, Anton Webern or Pierre Boulez. Fifteen years later music is still an effective and immediate counterpart for this painting, although much has changed in my appreciation of it, and Webern or Boulez no longer come to mind (strangely, Debussy does). For many years and countless viewings, I believed the canvas had no beginning and no end, and I sensed, without ever ascertaining it, that the color and form motifs repeated themselves with established periodicity, in horizontal as well as vertical directions. I believed Pollock had sliced twenty feet of a most spectacular wallpaper, that he had caught in midflight the playing of an infinitely recursive musical theme, a *tranche de vie* made up of vague beings twirling and dancing a mysterious, circular ritual. That is hardly the case as I now see it. There is, in fact, no period to the motifs, although color and form themes do reappear in a sort of arrythmic pulse that has neither geometric nor audiometric regularity. Forms are never repeated and the areas subtended by one of the pulse colors—pink, viridian blue, yellow, black, cobalt blue—are different from region to region of the mural. When you fold, in your mind's eye, the bottom half on the top one, or the right on the left, you realize how the work is devoid of symmetry. There is an unequivocal top-heavy verticality to the painting and it simply would not make sense upside down. Furthermore, *Mural* is also varied along the horizontal axis. About the middle three-fifths, the motifs have a considerable breathing space but at the extremes

Antonio R. Damasio is a Professor in the Department of Neurology, and Chief of the Division of Behavioral Neurology.

there is a crowding of material, as if Pollock wanted to cram these visual gestures in the canvas before running out of space. It also gives me the impression that the painting does have not one but two ends, as if Pollock worked from the center out, to both the right and the left edges. And yet, in spite of these different modes, the painting is structurally of one piece, not only thematically but technically–the same hues and texture appear to have sprung in different regions of the canvas at the same time, and apparently they almost were (after days of brooding and immobility in front of the empty canvas, Pollock is supposed to have filled it feverishly in a few hours). Even the signature is of the same textural vintage. A supraordinate concept overrides the whole painting and is one of the great sources of its beauty, of the pleasurable state it produces in the viewer.

Another first impression of *Mural* I recall is that it contained no recognizable figure, that all its signs were unidentifiable, and that a private calligraphy had made them more so. But at some point in my encounters with this painting, I started seeing human figures, some standing, full body, heads up, almost swaying, others caught contorted, in some hieratic representation of suffering, still others glimpsed only as faces or parts thereof, their states of mind or universal role not immediately discernible, the modern counterpart of a frieze by Mantegna, as a friend of mine suggested. I still see that very much, on certain occasions, but the intriguing point is that my readings, which can hardly be called naive at this point, can change with the light, or the mood, or my whim. At a distance, especially, I can make the painting retain its obscurity as far as direct representation of an external world goes. But at closer range, I can also see a forest, complex, dense, not especially dark, not especially frightening, populated by numerous animals but not by man. There are birds of all sorts, horses, donkeys, rhinoceros, wolves, giraffes, a cunning little vixen, some kind of curious flying fish, and marine mammals of the dolphin variety. The level of definition of these figures is so ambiguous that I do not always see the same ones although some images do latch on to memory and persist for future viewings. How many of these figures, human and not, Pollock himself saw will never be known. How many did he retouch after his free gestures begat them? How many did he deliberately create as he completed the picture?

Be that as it may, give or take the vagaries of my viewing mind, what I see in *Mural* today touches me both because of the aesthetic pleasure it permits and because of the intellectual mood it sets. It leaves me in awe because of the originality of its achievement (*Mural* is connected to the work of genial forerunners but it is primarily novel and path-breaking) and because it does speak to the human condition, even when it does not specifically mention war, death, famine, fear, pain, disease, tyranny, or oppression. *Mural* deals with human rights and human wrongs, after its fashion.

Pollock's painting celebrates a major right, freedom, but it deals mostly with human wrongs, with the torture of a mind imprisoned in itself, circling its obsessive few ideas in much the same repetitive approach; more able to see clearly in the subterranean of the soul than in the open floor of its consciousness; more ready to regain its lost equilibrium through impulse than through rational reflection on the condition that creates its suffering; and yet, capable of generating the kind of stirring beauty that cancels the wrongs thus celebrated.

How does Pollock's painting achieve that, how does it provoke us into considering such contents and states? To some degree, the answer may be gleaned from a discussion about the artist and the circumstances in which his work arose.

### Backdrop for a Painting

Pollock's *Mural* was painted in 1943 at the approximate midpoint of his career. He was thirty-one and would live thirteen more years. He had been painting since adolescence and had recently signed a contract with Peggy Guggenheim, the collector and art dealer who owned Art of This Century, a New York gallery devoted to modern art. *Mural* was Peggy Guggenheim's commission.[1] She wanted a large painting to decorate a wall in the foyer of her townhouse on East Sixty-first Street. Quite regrettably, the painting might have stayed forever on that very wall had Marcel Duchamp not pleaded with Guggenheim to have Pollock paint it on a canvas, should there be need to remove the piece later on. In fact, when Peggy Guggenheim moved to Venice in 1947, she discovered that her house in the Canal Grande (the Palazzo dei Venier di Leon) had no room large enough for *Mural*. And so the painting was saved and removed, first to the Yale Art Gallery, and later to its final destination at The University of Iowa, where it has been on permanent exhibition (except for the year 1982, when it was on loan at the Centre Georges Pompidou for the Pollock retrospective). In order to accommodate the twenty-foot stretcher for the *Mural* canvas, Pollock had to tear down a wall in his studio. After many days of inactivity in front of the canvas, he painted it rapidly and wanted to have it installed no less rapidly at Guggenheim's place.[2] Curiously, *Mural* was Pollock's only commission in a short but outstandingly successful career, and the largest of all his paintings.

The biography of Jackson Pollock has been analyzed in a variety of volumes. It is especially well covered in Francis O'Connor's catalogue for Pollock's Museum of Modern Art exhibition, and in the large catalogue of the Centre Pompidou retrospective.[3] This is not the place to discuss its details but some highlights are pertinent as a background to opinions we hold regarding *Mural* and Pollock's art in general: their base in personal gift and technical proficiency, their roots in the work of old and new masters, their link to personal and social suffering.

A sizable segment of the viewing public confronted with Pollock's painting in his own time concluded that the artist was neither talented nor technically proficient, that is, he could not draw and neither could he balance and color a recognizable composition. There are those who still think the same today. Pollock's biography denies this vehemently.

Pollock was finely schooled in art. He was an avid museum-goer and a constant reader of art books. He worked not only with Siqueiros but also with Thomas Hart Benton. Working with the former he developed an admiration for the Mexican mural painters and established a long and close mentor-disciple relationship. In his youth the painter he most admired was Piero della Francesca. Among the Americans his favorite was Ryder. Later, his admiration moved to the Surrealists, to Matisse and Miró, and, most of all, to Picasso. He followed the work of these artists regularly, at the Modern and at the New York galleries that showed them, and was quite passionately interested in the meaning of such work from a historical and social perspective. I also believe that his attraction to art and professional choice came from the realization, early in his adolescence, of his own pictorial talent, in spite of the fact that he often later doubted it.[4] As John Berger, an unbiased critic of Pollock, put it in writing about his paintings: "Their colour, their consistency of gesture, the balance of their tonal weights, all testify to a natural painter's talent. The same qualities also reveal that Pollock's method of working allowed him, in relation to what he wanted to do, as much control as, say, the Impressionist method allowed the Impressionists."[5]

Another attitude that greeted Pollock's work was that it was visually chaotic, referentially empty, historically and socially meaningless, nothing but a savage, irrational, uncultivated gesture by a young man from the brave new world, out of touch with the ills of that world.

Yet the social setting of Pollock's formative years, and his own psychological evolution, tell us otherwise. Pollock's twenties coincided with the Depression in the United States, with the turmoil of political developments in Europe and North America, with the social ramifications of the Russian Revolution, with the Spanish Civil War, and finally with the beginning of World War II. Pollock's knowledge of social upheaval was firsthand. These were years of extreme poverty for Pollock. These were also the years in which the young man's personality matured, in a decidedly unbalanced way. World suffering and personal grief coincided, and part of his response included turning to alcohol. By the middle 1930s he was severely addicted. In July 1937, when he was only twenty-five, he started formal treatment for alcoholism. Of special importance is the fact that in 1939 Pollock entered analysis with a Jungian psychologist, Joseph L. Henderson. This continued for eighteen months and was followed, after Henderson left for California, by another period of Jungian analysis under Dr. Violet de Laszlo which lasted into late 1943.[6] It is fair to state that Pollock was steeped in the human wrongs of his time and well aware of them in his own flesh. It is probably also accurate to state that Pollock believed art was an appropriate vehicle not only to alleviate personal suffering but also to express an attitude toward social and political ills. The question that remains, and to which we will turn later on, is whether or not his art was an effective vehicle to achieve such purposes.

### Expressing Human Wrongs

Pollock's career is generally divided into three phases. The first phase is seen as influenced by Benton, Picasso, and the Mexican mural painters Orozco and Siqueiros. It starts with formal figurative paintings, such as *Going West,* and moves through a variety of successively more abstract and symbolically rich works, such as *She-Wolf, Moon Woman Cuts the Circle, Pasiphaë,* and *Guardians of the Secret,* painted up to 1946. Only a few paintings from this phase used the "automatic" technique. The second phase is characterized by the automatic "drip" paintings and encompasses work from 1947 to 1952. The short and less productive late phase continues to his death in 1956 and returns to symbolism and figuration.[7] In theory, then, because of its 1943 date, *Mural* belongs to Pollock's long first phase. But in reality *Mural* is based less on the symbolism of the first phase than on the automaticity that characterizes the second. In a way, *Mural* announces Pollock's development and especially foretells one of his future major works, *Blue Poles: Number II.* The roots of these components can be traced in the artist's biography.

The two most often cited sources for Pollock's symbolism are the Indian and Mexican cultures, on the one hand, and Jungian psychology on the other. Without a doubt, Pollock had extensive acquaintance with Mexican culture, in no small part through direct contact with its great painters, but also through his travels in the southwest. But perhaps the most effective way in which he became aware of primitive art symbols, especially of the native American Indian, were the multiple exhibitions organized by the Museum of Modern Art in the thirties and forties dealing with primitive art. In an essay in *Abstract Expressionism: The Formative Years* Hobbs lists five major exhibitions: *American Sources of Modern Art,* 1933 (Aztec, Mayan, and Incan cultures); *African Negro Art,* 1935; *Prehistoric Rock Pictures in Europe and Africa,* 1937; *Twenty Centuries of Mexican Art,* 1940; and *Indian Art of the United States,* 1941, and comments that New York artists hardly needed to travel to the American Museum of Natural History to complete their education in this respect. Pollock is likely to have attended several of these exhibitions and apparently owned the catalogues for some of them.[8]

Pollock read about Jung even before he started analysis and was acquainted with the anthropological elements of Jungian psychology. It is also known that he brought numerous drawings to his analyst and that he actually insisted on having them used as the point of departure for his analysis sessions. He probably had available, on a regular weekly basis, a considerable amount of thoroughly scrutinized visual and verbal symbolic material that he may have made use of consciously or unconsciously. He might well have been at the height of such a secondary utilization of those materials in 1943 when he painted *Mural.* (To evaluate the possible significance of this fact it is helpful to note that Dr. Henderson later sold eighty-two drawings and one gouache that Pollock had brought to the office in only eighteen months. The number of works he left with Dr. de Laszlo is not known.[9]) But the Jungian emphasis prompted by his biographic data has obscured the role of Freudian thinking and Freudian symbols, which were widely disseminated in the cultural environment of the thirties and forties in New York City. In point of fact, William Rubin's theory – that the far more accessible and practical aspects of Freudian psychology may have played the key role in Pollock's artistic production – is quite appealing. I suspect, in addition, that Freudian and not Jungian psychology also played the key role in his attempt to cope with his own neurosis. Freud and his symbols are also likely to have reached Pollock through the work of the European Surrealists and through Picasso (the Minotaur is an example). Picasso's imagery was an acknowledged influence on Pollock and Freud dominated it. This can be noted in the small drawings of the late thirties and early forties (the drawings used in the analysis sessions are rarely exhibited but two of them can be viewed in the San Francisco Museum of Modern Art and bear the stamp of Picasso). Pollock the symbolist was not as much a man of his time as a follower of forerunners who had decided the unconscious was the true subject of painting. The automaticity approach that he later embarked on maintained the unconscious as a target but drastically changed the means to access it.

## AUTOMATICITY

Pollock admired and often emulated Picasso but Picasso's shadow was also an unbearable burden for this sensitive analysand. It is conceivable that Pollock ended up, in very Freudian terms, killing this influence by acting out a rejection of the very figuration which he admired but was unable to compete with. It is reasonable to venture that such a rejection started with the automaticity of *Mural* and finally succeeded in the unabashed, free-flowing gestures of the "drip" paintings four years later.

The point to be made here, then, is that the automaticity approach begins well before the generally accepted date of 1947 and that prior to that date no other single work of Pollock appears to represent it better than *Mural*. Naturally, I do not want to suggest that the very origin of automaticity lies with Pollock's rejection of Picasso's influence. For instance, Pollock was aware that unintended gestures could, on occasion, produce striking images. Siqueiros was known for making use of accidents and for turning casual splashes of paint into meaningful areas of the canvas.[10] But it must have taken considerable intellectual elaboration to go from the clever recovery of a mistake to the notion that an uncontrolled gesture might be the source of a useful representation, one that would be in contact with unwilled but no less real contents of the mind. This is the intellectual trajectory that Pollock appears to have followed, as is well indicated by his decisive statement that nothing in his painting was accidental, not even the many components that had occurred by alleged "chance."[11] I believe that it is in regard to his theoretical development and to its practical use that we must give credit to psychoanalysis in both Jungian and Freudian versions. It is highly unlikely that Pollock would have reached this solid trust in the power and wealth of unconscious processes and in the ability of those unconscious processes to guide the production of visual art, had he not experienced a considerable insight into those processes by means of his sessions of analysis, of his reflection on those sessions, and, quite probably, of the special states of mind that his alcohol abuse must have placed him in.

It is important not to mistake Pollock's approach as the mere intent to use "unconscious material" as a theme of painting. The Surrealists as well as Picasso had turned the "unconscious" into the major source of their painting and struggled to identify, through self-analysis, unconscious subject matter that later found its way into the canvases after deliberately reasoned intellectual elaboration. Pollock obviously did the same in his early years, sharing this approach with other Abstract Expressionists (e.g., Rothko, Hofmann, Gottlieb), who not only wanted to paint from "within" but were convinced that the symbolic lexicon of primitive art helped them view the inner landscape more clearly. Their theoretical mentor, John Graham, sums it up comprehensively: "The purpose of art in particular is to re-establish a lost contact with the unconscious . . . with the primordial racial past and to keep and develop this contact in order to bring to the conscious mind the throbbing events of the unconscious mind."[12] The novelty, in his automaticity period, was in the short, circuitous route he established between unconscious and canvas, and in Pollock's belief that it would provide no less rich and valid a revelation than a more re-reflected, less turbulent and volcanic approach.

Pollock was not the inventor of automatic painting, only its most successful practitioner. Hans Hofmann, in 1940, produced some drip paintings that even resemble what Pollock would later do. Pollock's wife, Lee Krasner, was studying with Hofmann at the time and their studio was next door to Hofmann's. (Incidentally, the relationship was probably not close. When the art dealer Sidney Janis first visited

Pollock's studio in 1942 and dropped in on Hofmann's studio afterwards, mentioning Pollock's work, Hofmann is supposed to have asked, "Who's that?").[13] Years before, Max Ernst had used a drip technique and even invented a device to "drip-paint."[14] Pollock probably learned about that too, from Ernst himself, or Peggy Guggenheim (Ernst's wife), or André Masson. But even if Pollock knew about such a technique, it was his own emotional and intellectual condition, his *illness* so to speak, that revealed to him the full potential of the method. As for the immediate motive to experiment and finally endorse the automaticity method, I believe it came from the silent bullfight he carried on with Picasso. Pollock often complained bitterly of his frustration in discovering that many of his own achievements were nothing but pale versions of Picasso's, that the man Picasso would always arrive at the prize catch before he did: "Damn that Picasso; just when I think I've gotten somewhere I discover that bastard got there first."[15] Considering that Pollock had a keen sense for what painting had accomplished historically, and no doubt strived to produce something truly new, perhaps the rest of what painting could still be expected to achieve, it must have been a source of great exhilaration to come, at long last, into the exhaustive exploration of a technique that permitted him to supplant Picasso, to make him finally surrender, in professional terms. When Pollock joked that he had developed automaticity "to get rid of Picasso," he really meant his joke. We can see *Mural* as the dress rehearsal for the developments that were to be.

It is difficult to imagine the Jackson Pollock of *Mural* and of later years had he not been through psychoanalysis, although Pollock did abandon the therapy sessions after 1943 and was often treated in biologically oriented alcoholism centers. In the thirties and forties, as well as for several decades to follow, psychoanalysis, in one variant or another, was a choice approach for the correction of personal wrongs. Analysis provided, if not a scientific form of treatment, certainly an intriguing system of beliefs and an intellectually interesting formula to interpret neurotic suffering, deviant behavior, and even social pressures. There is not much evidence that it did a lot of good for Pollock's psychiatric symptomatology, but the same cannot be said about his work. In fact, his first analyst confessed, disconcertingly, that he experienced such a strong countertransference with the painter that he made no attempt to treat his alcoholism![16] It is also difficult to imagine the Pollock of *Mural* and of later paintings without some of the effects of alcohol—a clouding and distortion of mental contents but also, at times, a disclosing of unsuspected relationships, and a heightened, clear, unrestricted view of ineffable memories. Let me make clear that I do not believe that alcohol or drugs are either necessary or sufficient for artistic expression. More often than not they probably hinder creativity rather than promote it. But on occasion they can help great artists by enhancing imagination and problem-solving and thus making the mind richer before or during creation. Whether or not, in the long run, the balance of drug effects is positive for the artist clearly depends on numerous factors (the artist's intelligence, emotional control, the amount and duration of drug intake, etc.). Finally, it is impossible not to sense, somehow, that the bleakness of the times was indelibly embodied in Pollock the man and in his art, in the torture of identifiable symbols or in the desperate rejection of symbols and of reason.

## THE CONDITIONS AND LIMITS OF A TECHNIQUE

Pollock's technique caused great scandal at the time and is still not acceptable to those who consider it an uneducated and primitive celebration of chaos. Those characterizations may apply to many artists who attempted Pollock's approach unsuccessfully but they certainly do not apply to him. The visual mind of the young man for whom Piero della Francesca was a revered painter was quite sophisticated. Pollock was also a splendid draftsman. Last but not least, Pollock was insightful. So that when Pollock took leave of his rational senses and let his unconscious go straight to the motor control of his paint-pouring arm, that was an unconscious that had known the landscape and human figure of the Renaissance, the stepwise perceptual breakdown of Cubism, the full-fleshed painting of twentieth-century American realism, and the symbolism of so many European artists painting in France in the first three decades of the century. His motor control had been through it all, in school as well as in daydreams and perhaps in alcoholic nightmares. When the "nonrational" connection was established, the results were harmonious, often beautiful, and so rich that they provide a constant source of pleasure. His insight on the process was remarkable, as his own words demonstrate: "When I am *in* my painting, I'm not aware of what I'm doing. It is only after a sort of 'get acquainted' period that I see what I have been about. I have no fears about making changes, destroying the image, etc., because the painting has a life of its own. I try to let it come through. It is only when I lose contact with the painting that the result is a mess. Otherwise, there is pure harmony, an easy give and take, and the painting comes out well."[17]

Because of the special conditions in which it emerged, Pollock's approach remains his own, dependent as it is on his spiritual condition. His approach and technique failed in the hands of other painters and it is not easy to imagine its successful practice by other artists or even by Pollock himself, beyond a relatively short period. Five years before his untimely death Pollock had largely abandoned it.

There are considerable limits in the automatic approach to painting. As less conscious control is exerted on the painting and as more free-flowing unconscious motor activity takes hold, rhythmic, stereotyping actions come to dominate the canvas. The dimming of higher control reveals deep cerebral rhythms, primitive pulses of brain activity, that are normally inhibited by conscious cognition. There is no necessary chaos in that activity, just a lower, more primordial type of cognitive and neural organization. Those rhythms are characteristic of the function of lower brain levels and normally express themselves fully only in sexual activity, dreams, or in altered mind states caused by brain disease, for instance in autism, in psychoses such as schizophrenia, and in the perseverative, stereotypical symptoms caused by damage in frontal cerebral cortices and related brain regions. Chronic alcoholism can cause such states either by direct brain damage or by inducing transient cerebral dysfunction, and I am persuaded that Pollock's condition played a major role here. Such low-level rhythms are ideal to depict emotional states, feelings, drives, forces, pain, pleasure, joy, gloom, but are hardly adequate for the direct representation of figures, actions, or values. Incidentally, the suggestion that Pollock had schizophrenia, made by Dr. Henderson and by Wysuph, is entirely unacceptable. The diagnosis is just as incorrect as Jung's own inept classification of Pablo Picasso as schizophrenic. In strict clinical terms Pollock had a severe neurosis, and his behavior had sociopathic features. He also had a severe alcohol addiction. The latter is likely to have caused some gradual brain damage and, given its magnitude, certainly conditioned brain dysfunction as well as a disruption of "normal" cognitive function. Again, let me make a qualification of the sort I outlined for alcohol and drugs: psychiatric illness is neither sufficient nor necessary for artistic expression. Some artists may produce great art *before* they become psychotic or *after* they regain a normal state of mind, but *not* during active psychosis. The situation is different with neurosis, even if severe. Neurosis is a frequent contributory factor in the production of the most humanly significant art. The suffering caused by neurosis directly or as a result of the social consequences it carries can provide great artists with experiences that will find a way into the substance of their art. Much the same reservations apply to the results of focal brain damage as caused by a stroke or chronic alcoholism. Mild degrees of abnormality, for instance in visual or auditory perceptions, can provide artists with novel experiences that can be used artistically to great advantage. But when dysfunction reaches a severe level in any of the cerebral systems that subtend cognition, there is no evidence that valid artistic productivity can be maintained.

The technique is thus limited, capable of suggesting moods, affect, general drifts of the human mind and its condition, but incapable of coping with the problem that the unconscious also contains figures that perform actions according to values, in specific times and places, and that there are inextricable and important specific relationships between those figures and acts. It is perhaps unfair to ask painting to bring us closer to a more clearly referential level of cognitive processing, although painting certainly can and Pollock might have. Painting or music should not have to compete with photography, let alone with the novel, film, or theatre. And yet, it is important to note that Pollock's most personal and novel approach had a limited expressive capability.

## POLLOCK'S TECHNIQUE IN THE PERSPECTIVE OF COGNITIVE SCIENCE

Modern research on cognition has shown that the brain utilizes largely different neural mechanisms to acquire and process different types of information. For instance, the personal information that relates to our own experience of a given life episode ("contextual" or "episodic" knowledge) is retrieved differently from that which is shared by most of us, to a larger or greater extent ("generic" or "semantic" knowledge). Similarly, the brain units involved in processing information based on propositional data ("declarative" knowledge) are different from those that manipulate information according to a problem-solving strategy or from those that learn a skill ("procedural" knowledge).[18] Pollock's *Mural* and most of the paintings for which he became famous are based on "procedural" knowledge, a knowledge of "how," based on the access, by motor activity, of moods and states and skills with which unconscious processes manipulate their contents. But the contents themselves are never manifest, the knowledge of "that" is not specified. The attitude is diametrically opposed to that of Robert Arneson: *Minuteman* could not be more "declarative" in its exposition of factual data, judgments, and qualifications, and quite different also from the early and late phases of one of the most remarkable Pollock contemporaries, Philip Guston.

Even the types of movements Pollock discovered to perform his paintings are intriguing from the neurologic and cognitive standpoints. Pollock used movements of the whole arm, trunk, and occasionally of the whole body, but *not* fine movements of the hand and fingers. Neurophysiologically, it is now known from studies in both humans and monkeys, the cerebral units which control the grosser proximal movements of limb and whole body are entirely different from those that operate the fine motions of individual fingers (in writing or drawing) or of the phonatory apparatus (in speech).[19] How interesting then, that Pollock explored so successfully the phylogenetically more primitive machinery of whole body movements, the ones more suited to access and transcribe the phylogenetically more primitive structures of our mind.

POLLOCK'S *Mural:* SUCCESS OR FAILURE?

Sitting in front of *Mural* and enjoying its sight once again I have no doubt about Pollock's success. Did he not create stirring and original beauty? Does that beauty not diminish and transcend the pain that moved it to be? The answer is affirmative on both counts. And yet the technical limitations discussed above suggest that Pollock's work may have been personally effective and unquestionably linked to the ills of his time but did not express the human condition to which it speaks as clearly and as forcefully as it might have. I propose that, great as his achievement was, it *could* have been greater, considering the dimension of his talent and the fabric of his person.

John Berger goes further and more harshly with a similar thesis. Although he admires Pollock's talent he believes Pollock was a failure. His argument is that Pollock initially borrowed and was sustained by the intellectual fervor of the Mexicans and of Picasso but had to abandon their course because their themes were not "applicable to his own view of his own social and cultural situation." And he adds: "Finally, in desperation, he made his theme the impossibility of finding a theme. Having the ability to speak, he acted dumb."[20] I subscribe to this view only in part. I agree that Pollock turned his rejection of a theme into *a* theme, and I can even concur with the harsh judgment that his choice was less articulate than it could have been. But where I differ is in the assumption that Pollock's choice took into account an analysis of the social and cultural conditions of his time. That his actions were inextricably linked to a unique social and cultural context, I have no doubt. But the final choices, if choice is the appropriate term, that dictated the shape of his art, came from far more personal, less rational, and less choate quarters of his being. The peculiar combination of his illness and his intelligence allowed him exceptional entry into a generally forbidden landscape of the human condition. The landscape was uniquely private and uniquely remote and consequently the intelligibility of the art it provoked is limited. Therein lies, in my opinion, the paradoxical combination of Pollock's great success and relative failure: by striving for universality within his ailing, insulated self, he risked being mistaken for a paragon of pure aesthetics.

## NOTES

1 See Peggy Guggenheim, *Confessions of an Art Addict* [reprint of *Out of This Century* (1946)] (New York: Macmillan, 1960), 106–7.

2 Ibid.

3 See Francis V. O'Connor, *Jackson Pollock* (New York: The Museum of Modern Art, 1967), 11–74, and the catalogue of the recent Pollock exhibition at the Centre Georges Pompidou, *Jackson Pollock* (Paris: Centre Georges Pompidou, 1982), 213–309.

4 O'Connor, 14, 15.

5 John Berger, "Artists Defeated by Difficulties," in *Permanent Red* (London: Methuen and Co., 1960; reprint, New York: Writers and Readers Publishing Cooperative, 1979), 66–70.

6 Pollock's years in psychoanalysis are discussed by William Rubin in "Pollock as Jungian Illustrator: The Limits of Psychological Criticism," *Art in America* 67 (Nov. 1979), 17; by Judith Wolfe in "Jungian Aspects of Jackson Pollock's Imagery," *Artforum* 2 (Nov. 1972), 65–73; and by O'Connor, 23.

7 For discussions of Pollock's stylistic development, see Robert C. Hobbs, "Early Abstract Expressionism: A Concern with the Unknown Within," in Robert C. Hobbs and Gail Levin, *Abstract Expressionism: The Formative Years* (Ithaca: Cornell University Press, 1978); O'Connor, *Jackson Pollock*; and Centre Georges Pompidou, *Jackson Pollock*.

8 See Hobbs in Hobbs and Levin, 14.

9 See Rubin; Wolfe; and C. L. Wysuph, *Jackson Pollock: Psychoanalytic Drawings* (New York: N.p., 1970).

10 O'Connor, 21.

11 Ibid., 80.

12   Quoted by Hobbs in Hobbs and Levin, 13.

13   L. De Coppet and Alan Jones, *The Art Dealers* (New York: Potter, 1984), 36.

14   Guggenheim, 107.

15   Quoted by Rubin, 88.

16   Joseph L. Henderson in "Jackson Pollock: A Psychological Commentary," an unpublished essay [1968], cited in Wysuph, 14.

17   O'Connor, 40.

18   Antonio Damasio, "The Anatomic Basis of Memory Disorders," *Seminars of Neurology* 4, no. 2 (1984), 223–25.

19   Norman Geschwind and Antonio Damasio, "Apraxia," in *Handbook of Clinical Neurology*, 2nd ed., vol. 1 (Amsterdam: Elsevier, 1985).

20   Berger, 6.

# POLLOCK AND CANVAS

Jorie Graham

## Part I

When he leaned down over
   the undefeated soil
to make it end somewhere,
   to make it beautiful
( go nowe forthe, thou litel song upon
   my message ), when

he leaned down through the space
   which separated him from it,
down through the way and the life,
   and the garment of minutes ( and sey that I
give her ) and the garment of light ( hert body and
   minde ) parting the past from the future with his leaning,
a flare, a tiny quick
   freedom ( let no waves

let no winde, let no stormes, let not the salte
   see. . . . ), what he chose—can you understand
this—what he chose ( go forthe
   in hast )
what he chose
   through the see no evil, through the eye for
the eye,
   choosing to no longer let the brushtip touch,
at any point,
   the still ground,

Jorie Graham is an Assistant Professor in the Program in Creative Writing, Department of English.

was to not be trans-
    formed but to linger
in the hollow, the about-to-be, whispering *Yes*
    *I understand you* whispering
*tell me then what will render*
    *the body alive* whispering ( leaning down
further ) *is there anything finally opposite*
    *to life* ( his brush

hovering, his brush able to cut a figure
    on the blank and refusing ) whispering *suppose the imperishable . . .*
whispering *may not the same be said for . . .*
    the leaning out itself a kind of whispering . . .
The king can neither ride nor walk, neither lie nor stand, he
    leans but cannot sit and sighs
remembering. There is a lake called

_____. There is a ritual silver bowl
    found at _____ in a bog.
On the outside deities, unidentified, and within
    a series
of scenes. . . . There is a lake, they bring him there for the
    air, for his painful open wound, he calls that his
hunting day, what can he catch there with his wound so painful
    that would provision
his home?


PART II


1.

Here is the lake, the open, he calls it his day; fishing.

2.

The lake, the middle movement, woman's flesh, maya.

3.

And here is the hook before it has landed, before it's deep
                                        in the current,

## 4.

the hovering–keeping the hands off–the gap alive,

## 5.

the body of talk talk between the start and beauty,

## 6.

all limbs this one sucked alive by delay and brought to stand here
in the room
among the rest of the forms

## 7.

this girl all accident all *instead-of,* of the graces the

## 8.

most violent one, the one all gash all genitalia

## 9.

( between the creator and the created: a flash: a girl: )

## 10.

( the most violent one ) ( *one cannot produce depth only the sensation of depth* )

## 11.

( without embarassment, without shame ) the most violent one–

## 12.

as in *I can* ( the hook hissing mid-air ) *control the flow of paint, there is no accident no beginning no end. . . .*

## 13.

Oh but we wanted to paint what is not beauty, how can one paint what is not beauty. . . .

## 14.

And I will cover thee with my hand when I pass by

## 15.

And will take away my hand and thou shalt see my back my

form—The most violent one, standing there with her hand on her hip,
gorgeous gap

between the mind and the world, water, water,

the line being fed out the line without shape before it lands without
death

saying a good life is possible, still hissing, still unposited,

before it lands, without shape, without generation, or form that bright
fruit

( a part of the place but cut out from the place )—

not in the wanting,

not motionless but not in the wanting yet, the image,

the unsaid billowing round the hook, updrafting, caressing,

the light whispering never ( can you hear it ) have we been here

before can you hear it never never green hook in the sunny

day, young, beginning to sink,

down through the day the netting of chance her body

as the young god stole down through the suffering to come up with a
meaning a

form

## 28.

which is nothing more than a desire for clearly matched theft and
                                                                    punishment

## 29.

and the streames of hir heavenly looke shall all your sorrows
steer

## 30.

and down into the end finally still on the ground there beneath him.


PART III

Where does the end
    begin?
Where does the lifting off of hands become
    love,
letting the made go out into danger,
    letting the form slur out into flaw, in-

conclusiveness? Where does the end of love

begin? ( Where does that love begin? )
    And then He rested, is that where the real
making
    begins—the now—Then he rested letting in chance letting in
any wind any shadow quick with minutes, and whimsy,
    through the light, letting the snake the turning
in. Then things not yet true
    which slip in

are true
    aren't they?
Where is the border of *stopping* and *ending?*
    And the land was waste but the king did not die,
his brother died but something king did not die,
    molting,
not at any point
    dead.

The clouds *like transcripts* over the pond
( did not die ), the grammar the deepwater which mutters
    long before the sentence ( hissing, mid-air )
begins
    and keeps on keeps on, under the caught fish, lifted, silvery,
keeping the wound
    alive. The caught with its outline, promising, promising. . . .
*It is the window that makes it difficult* ( but here
    there is no window ) it is

the eyes that cannot see *the present,*
    that flit, naming, with a carpenter's
lateness.
    The exterior of x is the body. . . .
The exterior of stopping is ending. . . .
    Look down here into this open sepulcher
( unstretched ) what has he planted? What's coming up?
    Is it a shape a dead thing?
We used to think that shape, a finished thing, was a corpse
    that would sprout–Easter in every heart–what do we
think

now?
    What we want is to paint nothing how can one paint nothing.
The look of spontaneity
    comes up, the figure. Has it a name? Can you nail it?
–arms, eyes, is it a woman is it three women moving towards
    one man, is it what we did and why
why
    this girl this girl

rising in the mind in place of the mind
    shedding her garment like a sense of earlyness, shedding the
                                        next one
as the possible slips off the shoulders of the true,
    bright shoulders rising up ( birdscreech, daybreak ) likewise the
                                        next one
and the next, shedding your hands on her,
    your wish, altogether, shedding your eyes on her,

sticky, as petals drop off, all at once, just after rain, just as the first
                                                      light strikes

    and the meaning of the rose rises up,
( shedding the meaning of the rose )
    and the memory of the rose rises up
( shedding the memory of the rose )–

( the hands lifting off, the mind lifting off, the wish lifting off, all at
                                        once now )

Oh she would be a readiness, a first clearing, a sound
    beginning at the end of sound, an escape from . . .
escape from. . . . But can she step free into
    that chapel say I
do, can the girl come clean of the mother's body
        ——the legs are still up there where does she end–
you can't pick her out can't choose a thing here–
    what's the title, the scales won't wash off,
the shimmering scales won't and she

stand up clean on the shore and walk towards you, no,
        ——A shell he said, a nut, a plum, a pear a
kidney a carrot a treetrunk he said a bird a
bird a lark a shore a bulrush he said a
mountain a bone——( is it enough, will it provision his home? )

                                    . . . . The moment
    a figure appears on the canvas she said
the story begins, the story begins the error sets in,
    the error the boredom she said the story talking louder
than the paint she said, the boredom the hurry, she said
    ( without embarassment, without shame )
( and you must learn to feel shape as simply shape whispered the
    wind, not as description not as reminiscence not as what

it will become )
    ( down past the birds the daybreak the glass
in the landfill glimmering, reminding ) ( down past the blind girl on
                                        our corner now

turning to face the wind, waiting for the light
to change )
    ( and I will take away mine hand, He said,

and I will take away mine hand and thou, thou. . . . )

# ROBERT ARNESON

American, born in 1930

*Plate 3*

*Minuteman,* 1982
Glazed ceramic
48 x 31 x 15 in.
(121.9 x 78.8 x 38.1 cm.)
University of Iowa Museum of Art
*Museum purchase*

*Detail: left profile*

# REPRESENTATIONS OF A PIECE OF FLESH

DAVID HAMILTON

W henever led to the chance, and especially indoors, I'm what Mar-
shall McLuhan has called "a print-oriented bastard." So for me, I'll
confess, the Iowa Museum of Art is usually what I walk past on my
way to and from the library. Occasionally I go in, but I am more likely
to keep my eye on the river beside it. A luxurious willow has been
taken, sadly, from the bank by the museum (a fine place to pause in
the summer), but ginkgoes and flowering crabs still line the path.
Cedar waxwings have their season, especially among the crabs, and
ducks are all but ever present. Last summer, when I made more of a
point than usual to explore the museum, on the mission I'm here to
unfold, the ducks were bringing along at least two hatchings of
chicks. Several flotillas meandered with the river as I made my way indoors. Could I cope with a contemporary sculpture, I wondered?
Could I manage, in effect, to read that as well as I knew to watch a
river or read a poem? Remembering the advice of a Shakespeare professor, not to scorn beginning with "a firm grasp on the obvious," I
walked into the museum to locate the obvious in a work by Robert
Arneson.

*Minuteman,* Arneson's glazed ceramic sculpture (1982), seems intended less to grace a museum than to browbeat its audience. In a library, I thought, creations as daunting as this keep their place between covers. We approach them by way of a certain ceremony of acquaintance, proceeding through the catalogues, corridors and, frequently, through a misleading introduction. But this thing glittered all
out in the open. If anything, it seemed too straightforward.

The work is a vigorous antiwar statement in the form of a head,
most likely a warrior's, hacked off crudely below the base of the neck

---

David Hamilton is a Professor in the Department of English.

and impaled on a cross. The upright member of the cross bears the inlaid pattern of a missile. Hence the name, *Minuteman*, contains at least two references – to the contemporary armament, and to a member of a Revolutionary War militia, both set companionably against the primary symbol of Christian civilization.

The head of *Minuteman* is significantly larger than life but the cross is short; you stoop to view the face eye to eye. Its sockets are empty. The glaze includes a variety of colors, none of them particularly healthy. There are splotches of yellow, some gray, patches of brown and of rust; here and there a sickly pink, such as I associate with dolls, obtrudes. Overlying some of that are drips of black paint, as from the hand of Jackson Pollock. The head itself, massive, bulging, brutalized, and bald, suggests the heroic.

What first commanded my gaze though were the wounds. Three bullet holes cluster to the left of the man's crown. Blood wells in each. An unspecified blow has caved in his right cheek, twisting the nose back across it and forcing the eye above into a squint. The mouth seems to trace a private satisfaction. A fourth bullet hole opens on the lower right behind the ear. Blood pours from both eyes and the nose and drips from the base of the neck. Three grooves run laterally across the top right side of the head; one has the softened contours of a drainage ditch but the other two could have been worked with a chisel. The neckline is ragged as if the instrument of decapitation had been a bayonet.

The obvious damage done this character has a second component in that his head bears designs and words as well as wounds. The man's forehead, for example, displays a target. The three clustered holes above and to the left would have to have been inflicted by a rather poor shot, but they do form a group, as marksmen would put it. The words seemed especially inviting to me; I took them as signs of advertisement, mockery, and warning in proportions that are anyone's guess. In a sense the words are the more severe wounds – some are carved deeply into the flesh – but whether assaults on his flesh or tattoos proudly born, it is difficult to say.

They don't mince words, however. "KILL" says one, then "Butcher Slaughter Human Beings Indiscriminately." Also, "Attack," "Rat-tat-tat," "Massacre," and, once again, "slaughter." Finally, in smaller capitals more faintly engraved, "OFFICIALS DENY KNOWLEDGE." That last remark, on the base of the skull, lies between a couple of sketches, one of a World War II GI aiming his rifle, its barrel creating a line for the words "Attack" and "Rat-tat-tat," the other, higher on the head, a less distinct sketch of bodies in a pile, perhaps a reminder of Goya. All these details are simple enough to recount, and my first impression, surely, was of a blunt antiwar statement, undistracted by any subtlety.

Frequently art grips us because it is direct, saying exactly what needs to be said, occurring, it seems, only a millimoment before we would have realized the same thing ourselves, as if the idea lurked in our own minds on the very verge of expression. Once expressed, it is obvious; and once obvious, compelling. I feel something of the hope for that effect in this work. But "the aesthetics of directness" usually depend on a quick effect heightened, often, by understatement, as in, for example, Hamlet's offhand remark on the fate of his former friends: "So Rosencrantz and Guildenstern go to it." This piece is too baroque for that. One feels the brunt of the message quickly and then becomes diverted tallying the wounds and sayings. Through all that tallying, the whole loses its force. Hence I worry that I haven't seen enough in Arneson's work and find myself deflected toward what seems at first a merely incidental part of the composition.

Below the impaled head and on the left arm of the cross lies a smaller lump of flesh, exposed like a bluegill on the bank of the river. It's a curious distraction. Not only has the head been clumsily re-moved but the body brutalized further. This single piece of flesh, bloodied like the other wounds, underscores that gratuitous violence. My inclination was to police the site, to pick up the smaller piece and throw it in the trash. But one might as well dispose of the head, which could as easily require burying, or for that matter dispose of any flesh whatever, our individual need for burial being only a matter of time. That small lump reminds us how close we are to treating all flesh as waste, and so it becomes oddly touching.

A more compelling direct statement might have had the work con-sist only of that extra lump of flesh. Label it *Minuteman*, (Minute man, My-nuked-man) as if it alone were left once Christian militancy has had its say. Or place it alone on the arm of the missile-inscribed cross. What would be subtracted from our immediate view would return to our minds, variously but powerfully, as we stood contemplating that small remainder, which would also remind us. We would each be abandoned to our thoughts, imagining, privately, the message of a poor piece of flesh.

But it is unfair to prescribe a classically spare or minimalist style that seems far from Arneson's intent. I thank him for allowing me to imagine that possibility, which I prefer, but let us turn now to a second way of reading his work. Let us try to see it less as a blunt antiwar message than as comedy.

This second and probably less obvious reading begins with the words, especially "Rat-tat-tat." Might not that be openly comic? Only kids playing war say "rat-tat-tat," and these days they probably mimic more of an explosion, a World War II machine gun not being their weapon of choice. We needn't press too far, therefore, to discover a comic-book effect, with words, noises, and images of violence splattered on, say, a warrior from the world of Mad Max, a Charles Bronson toughguy-cum-brute who increases in strength the more he is beat up. His multiplicity of wounds, both physical and verbal, fill out the world of the comic grotesque. Who, after all, bears slogans etched deeply into his flesh? Who brandishes blood from as many wounds as these as if each were a Cartier watch? And whose twisted mouth could suggest a smile more readily than a villain savoring his fate? On what kind of flesh does someone sketch the elements of carnage, casually, as if doodling on yesterday's paper? The grotesque is often comic, an attitude that stems from its excess. There is even a tick-tack-toe game begun on the backside of the cross, adding a touch of the commonplace and of idleness, as if Kilroy had also been there.

One question is what to make of a comic response to the apparent theme of warfare/warfear, which in part motivates this work. To make much of this question, I seem pressed to read Arneson's mind, an improbability at best, which I'll skirt by claiming merely to describe attitudes of his that I am beginning to suspect. Those attitudes include an element of nervousness and a certain doubt that the audience will get the point.

We are all familiar with laughter as companion to horror, as to embarrassment; and horror itself is embarrassing, especially in a peaceful museum with its hushed corridors, its variety of attractive objects evoking other moods, usually more thoughtful than threatening, and this within an almost pastoral setting on the bank of a calm river. It's almost a rudeness to impose this object on that setting, and the comic elements, seeking to defuse the affront of violence, come close to announcing a failure of nerve. Violence is written all over the piece, which cannot easily settle into this place, and so the comic stylization allows us to take it less than seriously. We can say "rat-tat-tat," smile at a companion, and comment next on the luster of bright blood. Well, bright red glaze on the ceramic; we're not likely to make that mistake either.

Arneson's comic relief accords oddly with fearing we may not get the point, but the work is relentless in multiplying its evidence. Perhaps that, too, signals nervousness. Rather than pausing to absorb a serious point, we dodge off to another and yet another gesture. The work is full of "don't you sees," and "I meant to says," and "let me put it this way" and then "that." It's as if the artist doesn't trust us to take his message seriously were it reduced, possibly, to a missile-engraved cross on the suggestion of an ashen landscape. That alone would be a political statement, not novel, but demanding. It would embody the further virtue of laying blame where it belongs, on social organization in its larger dimensions rather than interposing an incidental, fantasy warrior.

But perhaps the version I've just suggested would be missing Arneson's point, which could be to make an eye-catching sculpture in clay, of course, one that can attract attention amid the cross-stimuli of a museum or gallery, one that can compete well amid the mishmash of the modern world, which seldom encourages political reflection. A certain luxuriousness of execution assists these ends as does a playful diversity of wounds toward which one can point and point with the mind's finger.

Perhaps, then, any message, as such, should be the least of our worries. In this case, and as a third way of reading, we could regard *Minuteman* as pure art, an orchestration of glazed ceramic forms. From this point of view its message is incidental. It's an old theme anyway, the horror of war, almost as old as summer ducklings on a river. The point may be less to stress the message than to display how Arneson handles it once more, artfully, and in ceramic.

Accordingly, one might begin by noticing again the persistent pink of the flesh. The blood from the wounds, from the eyes and the nose, is cherry red, like Marilyn Monroe's lipsticks. Here voluptuousness spills over, urging a peculiar pleasure. The multiplicity of wounds encourages this effect; pleasure lies in their reiteration. One crease across the skull won't do, take three. One bullet wound, hardly enough; suffer two more, then another.

Its divided form is another formal element of this composition. The single piece of flesh, dropped from the rest, urges a broader inquiry into the relation of part to whole and suggests the strange case of the divided sculpture, not a mounted warrior or a pietà in which the two figures join as a continuous run of marble or metal, but the odder situation of a main element with something slighter separated from it. This vulnerable bit of meat lies out on the end of an arm of the cross, almost disconnected.

Any broken form affords, I think, a curious double pleasure. We feel the momentary thrill of violation but sense equally the whole beyond the parts, forever perfect as an idea. Such feelings may account for our captivation by old manuscripts with lacunae, by stories unfinished, by all that ancient statuary missing limbs or heads, by ruins we flock to in buses or find voluptuously detailed in the drawings of Piranesi, by the odd piece of driftwood we find washed up by a river. Fragments are ineluctably poignant. Here we find another when our eyes fall almost accidentally on that extra piece of flesh. Including it in the composition is an aesthetic challenge.

As it is, likewise, to include the words. The interplay of material and verbal features is not strange in itself as any of the last few faculty shows has demonstrated or, for that matter, *The Book of Kells*. Nevertheless the representation of words in material form has an unusual aesthetic effect, making their reading anything but obvious. What is the point anyway of making words palpable? Arneson sets them in various ways, both more and less boldly. "Kill" and "slaughter" have been deeply engraved in blockish letters, while the others are more lightly suggested by pinpricks in the clay or in letters that portray an unaccomplished freehand. Part of the pleasure must be actually seeing these words and, beyond that, getting a feel for them. I felt an urge to fondle the gouges as one might finger a wound, and I wondered whether they should sound more or less tentative on the tongue in correlation with the force of their depiction.

But the subject matter of this piece is finally too blatant to suppose it incidental, as if Arneson had selected a warrior as only a random theme upon which to play his ceramic variations. Clearly this work is against war more than it is about composition. If it is to haunt us, I think its power will arise from yet another way of reading. We have considered an aesthetics of directness and another of grotesque, even burlesque comedy. A third way has been to mute the message in order to concentrate on arrangements of form. For a fourth, let us consider irony, a way of reading that draws out from the work the materials of its own refutation.

*Minuteman* makes several ironic suggestions, the most obvious being the resemblance of the head to Roman busts memorializing conquering generals. The rounded, vigorous head, the empty eye sockets, the forthright, confrontational demeanor, and the bust cut off where chest and shoulders begin to spread from the neck all indicate, say, the head of Trajan. This figure is notably uglier than the Roman original, a grotesque as we have said, and the relation of the two is inherently ironic, especially as Arneson's figure is also, among other things, heroic. Moreover, this character makes a defiant gesture: the more bloodied he becomes, the more impossible he seems to dispatch. In that light the irony deepens. Perhaps this contemporary figure offers something more enduring, even, than a Roman bust.

The wounds themselves are primitive. Nuclear war would hardly leave such a recognizable figure. The bullet holes, the furrows across his skull, his caved-in cheek; all those wounds suggest one-on-one combat, in which we still locate vestiges of glory. This figure for warfare inherits an ancient form. He is a warrior who persists. His energy has been around for longer than we have any sense of civilization, and it is not clear that he is dead. Whenever we think we have put an end to him, he crops up again with that same trace of a smile. However eyeless, he swaggers before us with his trace of a private satisfaction.

And the words as wounds reinforce his primitive bearing. It is as if he were an old stick bearing runes, the most ancient and minimal form of writing in our language, a code for blunt messages, secrets, and sayings. These we can read either as the vicious endowments of our culture rendering him mindless or as slogans he enforces. One has a way of becoming the other.

Wounds and words, wounds and words; reiterated they become a chant. How do we hear it? As background noise, a murmur, all sense abstracted, or as cruelly threatening? Massacre, butcher, slaughter, kill. Massacre, butcher, slaughter, kill. Material and verbal forms envelope each other. Here are rhythms for a playground game, for boot camp, for intoning at a gravesite.

What is this figure's particular pleasure? Having survived. Having fought as he has, inflicting as much as has been inflicted upon him. Frightening more sedentary sorts with a specter from the roots of our civilization. Or simply persisting as only our desires for food and sex, our discontent with social order, and, perhaps, our fondness for nature have also persisted.


Off and on over the summer I've come by the museum to look again at *Minuteman* and see what reactions I might have. This essay records much of what I have been able to think about it. My steadiest conviction is that this last way of reading the piece is probably close to what Arneson "has to say" with his sculpture. I've been told I might call him and discuss it, but I don't want to do that. It's in the public domain now, whatever he says, and we must make up our minds, which is what we mean by "interpret." Robert Frost once said, "I'll take credit for anything you find in my poems." For my part, I'm happy to credit Arneson with this grimly ironic warning. His unlovely figure is a part of our genetic heritage and culture. To see the folly and viciousness of war is easy. To acknowledge its seed in ourselves as we chant antiwar hymns asks more of us.

Toward the end of his last play, Shakespeare has Prospero look upon Caliban and say, "This thing of darkness I acknowledge mine." Without that acceptance Prospero can hardly transcend his disquieted state and still "the beating in his mind." Arneson's message I take to be similar. I wish, nevertheless, that the work had been different. I would have preferred just that lump of flesh. Or maybe – and I have in mind now a Mauldin cartoon – the cross, the missile enscribed on it, but with no head at all, only that piece of flesh beside the cross, like an afterthought, on the ground. As long as the human figure of warfare persists, we can harbor a dream of converting him to a man of peace. A more timely warning would deprive us of that hope, and that trace of flesh would make its own representation, foreshadowing disaster.

I can express that preference, but I wouldn't have found it without Arneson's creation. So I'll credit him not only for everything we find in his work but for much I bring myself to imagine.

Why should I leave off, though, without admitting that my preference for a more minimalist statement, for a less baroque, less frenzied message of warfear, continues unabated. Having thought of that, I believe it would have been stronger and am less able to celebrate this work as effectively political. Arneson is no stranger to spare strategies. A bronze skull from 1983, sexless, wasted, utterly without hope or comic deflection, offers an example. It is from a year later, though, which means *Minuteman* could be transitional and my remarks now only a conjecture of his own self-criticism. But to continue. It bears words too, and possibly other markings; I've only seen a photograph and can't confidently speak its character. If its title, *Nuclear Warhead*, is any indication, however, Arneson's sense of humor discovers in it a more chilling effect. That time, it seems, he didn't duck the challenge.

These thoughts lead me to a more complex conclusion. I'm ready to believe that Arneson's message in *Minuteman* is close to our ironic fourth reading of the warrior who persists. But the terms in which the work succeeds best, I believe, are closer to our third suggestion of an orchestration of glazed ceramic forms. It succeeds then not by being frightening–our fright is only conventional and polite–but by being eye-catching. Attractive in the most literal sense, it draws us into the pleasures of appreciation, where we notice this, notice that, see how one element complements another, and revel in observation, the busyness of our minds a reflection, for the moment, of the busyness of the art. All of which makes the figure itself more of a commodity, which is no more than we might expect in our culture and a truly disconcerting irony–if warfear truly demands our attention, and if this much glitter is what grabs it?

# ROBERT ARNESON'S *MINUTEMAN*

RICHARD M. CAPLAN, M.D.

W hat's the value of looking repeatedly at an artwork? What is the long-term residue of a three-minute look repeated, say, at ten weekly intervals, compared to a single "immersion" session of thirty minutes? That's an empirical question. (For example, one could devise a test to judge retention of visual detail among two groups of "equivalent" viewers one week, month, or year after each type of viewing experience. Maybe such research has already been done by some hybrid of a psychometrically oriented psychologist crossed with an art historian.) There is unquestionably an enormous importance to incubation and reinforcement, whether in writing an essay, playing an instrument, or studying a work of art. At least, that's the conclusion I've reached as a result of my being asked to view Robert Arneson's *Minuteman* and write my reaction to it. The challenge of studying the work and responding to it *because* I am a physician and *not* an art critic/historian was a challenge too great to pass by. I wondered what *would* happen if I studied a work intently, and how my physician-hood would enter into my reaction to the work. What follows contains my answer to myself and to you.

What merit lies in going back again and again to look at the same work? It depends on the work, of course. If good enough, it will reward the returnee with new observations and fresh interpretations. If there always seems more detail to notice and more response to savor, then the work is indeed great; if it provides no such rewards, then one will not give it the third glance—maybe not even the second. Although a critic may help the naive viewer by drawing attention to some of the details and associations, or through words lure a

Richard M. Caplan is a Professor in the Department of Dermatology, Associate Dean for Continuing Medical Education, and Director of the Program in Medical Humanities.

potential viewer to become an actual viewer, the work must make its own case, which it might achieve if the viewer will come to it with an open mind.

I was invited to read articles that provided information about Arneson and the California school of ceramicists. I did that, and also talked to the artist, but only *after* I had spent considerable time looking at *Minuteman*. (I will occasionally insert Arneson's comments as italicized quotations.) Learning details of Arneson's life, seeing other examples of his work (mainly via photographs), placing him and his work in a broader cultural and historical context – all indeed added to my interpretations and appreciation of *Minuteman,* even though the work proved richly provocative and rewarding without those extras. My reaction is similar to my feelings about the practice of medicine: the broader one's knowledge of people and society, as well as one's own personal and professional roots, the more effective and humane will be one's medical work and the fuller the enjoyment of it.

How shall I respond to thee? Let me count the ways. . . . I visited this work several times, took photos from several positions and distances, and studied it more intently than I had ever done with any other art object. I can now readily summon it to my mind's eye. Were I to write of what I saw, how I looked, and what reactions I had, then I would need several periods of close observation, along with periodic mental re-creations to stimulate internal mental associations.

The physician Arthur Conan Doyle, in writing "The Adventure of the Blanched Soldier," has protagonist Sherlock Holmes say, "I see no more than you, but I have trained myself to notice what I see."[1] It is this remark plus similar comments about the need for closeness of observation, and especially Holmes's demonstration of his skill at it, that continue to charm readers to this day. It is also what makes the Sherlock Holmes stories, although not literary masterpieces, such useful works in exemplifying for medical students and practitioners the necessary skill of close observation. It may properly be thought especially important for practitioners of dermatology, my own discipline, to seek and notice fine details because most of our diagnostic effort comes through interpreting visual clues. But surely this is as true for diagnostic radiology, and in fact almost any branch of medical work. Complete blindness is an extreme handicap to the practice of almost any medical discipline.

This point of view makes it useful for me, in my introductory lecture about dermatology to sophomore medical students, to project on the screen various works of art to help students understand that they can easily grow accustomed to noticing recurring details and patterns that help identify the style of the particular artist. This step—inspection—is the beginning of what physicians call the physical examination. One must *look* consciously and *notice* the detail. The same principles of observation that permit one to recognize an El Greco by the attenuated shape of the figures—or a Rubens by their plumpness, or a Mondrian by the colorful rectilinear arrays, or a Modigliani by the slim necks and almond-shaped eyes, or a Magritte by the visual non sequiturs—will also permit one to make a recognition diagnosis by observing the shape, size, color, amount and slope of elevation, texture, depth, sharpness of border, surface markings of individual lesions, and how they are distributed over the body. This comes after one has seen the patient totally with respect to such details as body configuration, manner of movement and gait, color of skin, rate and manner of breathing, strength and pitch of voice, and all the details that might be summed up by the phrase "body language." If I have done a really first-rate job of enumerating the details, I then stand a chance of doing a better job as a physician.

## THE HEAD

Is it totally unreasonable to "read" the crossed-hairs target on the figure's forehead as a transformed halo of traditional iconography? Probably. Yet to do so adds at once to the sense of distortion and outrage that accentuates the power of this work and invites a more careful look at the many other vivid details of this image that invite interpretations.

Is it only trauma that has produced the unseemly lumpiness of the skull? The distortion of shape (especially with words imprinted) suggests a reference to the pseudoscientific phrenology of Franz Joseph Gall, who taught in Vienna almost two centuries ago (and spawned an industry not yet eradicated by modern neuroanatomy and physiological psychology). His work proposes that attributes of intelligence, character, and personality reside in certain portions of the brain, producing variations in brain shape that may be "read" from the shape of the overlying cranium—as if the skull were formed by molding not-yet-solidified bone gently but precisely over the contours of the brain, the way an artist shapes papier-mâché over the contours of a clay mold beneath.[2] [*Fig. 1*] It is similar to the way culinary books

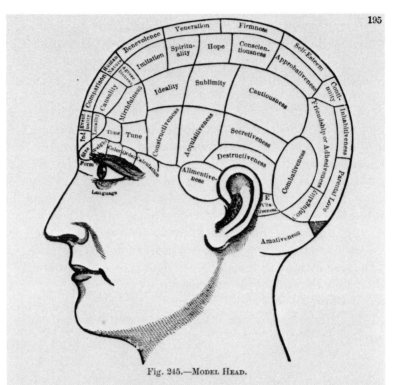

Fig. 245.—MODEL HEAD.

## NAMES, NUMBERS AND LOCATION OF THE MENTAL ORGANS.

1. AMATIVENESS.—Connubial love, affection.
A. CONJUGAL LOVE.—Union for life, pairing instinct.
2. PARENTAL LOVE.—Care of offspring, and all young.
3. FRIENDSHIP.—Sociability, union of friends.
4. INHABITIVENESS.—Love of home and country
5. CONTINUITY.—Application, consecutiveness.
E. VITATIVENESS.—Clinging to life, tenacity, endurance.
6. COMBATIVENESS.—Defence, courage, criticism.
7. DESTRUCTIVENESS. — Executiveness, push, propelling power.
8. ALIMENTIVENESS.—Appetite for food, etc.
9. ACQUISITIVENESS.—Frugality, economy, to get.
10. SECRETIVENESS.—Self-control, policy, reticence.
11. CAUTIOUSNESS. — Guardedness, care-taking, safety.
12. APPROBATIVENESS.—Love of applause and display.
13. SELF-ESTEEM.—Self-respect, dignity, authority.
14. FIRMNESS.—Stability, perseverance, steadfastness.
15. CONSCIENTIOUSNESS.—Sense of right, justice.
16. HOPE.—Expectation, anticipation, perfect trust.
17. SPIRITUALITY.—Intuition, prescience, faith.
18. VENERATION.—Worship, adoration, deference.
19. BENEVOLENCE.—Sympathy, kindness, mercy.

20. CONSTRUCTIVENESS.—Ingenuity, invention, tools.
21. IDEALITY.—*Taste*, love of beauty, poetry and art.
B. SUBLIMITY.—Love of the grand, vast, magnificent.
22. IMITATION.—Copying, aptitude for mimicry.
23. MIRTH.—Fun, wit, ridicule, facetiousness.
24. INDIVIDUALITY.—Observation, curiosity to see.
25. FORM.—Memory of *shape*, looks, persons.
26. SIZE.—Measurement of quantity by the eye.
27. WEIGHT.—Control of motion, balancing.
28. COLOR.—Discernment, and love of colors, hues, tints.
29. ORDER.—*Method*, system, going by *rule*, arrangement.
30. CALCULATION.—Mental arithmetic, numbers.
31. LOCALITY.—Memory of place, position, travels.
32. EVENTUALITY.—Memory of facts, events, history.
33. TIME.—Telling *when*, time cf day, dates, punctuality.
34. TUNE.—Love of music, sense of harmony, singing.
35. LANGUAGE.—*Expression* by words, signs or acts.
36. CAUSALITY.—*Planning*, thinking, philosophy
37. COMPARISON.—Analysis, inferring, illustration.
C. HUMAN NATURE.—Sagacity, perception of motives.
D. SUAVITY.—*Pleasantness*, blandness, politeness.

*Figure 1.* Phrenological diagram, from Nelson Sizer and H. S. Drayton, *Heads and Faces and How to Study Them: A Manual of Phrenology and Physiognomy for the People,* p. 195.

depict in outline a side of beef with areas marked tenderloin, round steak, chuck roast. Modern parodies of the "science" of phrenology still appear in which the head is shown with areas marked honesty, lust, greed, and so on. It's hard *not* to think of such a relationship if one has seen such drawings or parodies, simply because Arneson elected to inscribe words there. ("Had you ever studied or been interested in phrenology?" *"What's that? . . . Oh, that . . . I used to be amused by the stereotypes . . . maybe it was when I was young and used to copy comic books."*)

Are these inscribed words irrelevant to the work? Hardly. These words are not random; they carry great emotional power, suggesting underlying urges or explaining to the viewer what has happened to this figure: kill, butcher, slaughter, human beings, indiscriminately, attack, rat-tat-tat. Arrange those words spatially as Arneson did and then read them from the top down in our usual manner of reading a road sign or a poem:


KILL
BUTCHER
SLAUGHTER
HUMAN BEINGS
INDISCRIMINATELY
ATTACK RAT-TAT-TAT


Modern neuroscience has shown that for right-handed persons the left side of the brain controls language while the right side deals more with visual imagery and the integration of emotional responses. Most of the quasi-phrenological writing in *Minuteman* is on the figure's right side. A paradox. (Is Arneson right-handed? *"Yes."*) Still a paradox.

(These physical wounds that spell out words or messages recall the macabre, profound story by Kafka, "In the Penal Colony."[3] There, a fantastic device exists that spells out in words the answer to the riddle of life on the chest of its occupant as its great needle, sewing-machine-like, impales and kills the victim, who at death is assumed to enjoy a bittersweet moment of exaltative insight.)

The head is misshapen: by abnormal structure of Arneson's model? by an attempt to suggest trauma? by artistic license of the sculptor seeking to produce an emotional effect? Surely the last of those, if not others. But there is far more abnormality here than just the overall shape. Three penetrating wounds of the right frontal area are depicted, of similar size and age, round, and each hole revealing a base of bright red "blood." Almost surely these represent bullet wounds. But look to the rest of the skull–there are no exit wounds! They would be larger, shaggy, and revealing an outward protrusion of brain, bone, or skin fragments. Instead, a similar wound of entrance appears on the neck below the left occipital (rear) area, and once more, no corresponding exit wound. This figure's head is only *absorbing*, not transmitting, insult.

One sees a variety of wound types: linear crush-marks on the left parietal (side) area; the ears asymmetrical, with the left one crimped, its cartilaginous frame mangled. A fragment of what appears to be skin lies on the crossbar below the right ear. If it was meant to appear as flesh having come from the figure, then it would have been *cut* from the lower right side of the neck–cut because its edge is sharp. But at first glance it looks as if chipped off the clay statue, perhaps by accident, or vandalism. That piece and the necessary speculation draws the viewer's attention from the image to the clay of which it is formed. If meant to be a piece of flesh, rather than an unintended piece of chipped statue, what does it portend? But now I see that it must represent flesh, for the edge of the neck above, where this fragment would fit, is coated with a glaze of red "blood." What is the emotional effect of this separated piece?–to intensify the horror of mutilated, separated body?

The blood in the wounds is bright–arterial red, shiny like fingernail polish (or ceramic glaze). But presumably that same liquid, guided by gravity, has run down the neck and onto the upright of the support, and there, though still shiny, it is a deep blue-black. Is this artist forensically oriented, knowing the dried blood will look older and darker in contrast to the bright fresh blood? If so, what prompted him to the ambiguity regarding the age of the shed blood? Ah yes, art can revel in ambiguity, whereas science tries to dispel it. The artistic convention of trompe l'oeil comes to mind, but this work doesn't seem to be trying for such precise representation as to fool the eye into thinking it is looking at a real head. Are the profuse spatters of glaze or paint to represent blood, or otherwise unspecified gore, or the impaction of flying debris against the skull? Have those dots been put in place one at a time (Seurat's pointillism technique) or were they flipped from a brush (Pollock's spatter technique)?

A mixture of wounds, then: the "bullet" holes seem especially conspicuous, the left fronto-parietal area shows blunt trauma, while the front of the neck on the lower left reveals a slim horizontal wound such as would be made by a knife stab. Blood drips from it. Across the occiput the word "massacre" stands forth, but these letter outlines were incised into the skin, and flesh (and maybe bone) are not gouged away as is true for "kill" on the upper right side. The absence of blood suggests that the letters were inscribed after death. But were these letters conceived as written in flesh or in clay?—again a confusion or blending of the represented figure with the substance of which it was made.

There is no hint of hair—not scalp, brows, lashes, or beard. Has it been lost through singeing, as would happen from a direct exposure to great heat? Or is this a figure reduced to its fleshy essentials, the "ornamental" character of human hair already lost? Could it be that the absence of hair serves to eliminate a clue about gender, permitting us to interpret the figure as either man or woman? I think not, for the heaviness of the underlying bony structure (such as the ridges above the eyes), the size of the nose, and the coarseness of the flesh strongly suggest a man.

Other colors present besides "blood red" include darker brown (frontal crown and behind right ear), lighter brown (splotches on forehead and face), and dirty brown (occiput, where lie the dots and tracks of a great many seemingly superficial wounds). Glazes applied to clay permit color effects not available to sculptors who work in bronze or marble, for instance. In a work like this one, constraint is necessary so that the colors fortify the general effect of physical damage, and intensify the emotional effect without suggesting an iota of decoration or ornamentation. The color must be used sparingly, but impressively, as Mondrian used it.

I am struck by the surprising placidity of the right side of the figure's face. It's most conspicuous if one covers the view of the left (battered) side of the face. Perhaps it's unplanned. If deliberate, though, it recalls crucifixions or martyrdom (as St. Sebastian) in which an amazing calm bespeaks an attitude of union with a glory beyond. The pains of mortality, those slings and arrows of outrageous fortune, are ignored in a beatific trance. I've been surprised at finding such an unstrained appearance in some other works where the expected human emotion would have been far different. For example, I recall a Flemish Icarus falling, head down with a face fit for a beatitude; or a medieval painting of Cosmos and Damian amputating a leg from a patient whose face expressed no pain; or the bland look on a platter-borne head of John the Baptist displayed to

Salome (and an equally bland look on her face). Such inconsistency of emotion and circumstance makes me wonder in any of these instances if my interpretation is failing to grasp something important about the work and the artist's "message," or whether the work is merely flawed.

The most striking physical injuries to the figure have happened to the left middle part of the face where the presence of the left eye is indeterminate; fresh, bright blood streams from that orbit. The left sides of the nose and lips seem decreased in their mass, and the facial bones and soft tissue of the left cheek are smashed inward. The blue-gray glaze prominent on the left lower cheek is not so much the true color of an ecchymosis (bruise), which would contain more purple, but rather, it repeats the deep blue-gray of the grave marker. Well, Arneson might not claim sophisticated anatomical or forensic knowledge. (Has he dissected corpses or victims of accidents or hangings as Leonardo, for instance, surely did? *"No, I never worked in a morgue or a hospital, and I wasn't a war veteran. My main connection is just being a patient having surgical operations."*)

His motive was to make an artistic, emotional, and (probably) propaganda statement, not to create a moulage of such fidelity that medical students might study lesions from it. No, one is not entitled to expect clinical verisimilitude from Arneson; on the other hand, my response to the work grows from the context of my personal knowledge and experience. Since much of that relates to the practice of medicine, all these clinical observations and comparisons seem inevitable, unless I try actively to suppress them—not even a very likely possibility. Besides, why should I make any effort to be deliberately untrue to my personal experience and thereby reduce the mental associations and the satisfaction of making diverse observations and sensing meanings from them? How much should I care about the artist's motives? His intentions are of interest, but not binding; once he has released the work, its effects no longer "belong" to him but to the viewer. This associative process may be a high-order variation of the child's game—"What does that cloud look like?"—but in Shakespeare's hand Hamlet plays that game with Polonius and as the cloud changes or is interpreted in quick succession as a camel, a weasel, and then a whale, we learn a great deal about them and their relationship.[4]

Sending and receiving messages—as social animals we do it always. If one were the last human on earth, and knew it, the inability to send a messsage to any person who might receive it and return a response would probably be the greatest part of the agony. To be human is to experience communication, shared meanings, relationships with others. Without that, who would wish anything but some hemlock to drink? Even though one might perhaps enjoy eating food, watching clouds, feeling warmth, basking in the warm sun (were it not nuclear or regular winter), or practicing auto-eroticism of fantasy and flesh, humans are, by genes and environment, gregarious creatures. From our earliest written history we have recognized that paradise in solitude is not paradise—witness the wisdom of Eve's creation in chapter 2, verse 18, of the Book of Genesis: "It is not good that the man should be alone."

## THE WORDS

The artist's election to use words prompts some special rumination. No reader of English can interpret or dismiss these marks as random wounds; these are *words* that wound. But are they externally readable labels, representing thoughts of this allegorical Everyman? Or has an explosion spat out debris that produced a series of wounds that could be read with the explicitness of words? Is Arneson, rather, saying to us, "I don't want you to misinterpret, and think that I'm showing you only a head that is wounded as if hit accidentally by a falling branch during a storm, or a man who fell over a cliff, or was mauled by a grizzly bear, but I want you to know this man was the victim of an attack by other men, who sighted at a target symbolically placed on his forehead, and set forth to kill, butcher, and slaughter him with malice aforethought"?

And yet, in spite of the intent implied by the forehead target, maybe this man, all men, are depicted as massacred not by a specifically directed hostility but—maybe even worse to contemplate, or more ironic—a mindless, thoughtless attack against "human beings indiscriminately," just as a berserk sniper with a machine gun that barks rat-tat-tat may mow down a line of unfamiliar people ambling on the street, or sitting in a restaurant, or perhaps, living in a nation felt by another nation to be its enemy. Such behavior in the case of the sniper is the acting out of a paranoid rage directed by one psychotic person not at a group of persons individually known to him, but at persons whose guilt consists only of being persons. They are as anonymous as ducks in a shooting gallery or on the wing, and as guiltless. But a similar paranoid rage can now, through modern weapons, be directed by one or a small group of leaders in one nation aiming an attack at an essentially anonymous group, now a nation called "the enemy."

Are the words and their explicitness, so contrary to the manner and intent of Magritte's use of words in his titles (see below), an *excess?* Do they bespeak an inadequacy on Arneson's part—that he could not evoke by the nonlinguistic image(s) alone a sufficient power or focus for the anger or concern he felt? He seems to want certainty that the viewer receive his message. He wants to eliminate the possibility that a viewer, for whatever reason (inattention, repulsion at the horror of the wounds, unsophistication with iconography, or lack of instruction or practice at interpreting and reacting to works of art), might miss his message. Everything depends on its not being missed.

Artists have often used words in their works. Sometimes the words were simply present in a scene being painted (shop signs in a Parisian street painted by Utrillo); they were not meant, necessarily, to convey any special mood or message—at least, not consciously. (Never again, after Freud, can we fail to wonder at what the "unconscious mind" has inserted into art and the human behavior that produces visual images. That will remain true, I believe, even if psychoanalysis as a mode of therapy continues its present decline.) If, however, Lichtenstein puts a comic-book "POW" into a painting, its meaning as a word can't be ignored, nor can "LOVE" on Warhol's statue created for downtown Philadelphia, "the City of Brotherly Love." Those letters and words are not merely abstract shapes that appeared by chance.

Michel Foucault has addressed the question of the kinship of language to visual art in the following terms, and thus supports the spirit of Magritte and others in "the antilinguistic program of modernism":

> . . . the relation of language to painting is an infinite relation. It is not that words are imperfect or that, when confronted by the visible, they prove insuperably inadequate. Neither can be reduced to the other's terms. It is in vain that we say what we see; what we see never resides in what we say. And it is in vain that we attempt to show, by the use of images, metaphors, or similes, what we are saying; the space where they achieve their splendor is not that deployed by our eyes but that defined by the sequential elements of syntax.[5]

It may be helpful to consider the analogous tension between "absolute" and "program" music. Liszt, for example, wrote an extensive scenario for his well-known tone poem *Les Préludes*, and so did Strauss for his *Death and Transfiguration*, yet we need not know a word of either story to hear and respond to the music. A detailed scenario (though not as detailed as the libretto of an opera) may guide the composer at his work, but the listener need not know the story to enjoy the work. The listener may respond to the music by creating his own scenario, which might or might not relate to what guided the composer. One can enjoy an opera while knowing nothing of the plot, let alone the words being sung. After all, opera is commonly presented in a language not known to the majority of the listeners. And so, what if *Minuteman* is viewed by one who knows no English? Of what intellectual or emotional impact then is the Kill Butcher Slaughter Human Beings "message" of the right parietal area? (*"I've been using words for a long time. It sort of came from early Dada . . . Duchamps. Sometimes there are multiple meanings. Sometimes it's like a newspaper headline dealing with atrocity. I get a kind of layered effect of the words—it intensifies it. Certain words are universal, maybe "kill" is one of them. If the words aren't read, then it becomes a texture, adding scarring to the surface. . . . It's sort of like Oriental painting, with the marks along the perimeter giving it borders. The words then are just graphic elements . . . but it adds a layer of mystery."*)

To *interpret* the words on this or any work of art, or in fact to attempt to *interpret* the total work may be unsuitable, some might argue. Instead, they might say, one should only "receive" the work and simply let an emotional response happen, with no effort to understand it at an intellectual level and no effort to expand its meaning through ratiocination. ("A poem does not mean, but is.") I am willing to respond without intellectual analysis, but find no reason to reject such analysis. It has usually enriched, not reduced, my sense of pleasure in viewing. If others find their satisfaction diminished by interpretative efforts, then I extend them my condolences. Interpretation is a product of human intellectual capacity that no other life forms, as far as we know, can generate. So let it flourish, but not grow static, rigid, or prescribed by authority. As Foucault warns: "The death of interpretation is to believe that there are signs, signs that exist primally, originally, really, as coherent, pertinent, and systematic marks. . . . The life of interpretation, on the contrary, is to believe that there are only interpretations."[6]

## THE CROSS

The head is mounted not on just any pedestal. This one is unquestionably a cross, thus carrying the iconographic significance (for Western culture) of Christ's crucifixion, and by derivation, grave markers. (What symbol, if anything, I wonder, serves as the conventional marker where Islam or Buddhism, say, is the dominant religious tradition?) The gray-black color of this grave marker evokes melancholy, somberness, ashes, and contrasts with the usual image of great rows of white crosses in military cemeteries.

A grave marker surmounted by a helmet is a traditional emblem of a military grave. [*Fig. 2*] But in *Minuteman* a shock greets us – a surrealistic transformation of the helmet into a human head. (Biologically speaking, what is the skull anyway but a helmet to protect the mass of crucial Camembert that lies within?) But this head and neck are not just a portrait, perhaps, of a particular man buried below. This image demands to be read as generic man, just as the biblical Adam, whose name suggests to our ear a particular individual of that name, stands for all mankind once we learn that Adam in Hebrew is the generic noun, man. The upright of the cross carries the outline of a missile tip. That surely relates to the work's title and is not just decorative marking.

## THE TITLE

What should the title *Minuteman* add to our understanding of this work? Magritte assaults the "mystical, Platonic identification of words with the essences of things"[7]: "To the extent that my pictures have any value, they do not lend themselves to analysis. . . . I recognize only one motive for the act of painting: the desire to paint an image one would like to look at. . . . An image *limited strictly to its character as an image* proves the power of thought just as much as Bergson's *ideas* or Proust's *words. After* the image has been painted, we can think of the relation it may bear to ideas or words. This is not improper, since images, ideas, and words are *different* interpretations of the *same* thing: thought."[8] That is what causes him to be so noteworthy among painters in applying to his works titles which seem especially inappropriate, arcane, mysterious, or unenlightening with regard to his highly representational images. What must be understood is Magritte's deliberate antilinguistic effort to provide an image which will not "speak in its own voice," since that involves an auditory and linguistic metaphor, but will provide meaning and feeling directly through its visual means. Because it is so easy to relate the title *Minuteman* to several ideas that seem to attach to this piece, I believe Arneson is not in this instance following Magritte's example any more than he has chosen to follow Oscar Wilde's aphorism, "All art is quite useless." (See below.)

*Figure 2.* Unidentified German grave markers, World War II.

First, the title may refer to the Minuteman missiles in America's contemporary arsenal of nuclear weapons. This meaning suggests itself almost beyond contradiction when we note the shape of the missile or bullet tip displayed on the upright that carries the head. Maybe this title refers to the Minuteman of the American Revolution (probably, also, the origin of the missile's name). We must be careful not to diminish the size of the image or the issue by accenting the second syllable. What would have been the effect had Arneson given the work no title? That has been a frequent ploy in this century when artists have striven, as did Magritte, to foster the dissociation they may feel is necessary to release their visual images from the tyranny of words.

## CLAY

Arneson has been a leader in the movement, particularly developed and thriving in California, to use clay and ceramic techniques for "higher art" and not just for utilitarian pottery or decorative bric-a-brac. I have no direct experience with the full range of potential media that sculptors may use, but I gather that clay is particularly serviceable for its variety of molding and shading possibilities. It must surely be easy to handle and allows a prodigious range of textural effects on the surface, so that one piece may be as craggy as a Rodin, or as spiculated as a Giacometti, while another projects the smooth roundness of a Maillol or Brancusi. Because of its ready malleability, clay lends itself to visual puns and jokes. Arneson has perpetuated many of these; yet now he is demonstrating, with a work like *Minuteman,* that clay, in his hands anyway, can express the utmost gravity and profundity.

## THE FUNCTIONS OF ART AND CRITICISM

Oscar Wilde begins his preface to *The Picture of Dorian Gray* by telling us, "The artist is the creator of beautiful things," and he ends with the aphorism "All art is quite useless." In the middle of that preface Wilde says, "No artist desires to prove anything. . . . An ethical sympathy in an artist is an unpardonable mannerism of style. No artist is ever morbid."[9] Of course, Wilde epitomized and exaggerated the aesthetic creed that "art is for art's sake only," for which in his own time and since he has been considered a glorious eccentric. Certainly this work by Arneson expresses a great ethical sympathy. In order to express his anger and fear, he is willing to be morbid, presenting us an image that must strike any viewer as grim, ugly, macabre, ghastly, perhaps obscene, and certainly conveying the melancholy that Milton described as being "Of Cerberus and blackest Midnight born."

With this particular work Arneson clearly lies in that major stream of art and Western civilization in which the artist reflects and comments, often critically, upon society and the ways of human beings. It is sometimes difficult or fruitless to try to distinguish between an aesthetic expression of the artist's feeling, and outright propaganda. (Daumier and Diego Rivera spring to mind.) Such social comment and clear propagandistic function is most obvious in artistic media that employ words (poems, stories, novels, plays, or any of those set to music). In visual art, music, and dance, the media are usually more abstracted from the literalness of the ideas. The viewer may either receive the art work and experience an emotional response, or may attempt to translate the feeling, usually using words, into the "meaning" that he understands or thinks the creative artist intended, or both.

If Arneson seeks not only to move us, but to instruct us, persuade us, even prompt us to action, then he surely speaks from other than the ceramics-as-decoration tradition from which he and other contemporary workers in clay have emerged. If *Minuteman* is more than just personal reaction, just comment, but means to move the viewer to action, then Arneson and other modernists (see also, for example, Picasso's *Guernica*) have broken thoroughly with that strand of late nineteenth-century tradition that came to espouse art for no utilitarian purpose but only for art's own sake. We must understand that Oscar Wilde meant "useless" only partially in the sense of "non-utilitarian," for he certainly believed art useful (effective) in prompting a hedonistic, aesthetic rapture. A less radical statement of the same art-for-art's-sake idea comes from the American painter George Inness (1825–1894), who wrote, "The purpose of a painter is simply to reproduce in other minds the impression a scene has made on him. A work of art does not appeal to intellect. It does not appeal to the moral sense. Its aim is not to instruct, not to edify, but to awaken emotion."[10] Arneson unquestionably seeks to awaken an emotion in us. The gruesome details, the grim horror of what we see in the battered head, the ideas evoked by its decapitation and positioning on a traditional grave marker, the image of the missile tip and the very clear message of the words seem, to me at least, not simply to reflect the artist's personal anguish, but also to prompt the viewer to adopt the artist's position and "take arms against a sea of trouble."

Any artist, if effective, may produce for a viewer the resonating response analogous to what physicists call "sympathetic vibrations," when one string vibrates near another and induces vibration of the same frequency in the second string. That induced emotional response in the viewer who examines a visual image may at times replicate not only the artist's emotion but also the artist's attitude or even the impetus to act. All that induction need not be from an intentional instruction by the artist. Whether there was unrecognized, subconscious *intent* to educate or propagandize one cannot assert for sure – this side of being the artist's psychoanalyst – but that may be the effect anyway. In other instances it would seem to stretch credulity too far to presume that the artist was *not* fully conscious of his intent to move others – not only to share his emotional response but to *persuade* the viewer to adopt a particular attitude, possibly even a specific political posture.

(*"I've never been a decorative artist. I've always wanted to make works that dealt with the human condition. . . . There's satisfaction in exhibiting a work that can speak. I won't deny a propaganda quality to much of my work. But I don't want to be just an illustrator of horrible events. I'm very worried about a nuclear holocaust. . . . And I'm a public artist – I don't mean art for public spaces but art that's accessible, not private. I don't want my work to have private meanings. It speaks of the times. I'm different than a lot of artists who direct themselves toward 'the art world' – that's too narrow a place."*)

André Gide is reported to have described his childhood fascination with a kaleidoscope which he one day took apart to learn the secret that produced such fascinating visual effects. Once he discovered its internal organization and how it "worked," he no longer found it interesting. This story warns those who would be too scientific about images, or even art historians as they engage in "analysis" of a work. Dissection may provide information, but perhaps at the high cost of delight, spontaneous reaction, or naive enthusiasm. The scientific approach "takes things apart" but may not find much reason to put them back together in interesting or significant ways. Jacques Barzun recently drew a challenging distinction between culture and scholarship. He concluded that culture as he defined it has no place in academe; the essence of scholarship is to be analytical and study something in ever smaller units. To do so is to lose sight of, and feeling for, joy in the whole. He argues, in effect, that a fallen Humpty Dumpty can never be restored.[11]

This same important question is explored in a greatly different genre by Mark Twain, who describes his personal transformation when he learned how to be a Mississippi riverboat pilot. His glorious perceptions of the beauty, majesty, and awe of the river were lost forever, he claimed, as each visual image became functional, portending a swiftness of current here, a hazardous sandbar there. He went on to speculate that something similar may happen to physicians who, having learned to read the signs of the body's behavior and illnesses, can never again luxuriate in the direct sensuous experience of its grace, its stamina, and the physical attractiveness of its form and function.[12]

I would argue with both Barzun and Twain, or at least report from my own experience, that a broad knowledge of the clinical signs of disease – or of the cellular or chemical processes that guide or misguide the human organism to either health or injury and decay – adds to the sense of wonderment so naturally evoked by knowledge of the body's mechanisms for control and repair. Knowing more of what seem to be the facts of the physical universe justifies ever more strongly a belief in a force that established that universe with its legions of complexities and well-meshing parts. I see nothing antiquated or naive about the ancient belief that the physical universe stands as enormous, eloquent testimony to some higher power.

Even when I'm at my most analytical about a work of art I try to allow at least a moment to permit an emotional response to develop *before* I become conscious of my desire to analyze: what style? what epoch? what artist? what technique? what message? For example, a smile comes at once when I see a painting by Frans Hals, for I'm extremely fond of the mischievous expression he manages so regularly to impart – even in portraits of unquestionably stolid burghers. On the other hand, one doesn't find much friskiness in El Greco or Rembrandt. And even though the seventeenth-century Dutch clothing looks similar in Hals and Rembrandt, the stark contrasts of light and dark, and the rich gold colors of clothing or jewelry reveal the work is not by Hals but by Rembrandt. It is those same skills of discernment, as I said, that permit me to diagnose a skin eruption that has a violet hue, flat rather than dome-shaped low elevations, a gray trabeculation over the surface of the individual lesions, a scattering of the little bumps especially over the inner surfaces of wrists or front surfaces of shins – to diagnose it as lichen planus as quickly on entering the examination room as I spot a Rembrandt when I round the corner in a museum I've never before visited.

The case for analysis can be extended, however, that such criticism as that provided by an art historian or critic teaches one how to value the artistic work even more for knowing what the creative process is and how it manifests itself. Scientists, too, share the desire to explicate the world in its objectivity and its meaning. Any great scientist exhibits creativity and imagination, for otherwise there could be no hypothetical leaps so obligatory to the scientific process. Likewise, the subjectivity of science must be recognized. Decisions about which phenomena to study, which questions to ask, which experiments to perform, at what level of probability to repose one's confidence – these are all inherent in the scientific enterprise and require a sensitivity, a refinement of judgment as well developed and carefully nurtured as those of any critic or lover of the arts. The scientist must seek and observe sensory data, and then know how to interpret them in order to judge the elegance of the experiment and the extent to which its evidence argues successfully in behalf of a scientific theory or principle. Similarly, the viewer or art critic must behold, study, and interpret the image. The aesthetic satisfactions in science are enormous for those who understand the artistry of human thought and the natural universe.[13] Science is by no means totally exact and impersonal, just as art is not totally inexact and subjective. The scientist must exercise his creative imagination; the artist, precision of technical craft. For both there exists an enormous task of design and editing. That effort may be done somewhat more at the conscious level by the average scientist than the average artist – or so some persons might argue (but they may well be wrong). If one has engaged in both art and science, one knows how both are blends of conscious and unconscious creativity, inspiration, and craft.

In *Minuteman* I read warnings of power gone astray, disease/trauma, distress-to-horror-to-anguish-to-agony, the missile tip, the graveyard marker, the mangled and distorted head, the blood, the powerful feeling-laden words on the skull – all this informs me that the work bears a political message. Where should this work be displayed? Since it is unquestionably not decorative, but grim and profound, one would instinctively tend not to display it, say, in a physician's waiting room or in the average hospital. The fact that to do so strikes us as obviously inappropriate testifies to our recognition of the powerful psychological significance and emotional impact of the work. No, it must be in a museum or public place – its message needs disseminating.

Even though the content or emotion related to a work be bitterly sorrowful, such as that of a crucifixion or a *Minuteman,* the artist will still feel a great joy in fulfilling the creative urge. Doris Grumbach writes: "The analytic mind staggers before the mysteries and imponderables of the creative impulse."[14] (*I'm still trying to deal with all the negative emotions in this work. But yes, there's a joy and satisfaction in completing it. An awfully lot of the effort is in dealing with the materials abstractly—a kind of engineering labor. But still, it needs quality to be art.*")

## FROM FUNK TO FULFILLMENT

Arneson reached his maturity during the heyday of "Funk Art." I perceive that art movement to bear much in common with "theatre of the absurd," which grew from the ecclesiastical alienation and social disruption that followed World War I. They had in turn spawned Surrealism and Dada, that begat Funk, which included the impulse to make something and throw it away, as if only the creative idea and process count, not the materials or product. Idiosyncracy, eccentricity, bizarre images and behavior—those appear to be the aspiration of Funk Art. *Minuteman* shows Arneson capable of work far more thoughtful and mature, and willing to deal with issues far graver and more crucial than the hedonistic, superficial novelty that characterized Funk.

Indeed Arneson has produced many works that are humorous, even jokes. But not *Minuteman.* Beethoven, too, is well known for having a great wit that generated many jokes in his music. But I find none whatever in his Ninth Symphony. It contains many moods, and not just somber ones, for the work ends in a glory of exaltation and triumph. But there are no jokes; it is totally serious. Whether Arneson as a visual artist will ultimately deserve comparison with Beethoven will be addressable only many years hence.

Some might think that the words ATTACK RAT-TAT-TAT across the back of the figure's neck mark the work as a tongue-in-cheek effort only one step removed from the comic book. I will not deny the possibility of such an interpretation. But much time spent looking at this work convinces me that Arneson does demonstrate with *Minuteman* his capacity to express such high seriousness, through a command of his medium so sure and expressive, that this work can properly be considered a major statement of profound feeling and noble intent. This is not a joke, a cute satire, a piece of decorative ceramic. Neither is it a seventeen-foot-high marble *David;* but among its many messages are the implication that a work of the force and magnificence (maybe even the size?) of the *David* might yet come forth from clay and from Robert Arneson.

NOTES

1 Arthur Conan Doyle, "The Adventure of the Blanched Soldier," in *The Complete Sherlock Holmes* (New York: Doubleday and Co., 1956), 1180.

2 See Nelson Sizer and H. S. Drayton, *Heads and Faces, and How to Study Them: A Manual of Phrenology and Physiognomy for the People* (New York: Fowler and Wells Co., 1885).

3 Franz Kafka, "In the Penal Colony," in *Franz Kafka: The Complete Stories*, ed. Nahum Glatzer (New York: Schocken Books, 1971), 140–67.

4 William Shakespeare, *Hamlet*, act 3, sc. 2, in *Complete Works* (New York: Walter J. Black, Inc., 1937), 1150.

5 Michel Foucault, *This Is Not a Pipe*, transl. and ed. James Harkness (Berkeley: University of California Press, 1982), 9.

6 Ibid., 12.

7 Ibid., 7.

8 René Magritte, quoted in Harry Torczyner, *Magritte: Ideas and Images* (New York: Harry N. Abrams, Inc., 1979).

9 Oscar Wilde, *The Picture of Dorian Gray*, ed. Isobel Murray (New York: Oxford University Press, 1974), 1.

10 George Inness, cited in a discussion of an Inness painting used as a cover illustration for *Journal of the American Medical Association* 25 (14 June 1985), 3240.

11 Jacques Barzun, "Culture vs. Scholarship," *The Atlantic* 254 (1984), 93–104.

12 Mark Twain, *Life on the Mississippi, The Family Mark Twain* (New York: Harper & Brothers, 1935), 47.

13 See Deane W. Curtin, ed., *The Aesthetic Dimension of Science* (New York: Philosophical Library, 1980).

14 Doris Grumbach, "The Source of the Literary Imagination," in *Exploring the Concept of Mind*, ed. Richard Caplan (Iowa City: University of Iowa Press, 1986). In press.

# FACING THE HOLOCAUST: Robert Arneson's Ceramic Myth of Postmodern Catastrophe

Barbara J. Hill
John S. Nelson

Perpetrator, target; victim, survivor: these are four of the many paired faces presented by Robert Arneson in the form of a new *Minuteman* for our time. This work of ceramic sculpture assaults spectators with the abominations of war that postmodern Americans would sooner not see or understand. It seeks for a minute to destroy the distance between observers and victims, on the premise that mere spectators become the perpetrators and targets alike of the era's continuing atrocities. It laments a stupid, psychotic insistence on self-destruction. Yet it also seduces people who prefer to think of themselves as bystanders into recognizing their participation in current troubles. It attempts to realign their perspectives, so that they will act to reorder their realities. Devastatingly, it indicts—but more urgently, it invites—our survival.

Facing the holocaust, the Arneson bust embodies the psychology of postmodern war as mass slaughter. It personalizes the misshapen politics of the age as a bludgeoned and brooding head of humanity beholding and beseeming the horrors of our time. It condenses the numbing holocausts of the last—and perhaps of the next—hundred years into a single skull, tense with images of callous aggression: bleeding but abstracted bullet holes, shards of flesh on a cold iron cross, machine-gun massacres, mounds of bodies, a nuclear missile with a human target, slogans of death and destruction, a sad and shaven head straight from the ordeals of a concentration camp, and many other fragments from the nightmares of our time.

But the very multiplicity of faces and images—fragments though

Barbara J. Hill is an Instructor in the Department of Political Science.

John S. Nelson is an Associate Professor in the Department of Political Science.

they be—can imply greater ambiguities. The skillful orchestration of diverse profiles into a single figure suggests the importance of perspectives and a postmodern insistence that no reality reduces adequately to one or two angles alone. The obvious reserve in depicting the results of violence—plus the evident avoidance of sheer shock and terror—invites careful thought about the confluence of fragments, images, and ideas embodied in the bust. The artful composition of brutality and the lurid glaze of blood project a rueful awareness of the aesthetic power of violence. The reliance on fragments might even acknowledge—though not necessarily accept—the claim of destruction or disintegration to be a favored art of our time.

Graphics and slogans in the style of advertising provide an ironic commentary on our savage condition but also on the savage wit of a satirist and polemicist such as Arneson. In fact, the whole design conveys the same ambivalence: simultaneously, the new *Minuteman* deplores but deploys the aesthetics of violence that mass communications seem to crave. The bust becomes a way to attract gazes both lingering and shifting. It coordinates disparate but connected elements in order to encourage reflection for far more than a minute, in a time when media and messages make that too rare for the common man.

Thus the new *Minuteman* faces postmodern America less at exalted levels of high art than at encompassing levels of ordinary culture and everyday politics. If these be times that try our souls, then Arneson assigns the first major challenge of response to popular art and the mythic eye. The new *Minuteman* dares us to see the contours, conditions, and intentions of the Everyman now. Initially with unease and eventually with outrage, the new *Minuteman* contests our cozy assumption that the catastrophes of war occur elsewhere, beyond our bounds of liability. He defies the politics of mass oblivion and mocks the abstractions of mass awareness. Facing the holocaust, his—and therefore ours—is an earthen portrait of politics as atrocities past and potential. But equally, it is an ironic reminder that visual arts play their own roles in producing such atrocities.

### Modes and Details of Destruction

The new *Minuteman* is a *bust:* of the modern human as failure and of the postmodern person as destroyer. Deftly, it says to us: here is your personality and history deconstructed, divided into its component aggressions and atrocities. Carefully, it encourages us to identify the remaining – artistically aligned – fragments and to contemplate their interaction. Bluntly, it asks of us: what is to be done now, buster? Thus it offers a composite portrait and question of twentieth-century motives and events.

Past a first, diffuse impression of atrocity and disaster, the bust focuses attention on the details of our depravities. So let us record the specifics of what we see in the sculpture, both to turn the eye toward Arneson's images of the holocaust and to set the scene for our larger responses to the new *Minuteman*. What we see, of course, need not be what Arneson intended. Far from the artistic equivalent of a Rorschach test, the work is not so abstract as to elicit sheer projections of our professional or individual personalities. Still, the bust seems to us a complex of ironies, ambiguities, and perhaps even ambivalences. These make the details worth recounting individually, as we encountered each aspect of the bust.

Viewed frontally, the bust is laid low on a thick, black cross with the cold look of metal. The sculpted head bulks large, possibly twice life-size. It stares at and through you, yet unseeing. On a level with the bust, its gaze is slightly downcast, perhaps, but amazingly and stubbornly empty. The hooded, eyeless sockets ooze blood vivid but dark. It is unsettling to think that they see only red or some bleak and internal blackness.

The right forehead furrows with thought or use, while the left lies more smoothly. The left side of the face is bashed from above and crushed from below: smashing and raking the left cranium, crumpling and tattering the left ear, shattering the left cheek and jaw, flattening the left nostril, and twisting the left side of the mouth into a hideous smirk. Are the lips merely mangled; do they make a grotesque grimace of great pain; or is their expression the sneering and demented smile of some devil within?

From the front, the right side of the face remains more intact. The right ear stands out whole. The right nostril flares with intensity. The right side of the mouth is implacable with determination yet slightly sensuous from a fullness of the lips. Nonetheless, the right half of the face suffers a myriad of cuts and scratches, plus three bullet wounds – surreally circular and red – grouped high on the right side of the cranium.

Wherever the skin has escaped more brutal treatment, it features the fine but jagged lines of scarring from dense brush, shrapnel, or the barbed wires of internment camps. From a distance, the flesh gives an overall impression of grim, light gray. Closer, it shows splotches of putrid pastels: pink, yellow, rust, and dark green fading into a military brown. The green and yellow of the scratches suggest mold, pus, and decay. The head is hollow; carefully aligned, we see from the right eye socket through the one back bullet wound to the floor or wall beyond. Is this the end of the American revolutionary and what he has wrought: the demise of the first among modern nations?

Centered above the forehead, between the bullet holes and the staving of the skull, is the crossmark of a rifle scope, projected onto or etched into the flesh. Name still in mind, we change angles to see what is easily missed at first in shadow: the outline of a ballistic missile, looming sharklike from the underside of the cross. The bottom of the fuselage rests on two stubby fins, making the missile unmistakable. This gives the cross an ethos of ancient pottery, displaying on its surface a stark hieroglyph. How much better to extend the missile's sleek lines as the eye initially imagines them, unbroken to the bottom: implying a greater force underground and only beginning to surface? This Minuteman points at the bust, which seems from the bottom (but not the top) to lean slightly to the right, perhaps just starting to topple from its pedestal. As a result, the missile aims toward or even slightly off the edge of the target's larger circle, not the smaller one at the center of the crosshatching. Might the Minuteman miss its mark? Might it be too late to matter?

From the front, the neck is shredded with scratches. On the figure's left, just above the clavicle, blood runs from the stab wound of a bayonet or knife. The neck broadens past the striking zone for broadsword or guillotine, to include the slightest suggestion of shoulders. Is the head decapitated, or does it offer the classic pose of a sculpted bust? The neck ends raggedly, and its blood streams down the upper arm of the cross. Are the streams less surreal red than vile green from an interaction of glazes, or do they imply what ambitions— surging from the heart—now run in futility toward the ground? Stray bits of flesh splatter the right arm of the cross. Seen from front or back, the head rises from its tombstone with the ghostly twist of smoke or dust, somehow thinner and more haunting than its massive substance should allow it to seem.

The right profile draws the eye, and the bust tells its story well by leading the observer to circle left. At a distance, the full right profile could be a composed but pugnacious Marlon Brando: immense with reserves of dignity, energy, and will. A step closer, and the scars resolve into words. Most vivid is KILL, only a little to the left of the three bullet wounds. Below, leading the eye down and gradually farther to the left – overcoming the direction in which the letters read – are BUTCHER, SLAUGHTER, HUMAN BEINGS, INDISCRIMINATELY. The first two words are faint, pin-pricked; the last three appear in block print, but smaller. By now, skin and skull seem to have given way to brain. Are the words cruelly carved into the tissue of a victim, or do they emerge from the mind of a perpetrator? Are they wounds or wills, messages or motives? Perhaps given their placement in or on the right brain, otherwise intact, the latter is more likely.

This impression is reinforced by the way in which the left brain also bears words on its back side. The smashed, victimized side aligns its words with alternating images of violence. High and slightly to the right of the great grooves created by clubs or claws loom again the letters of SLAUGHTER. Below them is a tangling of corpses, diagrammed to mimic the convolutions of the bared brain itself. And under that lie the still larger but more diffuse marks of MASSACRE. To the lower left, the eye spies a soldier firing a semi-automatic rifle. ATTACK says his posture, and RAT-TAT-TAT sounds his gun, in a kind of comic-book rendering of war to date in the twentieth century. The gun points in the general direction of a crudely drawn and X'd-out heart, on the back right of the neck. Is the new *Minuteman* broken-hearted or left without the capacity for sympathy and fellow-feeling?

Stooping to examine the soldier, gun, and heart leads the eye to a phrase spanning the left and right brains. Over the comic narrative for the soldier and gun, but almost hidden by the outbulging of brain or skull when seen from above, is the observation OFFICIALS DENY KNOWLEDGE – as though appearing for the thousandth time as the subhead to a news story. Now standing near to the lower brain and back of the neck we discern at the seat of deep primitive drives a face subtle and diffuse. Through color and contour, it conveys the impression of an old, apish animal – in the driver's seat of the new *Minuteman,* might we say? It grins of mischief, malevolence, even evil. Is it the monkey on our back? Is it the monkey of horror that capers through tales of evil, blighting human wishes in "The Monkey's Paw" and leering blankly from the jacket of Stephen King's *Skeleton Crew?*

Still lower, on the back left of the cross, appears a small grid for tick-tack-toe, with a game barely begun on it. Is this a sobering touch of realism: imaging common graffiti on a gravestone, in order to magnify the polemical impact of the sculpture? Or does this epitomize an irreverent humor peering playfully and ironically from other aspects of the generally grim bust? And if so, then is the monkey's face more comedic than it seemed initially?

Either way, the aborted game puts us in mind of another popular polemic against the nuclear politics of our time. In *War Games,* the computer that controls America's strike forces cannot distinguish its gaming from the reality of nuclear war. Brought by an adolescent to compare scenarios of nuclear holocaust with the child's game of tick-tack-toe, the computer learns at the last instant how futile any such war must be: played with adult intelligence and determination, it is a contest with no winners. When the computer stops playing at nuclear retaliation, the crisis ends in storybook style: life goes on–though we hope, this time, not as before. Like the Arneson bust, this film specifies no paths for improving our present situation, save to recognize its urgency. When the great temptation is to turn away, because we know of nothing constructive to do, that can be a kind of progress: modest, but the only kind now possible.

Stepping further around, we behold the full left profile. The three gashes seen glancingly from the front now show themselves both deep and wide: not quite like tire tracks or claw marks, but something in between. Now there are no words visible, only devastation. This brutalized visage recalls a famous passage in George Orwell's *1984.* O'Brien gloats to a nearly broken Winston Smith that the essence of totalitarianism is utter power, which in turn is utter cruelty. When Big Brother is omnipotent:

> There will be no distinction between beauty and ugliness. There will be no curiosity, no enjoyment of the process of life. All competing pleasures will be destroyed. But always–do not forget this, Winston–always there will be the intoxication of power, constantly increasing and constantly growing subtler. Always, at every moment, there will be the thrill of victory, the sensation of trampling on an enemy who is helpless. If you want a picture of the future, imagine a boot stamping on a human face–forever.[1]

Here words have little to add, at least about what we see. Instead, they twist toward what we do not–and perhaps cannot–see, save with the mind's conceptual eye: the human nothingness of nuclear annihilation and the postmodern perplexity of political art.

In prose, Orwell struggled with the same paradox of polemical art that seems to confront Arneson's *Minuteman.* What is the worth of art that distracts from an urgent politics of life and death, yet what is the way that art can remain worthy when yoked to political purposes? How can art speak persuasively against violence without degenerating into ineffectual polemics on the one side or cultivating a violent aesthetics on the other? How can art render the holocaust, when the very notion of art is denied and when every product of art is exploited as part of the politics that pushes us from cruelty to brutality – and on toward the apocalypse?

If the carnage incarnate in the face before us seems insignificant compared with that implied by the new *Minuteman,* can any sculpture do better than to point obliquely toward what must remain unseen? Politics often calls on art to portray what we otherwise cannot share, to make manifest what we find most urgent but elusive. Such art seeks to move, even to compel us. Now, however, it must seek equally and simultaneously to make us think in a more reflexive and sophisticated manner than before. It cannot lead to deeper understanding and restraint of human violence by immersing us in ever more violent images. It cannot occasion more accurate and complicated responses to our situation by producing forms that are easily co-opted or dismissed by political devices of image management. Nor can art close itself to all experiences and purposes except a few approved on narrowly political grounds, yet expect to remain art in the fullest sense – able to contribute the fresh and sophisticated apprehensions that we now need most.

To us, this is the main problematic of the new *Minuteman.*

## POLITICAL ART AND POLITICAL SCIENCE

These things the two of us see and say as professors of politics, educated in the disciplines of political science and philosophy, specializing in the issues of international relations and political theory.[2] No part of our academic field now attends significantly to visual art, no matter how laden with political purposes or implications.[3] In fact, no aspect of our academic profession readies us directly for distinctive responses to any of the fine arts.[4] Still, our view of Arneson's *Minuteman* as a work of political art stems importantly – if indirectly – from our professional interests and training. Before we explore more fully the features and effects of the new *Minuteman,* let us explain briefly some inspirations we draw from political science. Relatedly, let us identify what studies of political art can contribute to studies of politics. Both subjects help us clarify the methods of interpretation that guide our response to Arneson's *Minuteman* in terms of the problematic of political art in a violent and nuclear age.

Scholars become interested in politics for a variety of reasons, but a casual acquaintance with specialists in international relations reveals that they concentrate on war, revolution, and other conflicts with global implications.[5] Similarly, the major theorists of politics in our time include many who portray ours as an age of awful troubles: genocide, pollution, military confrontation, nuclear proliferation, chemical warfare, biological engineering, resource depletion, population explosion, national chauvinism, racism, religious fanaticism, imperialism, mass society, terrorism, totalitarianism, and more. Some theorists see these troubles as crises that threaten our continued existence as fully human beings yet remain too severe to recognize in daily life. They loom too massive to comprehend in terms that we can assimilate to concrete objects, familiar experiences, and specific events. Moreover, they long ago became too severe for ordinary remedies of political action, especially by individual citizens. Or so political theorists have suggested.[6]

Such concerns of atrocity, catastrophe, conflict, and disaster seem central to the new *Minuteman*. How should we respond to them in the Arneson bust? How might we fathom its political implications, especially? Its themes echo the interests of political scientists, particularly in the two parts of the discipline that the two of us represent most directly. Yet our discipline does not study visual art, either for insight into these aspects of politics or for ideas about their apprehension by humans.

This is all the more sad, if not strange, because political science since the First World War has shown ever greater interest in precisely those phenomena best addressed through examination of visual art. The more political science interests itself in political symbolism, of course, the more the study of visual art can teach the discipline. Thus such art has become crucial to the formation, transmission, and effects of political attitudes, because it has become one of their main modes of expression. As studies of political communication, culture, and socialization have moved into the mainstreams of political science, the reasons to concentrate on visual arts have increased.

Intent upon enhancing their status as scientists, however, professional students of politics generally avoid art of any kind. This is justified by tenets of "behavioralism" and "empiricism."[7] They insist that scientific studies of politics attend only to overt behavior, presumably by individuals, because only it can be observed in a direct and rigorous fashion. Were it possible, such "direct observation" would eliminate all distance between the object or behavior and the observer. Thus it would eliminate the room required for the mediation of art, and it would preempt any need for interpretation. To say this is to suggest how impossible and misguided behavioralism can become,[8] as well as how easily it slides into ignoring the arts as political media. So it is not surprising that our discipline of political science provides little more than a thematic basis for responding to Arneson's *Minuteman*. Were the concerns of the bust not so overtly political, political science would suggest even less about it.

As a set of styles of research, though, behavioralism hardly needs to rely on impossibly direct observation in order to focus on outward appearances and actual deeds. Instead, it could emphasize some of the same features of surface shapes, motions, and images that figure so prominently in the visual arts. Oddly, behavioralism has turned political scientists away from the intense observation of personal behavior that we associate with ethnology, the study of animal behavior.[9] Behavioralism has also led to neglect of rigorous interpretation of the body languages of facial expression and physical gestures, when these would seem good targets of aptly behavioral research.[10] From this perspective, art on the order of Arneson's *Minuteman* can teach us much about behavioral vocabularies of politics.

Even beyond behavioral levels, the study of artworks surely should assume a more important place in studies of politics than it has in the past. For example, we have already noted in connection with Arneson's sculpture some of the ways in which visual arts – along with musical arts – have become especially important in mediating between the elite and popular subcultures of America and other postmodern societies.[11] The increasing tendency of political science to emphasize the role of political culture, both as a causal force and as a contextual variable, makes the study of such arts more pressing than before.

But the two of us were in no position to produce a new project for our discipline on this initial occasion of responding to Arneson's *Minuteman*. So we simply approached the bust as two people with a keen interest in its apparent themes yet no special knowledge of its artistic context, medium, and techniques. We warmed to the task by a brief trial consideration of the Jackson Pollock *Mural* central to the reflections of three other essays in this volume. This allowed us to begin thinking before the Arneson sculpture became readily available for viewing, and it served repeatedly as a source of comparison when our responses to the sculpture gradually took shape. We looked intently at the bust for several extended periods of time. While looking, we talked about our perceptions and how they might be changed through alterations that we could imagine in the sculpture. Between sessions of apprehending the new *Minuteman* and for several months thereafter, we discussed intermittently its impact on our individual senses of self, our conceptions of politics, and—as you already know— our notions of political inquiry.

We became sufficiently entangled in the effects of the bust that each of us dreamed about it. The sage instigators of this experiment in responding to visual art supplied us with a fine batch of readings on the sculpture, other works by Arneson, and recent ceramic art in America generally. Not wanting these reports and commentaries to preempt or otherwise structure our responses, however, we reserved them for comparison with our initial ideas, once fully formed. After three months, we felt ready for the secondary materials and read them all. They produced a growing sense of satisfaction at the convergence between some of our views and those of the experts, for the readings confirmed many of our suspicions about likely inspirations, intentions, and trends in Arneson's art. More important, the readings fed a sense of excitement at the connection between our main ideas about the bust and our other recent concerns as political scientists. For we found, first in the bust and then in the readings, impressive evidence that Arneson's apparent project of political mythmaking carries through the dynamics and encounters the problems of *facing* that we discern also in three literary genres of popular culture: science fiction, fantasy, and horror stories.

Two years ago, our interest in science fiction led us to start a weekly luncheon where several political scientists discuss political implications of the science-fiction books, films, and television shows that sometimes entertain them away from work. Gradually, the discussions have come to encompass such related genres of popular culture as fantasy and horror fiction. As the literary theorist Northrop Frye noted long ago, an obvious commonality of these genres is their postmodern—that is, ironically self-conscious and reflective—engagement in myth.[12] Accordingly, talk at the sf luncheon turns recurrently to tasks, techniques, and troubles of political mythmaking in twentieth-century America.

From these explorations of myth and its intentional making, with special reference to politics, came three ideas that reemerged forcefully in our contemplation of the Arneson bust. They are syzygy, facing, and the paradox of mythmaking both personal and purposeful. Perhaps by explaining these three notions and their reverberations in the Arneson sculpture, we can best convey our response to the new *Minuteman*.

## SYZYGY

We draw the notion of syzygy from Frederik Pohl's recent novel of that name.[13] His novel can be read as an examination of the dynamics of political thinking and communicating central to science fiction as a kind of reflection about politics in postmodern societies. A syzygy is a tense and sometimes temporary alignment or linking of objects ordinarily disparate in kind or opposed in movement. In astronomy, it is an unusual and potentially consequential conjunction of heavenly bodies. The word comes from the Greek word for yoking animals to pull in tandem; and it is echoed in *syzygos*, the Greek word for spouse. Pohl's book suggests that the prime challenge to present thought and communication about politics is to render simple, tangible, and accessible the abstract, complicated, and often technical troubles of our time – so that citizens can comprehend them and act collectively to address them well. As we read the book, it contends that science fiction responds to this challenge through syzygy: through extraordinary alignments of characters, ideas, situations, and stories that render the abstruse and seemingly distant troubles of advanced societies immediate, understandable, and actionable.[14]

Arneson's *Minuteman* strikes us as a syzygy of the profiles and images of postmodern catastrophes. We distinguish seven dynamics of syzygy: (1) extrapolating, (2) patterning, (3) focusing, (4) concretizing, (5) facing, (6) loosening, and (7) committing. All seven are evident to us in the new *Minuteman*.

A first dynamic is *extrapolating*. It takes what is experienced or thought and extends it to some further realm. Is one tale of the twentieth century the expansion of war beyond all previous bounds? Then will it not reveal the perpetrators to be the targets, the survivors to be the victims, and vice versa? By extension, will it not portray the embattled warrior as an extrapolation of the malicious monkey? Extrapolating differently, the new *Minuteman* infers from the events of our times a next step in human self-destruction. Extrapolation is a dynamic of syzygy because one of the major reasons to bring disparate or disjointed things into alignment is to see what comes next, what can be expected to follow. In this light, extrapolating involves outcomes or implications. But it also figures in syzygy as a generator of further things from given things. Thus it can produce new align-ments, as well as fathom the repercussions of those already achieved.

A second move is *patterning*. It takes given events or information and forms them into a figure, typically one that we can recognize from previous experience. Arneson's *Minuteman* discerns in the con-flicts and violence of our time a recurrent complex of motives and re-sults. Similarly, the bust portrays a form of interdependence between aggressors and victims.

Extrapolating and patterning appear parasitic on one another. We pattern in order to extrapolate, and we extrapolate in order to pat-tern. In one respect, moreover, patterns are extrapolations that pre-sent themselves as filling in the gaps left by the particulars already given. Similarly, extrapolations are patterns, in that the extension from old to new either states or creates a pattern of relationship be-tween old and new. But these remain distinct dynamics of syzygy be-cause we sometimes pattern without extrapolating and extrapolate without patterning, in their fullest senses. Thus Arneson might have sculpted a bust to express the atrocities of major twentieth-century wars through the one in Vietnam, without extrapolating to a nuclear war possibly to come. So also might Arneson have sculpted a bust tar-geted by a ballistic missile, without seeking to evoke a pattern of human aggression in wars to date. Extrapolating proceeds by applying a rule or operator to transform something given into something else. Patterning seeks, expresses, or applies a complex of rules to manifest or account for some figure.

A third dynamic is *focusing*. Beginning with a set of particulars, art may pattern them and may extrapolate to additional particulars. The new *Minuteman* does both. Further, it identifies some parts of the re-sulting pattern as especially important. By the boldness and place-ment of the letters, the bust directs attention to one basic end more than others: KILL. The pointing missile, the prominent target, and the name of the sculpture emphasize the threat of nuclear war over the images of previous atrocities. More strikingly still, though, the bust presents no profile bereft of violence portrayed through obvious, in-trusive art: focusing on what we have called the problematic of polit-ical art in our time.

*Concretizing* is a fourth dynamic. It makes specific, urgent, and ac-tionable what has been focused. Through the medium of ceramics, the new *Minuteman* takes a particular shape compelling to Ameri-cans, especially. It dramatizes our danger by grievous wounds, bril-liant blood, and a black tombstone. It manifests a general assertion of ties between the intentions and disasters of our time by presenting a tangled mass of slaughtered bodies as the convoluted ridges of a human brain.

To be sure, concretizing can be understood as a way of focusing: drawing attention to one thing by presenting it in special and vivid detail. But there are other ways of focusing, and it can be accomplished while remaining at high levels of abstraction. Perhaps this essay shows as much. Still, the truly telling point is that concretizing need not involve focusing. Whole patterns can be concretized without calling special attention to a particular part. Another artistic polemic against nuclear war consists of an immense field of identical crosses, concretizing the jeopardy without focusing on a single aspect of its nature or sources.

## FACING

A fifth dynamic is *facing*.[15] If only by the nature of a bust, this is the aspect of syzygy most prominent in the new *Minuteman*. It is also the dynamic that we find most creatively and successfully carried out in the sculpture. Even so, it builds here on the preceding four dynamics. Furthermore, we think that Arneson's *Minuteman* faces well our troubles of war precisely because its facing leads skillfully to the last dynamics of loosening and committing. And in them, as manifest in the new *Minuteman,* we see a fruitful response to the postmodern problematic of political art. But before these claims can be explained and defended, we must clarify our notion of facing and how Arneson's *Minuteman* may be seen to embody it.

One connection is the old nostrum about the need and difficulty of facing hard facts. The challenge is to avoid turning away from unpleasant realities and possibilities. Once extrapolated, patterned, focused, and concretized, the question remains: are we actually taking things to heart? Will we apprehend their personal relevance? Will we remember them when the object of art no longer stands before us?

A second connection concerns *how* we can get people to face hard facts. We do it by giving people a face for the facts, a face to which they can relate as humans. The faces of objects are their sides or aspects which concern us centrally,[16] so at first this might seem merely another version of focusing. The key difference is that focusing identifies what ought to be important to people because of its (claim to) objective significance, whereas facing presents it so compellingly as to override people's tendency to turn aside if there are associated dangers and difficulties in responding effectively. People keep facing the concretized focus because it appears as a fascinating face. Animal faces can have this effect as archetypal images of deep psychological resonance.[17] Yet the greater the need for historically specific or otherwise individuated faces, the greater the impact of specifically human faces. Psychologists have long noticed that people have especially durable and nuanced memories for human faces, implying that the faces of persons engage special processes of memory and greater urgencies of motivation. When the challenge is to face new troubles that prove hard to apprehend, archetypal images play a part; but we see in Arneson's *Minuteman* that distinctly human, individuated faces can be more compelling still.

Thus the new *Minuteman* faces our history and possibility of war as a potentially terrifying reality in strikingly human terms. The bust also suggests a third dimension of facing: re-cognizing or character-izing. Faces are incredibly numerous permutations and complex combinations of many kinds and staggering amounts of information, yet we recognize them both regularly and rapidly. They stay with us and structure our human world; they characterize it. Recognizing through characterizing can itself have three senses or dimensions.

At a minimum, characterizing is describing. Pictures and words on the Arneson bust characterize warfare in the twentieth century by evoking its recurrent brutalities. We call this analytical characterizing, because the cognition is usually re-cognition or realignment. To identify different trees, we type each as a distinct kind. Sometimes it is a kind already familiar but not yet recognized as relevant; other times, it is a new kind, not previously acknowledged but now advanced as salient. Trees may be re-cognized as a forest; and a forest may be re-cognized as a type pertinent to our lives: tropical, temperate; wild, harvested; and so on. In this way, the new *Minuteman* faces war in the twentieth century by presenting our motives and acts anew, thereby re-cognizing our nuclear conditions.

More adventurously, characterizing is presenting or creating characters in a story. Narrative characterizing portrays actors who undergo events and undertake projects. Because the bust's progression of features conveys to leftward walkers a tale of twentieth-century warfare, the new *Minuteman* becomes a narrative character. The story straddles tragedy and satire, displaying several kinds of irony, including the self-ironizing that marks the black comedies of our day. As a result, the bust creates a complicated or even multiple personality. By tying the new *Minuteman* to many events, by making each profile a distinct face, yet by combining them well into one figure, the sculpture achieves a *rounded* portrait of its character—pun intended. By the same means, it also achieves the fundamental ambiguity about its character and the related ambivalence about itself as a vehicle for the character that typify postmodern narratives, such as John Barth's novels and Tom Stoppard's plays. So the new *Minuteman* faces the holocaust by suggesting fables of a holocaust character.

From other fables, we know that a third kind of characterizing is moralizing. The morals that summarize fables not only provide practical advice but also build (moral) character: Always remember your manners! Never listen to flattery! Thus the new *Minuteman* promotes a set of moral lessons about our self, our story, and our situation: War is hell; war is us. We are the perpetrators; we are the victims. There is nothing noble about war; in survival lies human dignity. The next and fully fatal step is nearly inevitable; awake individually to your jeopardy and act to avoid disaster.

Yet postmodern people also know that moralizing must remain suspect. It is often arrogant, narrow-minded, self-serving, and even perverse. Accordingly, the new *Minuteman* calls each of its evident morals into question: by concluding without commanding or exclaiming, by playing morals against one another, by counterposing the faces shown by different profiles, by making particular images ambiguous, by reminding viewers of the bias of artifice, and by including touches of humor and whimsy. For postmodern people, a self-questioning character who can still reach conclusions seems the most moral of all. The new *Minuteman* faces the holocaust by projecting postmodern morals for building the characters of diverse viewers.

Through this manifold facing, Arneson's sculpture promotes more intense and reflective responses to ours as a time of continuing and impending holocaust. The diverse faces of the holocaust somehow shaped into this single bust provide a humanly comprehensible and memorable form for pondering our American trajectory from the old Minuteman to the new. The sculpture aligns us with realities and possibilities that we find difficult to consider personally—because of their apparent distance from our daily lives and self-conceptions, their diffuse implications of incredible danger, and their evident immunity to any personal remedy. The bust dispels the distance by showing us our own images in the faces of the holocaust. It makes the danger more humanly comprehensible by weaving it into stories of our previous warring. And it combats the despair by renewing our hope be-

yond hope that the capacity to express a plight may imply some resource remaining to overcome it.[18]

## A Perplexity Met by a Paradox

Still, facing does not complete the syzygy performed by Arneson's
*Minuteman.* Aspects of facing hint at the two remaining dynamics, but
do not accomplish them directly or adequately. Together, the final dynamics of loosening and committing address the postmodern perplexity of political art that we two see as the main problematic of the bust:
how can art become political – that is, polemical – yet remain art? Our
politics appears to need the artistic resources of syzygy, but how can
they enter into politics successfully without becoming bad art: merely
giving new diversions or preaching old malignments? Together,
loosening and committing comprise the postmodern paradox of
mythmaking both personal and purposeful. Through its loosening and
committing, the new *Minuteman* contributes to mythmaking at once
individual and intentional – yet one that seems successful, at least
incipiently or partially.

A sixth dynamic of syzygy is *loosening.* We have already noted how
the new *Minuteman* seems to ironize and parody itself at some
points – through comic-book phrases, gravestone graffiti, and the like.
These are common techniques of loosening. They keep political art
from forgetting the difficulties of aligning art and politics.

Syzygy involves yoking particulars in tension with one another.
Hence it must reflect the continual possibility that the alignment will
disintegrate or turn unduly coercive, becoming illegitimate. More
subtly, it must also reflect the internal stresses of the alignment, including the tendency to misrepresent particulars by placing them in a
new order. This changes relationships accepted previously and thus
transforms the particulars themselves, so the syzygy must remain
alert to the potential for falsifying its elements or effects. Syzygy
loosens in order to stay self-critical as artifice: aware that its making
might become mismaking; determined that its aligning not seem tight
and inevitable; insistent that its limiting be ample and apparent.

Relatedly, syzygy loosens in order to free particulars for new alignments. Syzygists necessarily make new myths in part from the components of old ones. Moreover, such mythmakers must help to clear
aside competing myths in order to make room for new ones. Mythmakers are myth-destroyers and myth-remakers. The modern myth-

makers who helped to forge capitalist markets and democratic states had as part of the same process to remake medieval or mercantilist markets and feudal or monarchical states. Thus they needed to unmake the customs, institutions, and laws of the Middle Ages—which bound serfs to the land so that they could not migrate to cities to become an urban work force, which educated only clerics so that there were too few to form a skilled work force, which restricted finance so that commerce could not develop, which constrained trade so that markets could not grow, and so forth. They also needed to remake medieval ideas of contract, natural law, and earthly power into modern myths of political legitimacy, natural rights, and secular authority. Similarly, postmodern mythmakers need to unmake and remake modern myths by loosening them through irony, parody, and other devices.

Loosening works as well through incongruity: the yoking of strikingly disparate or evidently conflictual elements. This is less a matter of taking apart artifacts than of putting together alliances from components usually separate or opposed. The resulting alignment is loose: more a free happening than a tightly determined consequence. Postmodernism in art often relies on techniques of collage and bricolage to patch together objects that proclaim their manufacture, possible incompletion, or even arbitrariness. Thus does the new *Minuteman* partake of bricolage, as we commented earlier. Postmodernism in politics often relies on capacities of writing and speech to qualify commitments that musical and visual art are better at making urgent and unlimited.[19] Imagine political communication consisting mostly of photographs or skillfully shot and scored films: then the political value of clarifying captions and nuanced dialogue becomes evident. Even the partial speech of Arneson's graffiti endows the new *Minuteman* with a far greater capacity to convey ambivalence, identify ambiguity, and provoke reflection than the bust would otherwise possess.

Elegant, streamlined figures evoke tight alignments. By contrast with (postmodern) syzygies, they suggest (modern) systems that try to reduce virtually everything to a few tidy rules. By the twentieth century, we have reason to suspect comprehensive systems of totalitarianism—of utterly controlled and controlling patterns imposed contrary to interests in beauty, truth, and goodness. Loosening is a defense of artifice against assimilation to system-making; it strives to keep political art on track as mythmaking. The multiple profiles and ironic details of the new *Minuteman* resist reducing our time to some simple intention of atrocity or inevitable result of disaster.

A potential for surprise is the final feature of loosening worth recognizing here. Interacting faces and details of Arneson's *Minuteman* surprise viewers with unnoticed ambiguities and unanticipated interpretations. Such surprise enriches the character and the myth, but it also reminds viewers to stay alert for further developments. Through incongruity and novelty, then, syzygy is a kind of surprise which works only when loosening prepares the way for new alignments and recognitions.

A seventh dynamic of syzygy is *committing*. As spouses commit themselves to each other in marriage, syzygy encompasses commitment to shared action. The syzygy of Arneson's *Minuteman* as a political polemic thus echoes the well-known diagnosis of our political troubles by Yeats, who wrote of our time that "The best lack all conviction, while the worst / Are full of passionate intensity."[20] Arneson's bust demands that we re-experience the outrages of our time. It dispels old characterizations of victims as innocent bystanders and of soldiers as professional functionaries. It urges that we reject the roles of perpetrator and target, recognizing that we are both. By making the faces of the holocaust at once individual and communal, it commits us to fuller visions of responsibility and propels us toward more conscientious courses of action.

Given the needed loosening to allow the capacities of self-criticism and surprise crucial to political freedom and intelligence, postmodern people seek sophisticated knowledge of their myths as myths, rather than naive acceptance of them as given realities. The mythmakers, especially, appreciate the aspects of artifice and illusion that coordinate disparate elements into moving arguments, images, rhythms, and stories. How can postmodern people generally, and individual mythmakers particularly, manage the personal commitment needed for their art as myth to be meant and accepted as a presentation of political reality? How can the polemic remain persuasive politically—for the artist or the audience—when the art insists on cultivating awareness of its artifice and a capacity to criticize its political implications?

To display the postmodern problematic of political art as one of critical community is to recognize how it finds an answer in the paradox of mythmaking both personal and purposeful. Myths are intrinsically communal; a strictly "individual myth" is no more than a "merely personal belief," and often it is a delusional system of thought. From previous myths, moveover, we have become accustomed to assuming that they must be created collectively and therefore—as far as any individual is concerned—unintentionally. For example, we see no good sense in speaking of any myth of the ancient Greeks or Romans as individually authored. Particular tellings may appear in various texts by specific persons; but they appear also in other texts, and the particular tellers seldom pretend to originate the tales. Whatever individual intentions might have initiated the collective mythmaking have been stretched over too much intervening history to support specific ties between personal purposes and communal results. This is why talk of personal and purposeful mythmaking seems paradoxical.

But our communications and therefore our communities differ radically in the postmodern period. We can often trace the sources and paths of acceptance that have produced widely believed stories and commonly practiced patterns of thought. In consequence, individuals can intelligibly aspire to reorder our stories and perspectives. They cannot expect to succeed entirely on their own and in their own terms, yet they can personally and purposefully seek to make myths on the order of their individual intentions. When they recognize the kinds of dynamics of political art as political mythmaking that we have evoked here as syzygy, they become postmodern mythmakers: self-conscious syzygists.

The new *Minuteman* would seem to mark Arneson as one of them. It shows a sophisticated understanding of political art as mythmaking. Through the seven dynamics of syzygy and other devices, the new *Minuteman* challenges common myths of atrocity and apocalypse in our time. In the medium of ceramics, the bust poses a new myth of postmodern catastrophe. For us, it is a troubling but potentially effective way to face the holocaust.


## NOTES

1  George Orwell, "1984," in *Orwell's Nineteen Eighty-Four*, ed. Irving Howe, 2nd ed. (New York: Harcourt Brace Jovanovich, 1982), 178.

2  We thank Connie J. Nelson for sharing several insights into Arneson's *Minuteman*.

3  As two theorists of politics who sometimes write about visual and other fine arts, Benjamin R. Barber and Peter C. Sederberg pose notable exceptions to the rule.

4 Even so, there exist seeds of visual art and rhetoric in the persuasive display of data analyzed by various social scientists. This is evident from a pioneering book by political scientist Edward R. Tufte, *The Visual Display of Quantitative Information* (Cheshire, Conn.: Graphics Press, 1983).

5 How these phenomena dominate the research of specialists in international relations is evident from such key journals as *The International Studies Quarterly, The Journal of Conflict Resolution, International Interactions,* and *World Politics.*

6 See John S. Nelson, "Stands in Politics," *Journal of Politics* 46, no. 1 (February 1984), 106–31.

7 See Heinz Eulau, *The Behavioral Persuasion in Politics* (Stanford, Calif.: Stanford University Press, 1963); Eulau, ed., *Behavioralism in Political Science* (New York: Atherton Press, 1969); George J. Graham, Jr., and George W. Carey, eds., *The Post-Behavioral Era* (New York: MacKay, 1972).

8 See John S. Nelson, "Accidents, Laws, and Philosophic Flaws: Behavioral Explanation in Dahl and Dahrendorf," *Comparative Politics* 7, no. 2 (April 1975), 435–57.

9 See John C. Wahlke, "Pre-Behavioralism in Political Science," *American Political Science Review* 73, no. 1 (March 1979), 9–31.

10 John S. Nelson, "Education for Politics: Rethinking Research on Political Socialization," in *What Should Political Theory Be Now?*, ed. John S. Nelson (Albany: SUNY Press, 1983), 413–78.

11 See Bruno Bettelheim, "The Art of Moving Pictures: Man, Superman, and Myth," *Harper's* 263, no. 1577 (October 1981), 80–83; George Steiner, *In Bluebeard's Castle* (New Haven: Yale University Press, 1971).

12 See Northrop Frye, *Anatomy of Criticism* (Princeton: Princeton University Press, 1957).

13 Frederik Pohl, *Syzygy* (New York: Bantam Books, 1981).

14 See John S. Nelson, "Postmodern Myths of Politics, with Special Reference to Science Fiction," paper for the Annual Meeting of the Midwest Political Science Association, Milwaukee, 1982.

15 See John S. Nelson, "Horror, Crisis, and Control: Tales of Facing Evil," in *Imagining Politics: American Politics through the Prism of Popular Fiction,* ed. Lee Sigelman and Ernest J. Yanarella, forthcoming.

16 See Avrum Stroll, "Faces," *Inquiry* 28, no. 2 (June 1985), 177–94.

17 See Paul Shepard, *Thinking Animals* (New York: Viking Press, 1978); Elemire Zolla, *Archetypes* (New York: Harcourt Brace Jovanovich, 1981).

18 On political art and hope beyond hope, an excellent text for our time is Thomas Mann's *Doctor Faustus,* transl. H. T. Lowe-Porter (New York: Random House, 1948). See John S. Nelson, "Toltechs, Aztechs, and the Art of the Possible: Parenthetic Comments on the Political through Language and Aesthetics," *Polity* 8, no. 1 (Fall 1975), 80–116.

19 Perhaps the most compelling cases for the importance of speech to the art and politics of our postmodern period are the writings of George Orwell and Hannah Arendt: Orwell, "Appendix on the Principles of Newspeak," in *Orwell's Nineteen Eighty-Four,* 198–05; Orwell, "Why I Write," in *Orwell's Nineteen Eighty-Four,* 243–47; Orwell, "Politics and the English Language," in *Orwell's Nineteen Eighty-Four,* 248–58; Arendt, *The Origins of Totalitarianism,* 2nd ed. (New York: World, 1958), 493–95; Arendt, *The Human Condition* (Garden City, N.Y.:

Doubleday, 1958), 82–83, 157–68, 184–85; Arendt, *Between Past and Future,* enl. ed. (New York: Viking Press, 1968), 62–63 and 263–64; Arendt, *Men in Dark Times* (New York: Harcourt, Brace and World, 1968), 15–25. See John S. Nelson, "Politics and Truth: Arendt's Problematic," *American Journal of Political Science* 22, no. 2 (May 1978), 270–301.

20   William Butler Yeats, "The Second Coming," in *The Collected Poems of W. B. Yeats* (New York: Macmillan, 1956), 185.

Robert Hughes

Politics is probably the third subject to occupy the human mind. It
emerged after our ancestral exit from the Garden of Eden. One person alone thinks about God. Two people think about sex. Three
people, deprived, and you have politics . . . : thus the eternal themes
of Western culture announce themselves. We are all political animals. But these days, we have doubts about the value of political art.

The problem when talking about the reciprocal relations of art and
politics is how to limit the subject. Are we talking about state-spon-
sored art, or art that criticizes the state, or art that reflects on politics
in a neutral way, or art that adopts political metaphors to describe its
own aesthetic efforts and moral quandaries? Does art only have to
mention politics to be political? Or must it be charged with explicit,
didactic messages about the use of state power over human will? Does
it have to be left-wing to be any good? Can we imagine making aesthetically worthwhile political art that stands for the oppression of
women, or argues the inferiority of blacks, or encourages the exploitation of South American workers? And if we can't, why not, since
a good deal of respectable high art between 1600 and 1900 did just
that? Conversely, does the expression of virtuous political opinion do
anything to redeem a dull imagination? Can one regard Judy
Chicago's *Dinner Party* as garish vaginal Tupperware without being ac-
cused of antifeminism? Do we measure the quality of political art by
its social effectiveness?

Well, it is obvious that the heyday of state patronage of political ut-
terances in the visual arts is now over, and has been over since at least
the end of the Second World War. Most states, most governments,

Robert Hughes is the art critic for *Time*.

hold certain images of themselves. They propagate stereotypes of identity, of desirable conduct, of the citizen's relationship to authorities and strangers, which are meant to promote allegiances by giving people beliefs and enemies in common. Every state has an iconography of some kind. It arrives at that iconography by abstracting historical experiences, making them into totems, and then reducing those totems to signs; and finally, saturating everyday life in these signs to the point where response to them becomes reflexive. Moscow has socialist realism, with its benign, coercive images of production, progress, unity, and labor. New York has capitalist realism, with *its* benign and coercive images of consumption, progress, competition, and jogging. Each sees the other's as mere propaganda, and its own as a means toward truth, a gateway to reality. Each proposes an equally banal narrative of transcendence, to which the work of the artist has little to add, but the work of the journalist, the speechwriter, the advertising man, the public relations consultant, the TV producer, and the anchorman has everything. But if we want to know how these narratives are constructed, how these clusters of images are formed, we must recognize that they draw on the work of the artist to some extent – but not as much as they used to, before the advent of mass literacy, mass media, and (especially) television.

There is not much art, no matter how elevated and distinctive, which is 100% state-proof. States have a way of selecting peak experiences as trademarks. In the last fifty years this has been done, more and more, at the merely emblematic level of the 100 Great Thoughts; few major officials today, from the Kremlin to the Elysée Palace, from Peking to the White House, feel wholly comfortable without some lexicon of cultural uplift. Ballets and art shows are exchanged between the elected representatives of God and Satan, and though they may not do a lot of practical good in the easing of international tension they can't be shown to do any harm. When the Russians send their Matisses to Paris everyone is happy – the Russians because they own them, and the French because they made them. Cultural exchange is like the canary they used to take down the pit in nineteenth-century coal mines. It dies first, and when it falls off the perch you know the air is getting bad. There is also a subsidiary political use of existing art in the private sector: corporations here, in England, in continental Europe and Australia are always using it to burnish their corporate image and give the impression of benevolent responsibility to the public. The company that gave your aunt lung cancer now brings you the Impressionist Paradise.

But when it comes to the actual use of artists' images as instruments of State discourse, the contract can be fairly perverse and rarely predictable. Eight years ago I spent a few days interviewing Albert Speer, and at one point I asked him where he got the idea for the gigantic stadium he was going to build for Hitler at Nuremberg. Rather to my surprise, he fished out a copy of Goethe's journal of his travels in Italy, and read a passage about the amphitheater in Verona, where, as Goethe pointed out, every spectator would be induced by the uniformity of the architecture to forget his differences with his neighbor, to become of one mind and respond to the spectacle as with one heart. That is why Speer's favorite contemporary architect, in the closing years of his life, was Philip Johnson, whose corporate buildings he admired with real passion. Some classical forms—of art, of verse, of architecture, of oratory—are preferred by some dictators, but also by some republicans. Hitler loved the Pantheon, but Thomas Jefferson was utterly fixated on a Roman colonial temple in Nîmes, the Maison Carrée; the same Doric column, the same hexameter or iambic couplet, can signify dictatorial authority or democratic consensus, depending on its context. This lability of signs is something that governments have always exploited when constructing their propaganda. Equally, you can have State discourse which is entirely Romantic, which invests itself with the passionate, moving, instinctive rhetoric of the transcendent Self, and it can stand for tyranny too—as it did in the thirties, so that it has taken forty years to de-Nazify Wagner. And it is quite possible for a State to take some of its iconography of progress from the avant-garde of its time, and turn it to wholly repressive purposes. The best example known to me is the way Mussolini abstracted the language of Fascism, lock, stock, and barrel, from the rhetoric of Marinetti and the Futurists, and its obsessions with technology, mechanical force, war as hygiene, contempt for women, and so on. He sensed it would be popular, just as President Reagan sensed the benefits of identifying with a gun-toting bodybuilder named after a homosexual French poet. One cannot always predict the way the State uses the arts.

After George Washington died, the painters and sculptors of America diligently produced images of his apotheosis. Washington had been represented as a Roman senator, as a Roman general; he now began to take on the trappings of God the Father, the ultimate form of the pater patriae, the Father of His Country, enthroned in clouds, ruling from heaven, surrounded by allegorical figures of Virtue and Justice. Without these efforts our mental image of Washington today would not be the same. Because of them, we still find it a problem to think of him as altogether human. No president has been represented in quite this way since. The difference is simple. It is the rise of mass media, which conduct their apotheosis even more effectively while preserving the notional humanity of the god. Art put Washington on a pedestal; TV places Kennedy or Reagan in the corner of your living room, thus putting the masses on terms of adoring pseudo-familiarity with him. In the seventeenth century, when various despotic magnificoes from the Pamfili and Barberini families became popes in Rome, they shrewdly engaged Gianlorenzo Bernini to monumental-ize them with such public objects as the Fountain of the Four Rivers in Piazza Navona, a highly politicized image that signified the identity between the reigning family and the Holy Ghost, and the temporal power of the Church over the four quarters of the known world. Such sculptures were the mass spectacles of their day. The bronze of Mar-cus Aurelius would stand in for the real emperor, in the eyes of the entire population of second-century Rome. As late as the start of the nineteenth century you could imagine painting a fresco or carving a cycle of marble reliefs that would make relatively large numbers of people think differently about politics, because there were so few competing media and most people couldn't read. But the century of modernism is also the century of general literacy and mass photo-graphic and televisual replication of images. Print, radio, TV, and film generate heroes and dictate values with an insistence that painting and sculpture could never equal. They dominate societies as the fine arts never could.

Hence the almost total decline of official art in the modernist era. It has been supplanted. Your congressman does not use his campaign funds to decorate the highway dividers of Iowa with bronze effigies of himself on horseback. He hires a press relations officer and gets as much interview time on TV as he can. He papers the airwaves with as many commercials as his funds can buy. Pigeons cannot perch on commercials, as they do on sculpture; kids cannot deface them with their spray cans. And the penetration of mass media so far outstrips that of the traditional political or religious icon that there's no com-parison. (By the same token, one may observe, the religious revival of America has produced absolutely no religious art of the slightest con-sequence, nothing above the level of Hallmark-card kitsch, because Jimmy Swaggart and Cliff Robertson have television and do not need any icons beyond their own blow-dried, leisure-suited selves.) The au-dience needs to go, or be brought, to a work of art, and this necessity defeated art as an instrument of persuasion in mass societies. This fact was pointed out to me by Speer, who was talking about the difficulties of designing the great dome that was scheduled for completion in Berlin in 1950: seven times the diameter of Michelangelo's dome in St. Peter's, able to accommodate three hundred thousand Nazis for the ceremonial announcement of important events like the conquest of the world. One of the problems was that it was so big that clouds were going to form inside it and there was a risk of rain inside the structure. But the overwhelming difficulty was its size in relation to that of the man it was meant to glorify, the Führer himself. Inside it he was going to look like a mouse, a mere speck on a remote balcony. Eagle with the Führer in its claws. The demands of a mass audience overwhelmed those of political apotheosis. If only we had had television, Speer said—and of course he was right. It is only television that permits the kind of management of political reality that modern impresarios of the spectacle, like David Wolper, specialize in. Only television makes possible a career like Reagan's. No wonder the idea of government-sponsored public sculpture has shrunk, in our own day, to the harmless practice of putting cubes and bits of ironmongery in newly opened malls, in the hope that the diffusion of these harmless bulky artifacts will affect America's soul as fluoride does its teeth.

Today painting and sculpture only have very slight effect on political thought, one which is hardly even measurable most of the time. Sometimes there will be a controversy over a given monument—like Maya Lin's design for the monument to the American dead of Vietnam in Washington, the only rival in the late twentieth century to the great memorials erected in the twenties to the dead of the First World War—that great, grave slot disappearing into the ground, with the names of the dead ranked in democratic equality on its marble wall. Even granted that as an idea it owes too much to Richard Serra, and that it has been sadly compromised by the placement of the three bronze figures of soldiers, it is the sole political monument that I know of made in America since 1970 that works both socially and aesthetically, as a real focus of collective emotion.

We all have a private list of "political masterpieces." It would include such clearly polemical images as David's *Marat* and his *Oath of the Horatii*, Baron Gros's *Napoleon Visiting the Plague Hospital at Jaffa*, Goya's *Second* and *Third of May* and of course his *Disasters of War*, certain works by Gustave Courbet and Daumier and George Grosz, Picasso's *Guernica*, and so on—to take only the obvious, textbook ones.

Each has a different aim. It can be to praise a charismatic leader like

Napoleon, to present a scrofulous and cunning politician like Marat as a murdered saint, to denounce the cruelties of an occupying army (as with Goya) or the injustices of Fascism (as with Picasso), to comment on the pretensions and self-interest of a professional elite (as with Daumier's lawyers) or the greedy alliance of business, religion, and militarism (as with George Grosz). But in some way or another, the art we call political always aims to alter its audience's perception of its own social rights, duties, and opportunities, in relation to those of others. It may do this very crudely, as when Diego Rivera drew fat, skull-faced capitalists in top hats smoking Havana Montecristos while sitting on a pile of thin workers. It may do it quite obliquely, as when Barbara Kruger presents her odd slogans of self-destructive social clichés, done in homage to Flaubert's "Dictionary of Received Ideas." But it always tries to make the viewer think critically about social relations–including the language in which they come wrapped. These days especially, political art tends to be as much a critique of language as of formal politics.

Many works of art once were political but no longer are–Italy is full of frescoes painted to make dukes and condottieri look better than they were, but for most people the facts are lost and their social meaning has receded into pageantry. The past throws its charm around the political, softening or obliterating it.

On the other hand, there are works of art which, apolitical in themselves, may acquire political significance from the context in which they are put. A portrait of an old Jewish peddler by Chaim Soutine, seen in an American museum, may have no political meaning whatever. The same painting, seen in a German museum in 1935, would have been read very differently, as a specimen of what Dr. Goebbels called *Entartete Kunst,* degenerate art, an intolerable celebration of a despised race done in a visual language that did not conform to the doctrines of clarity, pseudo-classicism and coercive optimism that the Nazis were busy imposing on all cultural signs. We are in the habit of intuiting shifts in the political atmosphere of official Russian culture from the emphasis the Hermitage gives to eminently apolitical modern painters like Matisse or Malevich. There is nothing overtly or even secretly political about the early paintings of Mark Rothko or Jackson Pollock; and yet America's decision to send shows of Abstract Expressionism around the world in the late fifties, as proof of the superior freedom of expression granted to art in a capitalist democracy, was certainly a political act–though not exclusively so. The more totalitarian a regime, the more it seeks control of all discourse among its citizens, the greater the political loading of shifts of language that, in a more open society, would be seen as innocuous. That is why, as Philip Roth remarked, for writers in Poland nothing goes and everything matters; whereas, in America, everything goes and nothing matters.

There was once a natural alliance, now vanishing, between the idea of political art and one of the main cultural myths of our century, the avant-garde. Some artists had to be ahead of others—to be possessed by the will to push the limits of language, burst the bonds of convention. The term *avant-garde* began as a military metaphor. It meant a small scouting party that goes ahead of a main force, to reconnoiter and skirmish. The first man to apply it to the arts was the French social philosopher Saint-Simon, who declared in 1825 that "it is we artists who will serve you as an avant-garde . . . when we wish to spread new ideas among men, we inscribe them on marble or on canvas; what a beautiful destiny for the arts, that of exercising over society a positive power, a true priestly function, and of marching forcefully in the van of all intellectual faculties."

This was both new and not new. Saint-Simon was recognizing what already existed—the power of art to transmit ideas about life. But he was also saying that the artist may change social thought for the better and so bring about a better world, because what he makes has the iconic power of moral suasion. Europe would have Greek culture without Greek slavery.

From this point, one important aspect of the avant-garde myth develops—that it is inherently political—it implants radical ideas in the social consensus.

Gustave Courbet believed that; and he wanted to paint pictures that would change peoples' views of their own political fate. The same faith proceeds, growing steadily more utopian as it goes on, through the work of certain Dadaists and Surrealists, in the work of the de Stijl group and of International Constructivism generally, and especially in Russia. It permeates architectural thinking in the twenties, through the examples of Corbusier and the Bauhaus. Design a new kind of house, conceive a new order of city, and a new kind of social being would evolve to fit it.

The avant-garde hope was that human betterment would furnish the moral center of culture, as religion had provided it before. Except that Utopia would arise spontaneously—no need to enforce it, because people by nature prefer clarity to chaos, virtue to vice. Unfortunately this turned out not to be true. In terms of slaughter and suffering wrought in the name of ideology, the twentieth century has proven to be the worst in the entire history of humankind, and the weak hopeful propositions of art and architecture turned out to be utterly powerless against it. There is a very unequal relationship between art and reality, and Shelley was wrong—poets are not the unacknowledged legislators of mankind.

The great example of this tragic inequality was Russian Constructivism.

The October Revolution gave artists like Tatlin, Lissitzky, and Rodchenko their social metaphor. Here was process and transformation, the literal renewal of history. It combined in a special way with the worship of machine culture that had been diffused by, among others, Marinetti, who had enjoyed a great success with the cultivated middle class in Russia.

But the machine in Russia was not yet a dominant fact of life. Russia was still, overwhelmingly, a peasant agrarian economy. The idea of the machine was more a hypothesis than a fact. Hence the implications of machine culture seemed grandiose and mythic. In 1913 a writer named Shevchenko announced that

> the world has been transformed into a single, monstrous, fantastic, perpetually-moving machine. . . . Like some kind of ideally manufactured mechanical man, we have grown used to living by the clock—and the sense of rhythm and mechanical harmony cannot help but be reflected in our spiritual life, in Art.

To us this seems a hideous idea, all of a piece with the industrial world in Fritz Lang's *Metropolis,* and looking forward to Orwell's dystopic vision of 1984.

But people like Shevchenko thought it was a kind of millenium, which would be brought about by the help of Art. One should never underestimate what kind of nightmares an idealist can mistake for paradises. To help this state of mind along, art had to reveal the process of dialectical materialism. Its job was to produce formal metaphors of material substance, interrelationship, and force.

So Russian Constructivism was identified with Leninism—not by Lenin, who dreaded being depicted as what he called a "Constructivist scarecrow," but by the artists and their colleagues. No more Russian mysticism—instead, the display of materials and substance, which they called *faktura.* Instead of primitivism and saints and folk legends, the modernity of rivets, celluloid, airplane wings—in sculpture, stress resolved and made to name itself in open frameworks, not swallowed in mass. They hoped this would make art available to the workers—no more mystification, the old barriers between artist and artisan, architect and engineer, would be merged in a general idea of art-as-production.

Nobody shows this dream at work better than Vladimir Tatlin. He had been trained as an icon painter and as a marine carpenter. He could handle both the precious materials of old art and the common ones of daily work. Could you combine them in one ideal image of *proletarian* material? The stuff people laid their hands to every day? Tatlin thought so.

He had been to Paris and met Picasso and seen his Cubist constructions of tin and cardboard, like the famous 1912 *Guitar.* But he didn't want to make still-life sculpture. Because still life referred to ownership and he felt a truly socialist art should avoid reference to ownable things. Because any object that could be represented could also be owned – a bottle, a peach, a landscape, anything was potential property – he concluded that sculpture should be abstract. It would not depict property or the human body. Instead it would allude to what the body did, what its work produced.

We know what the fate of such ideas was. They were rejected by Lenin, who wasn't interested in modern art and knew that most Russians weren't either. They wouldn't have perceived such things as art, and sixty years later they still don't. And then came Stalin, with the results we know – the total suppression of every kind of artistic activity in Russia except the form of idealism known as Socialist Realism. In short, the Ice Age, which is still with us.

Now it seems clear that Constructivism in its various forms, particularly the Russian, was the closest modern art came to producing a *high* style with *exacting* visual and intellectual ambitions meant to produce *utopian* change in the lives of a *great many* people. Other areas of modern art – some in Germany in the twenties, some in France – had hoped for such changes. But Constructivism came closest to making something real out of its political activism, because for a short time it did have some backing from the new Communist bureaucracy. Hence its fate, which was to perish in the gulag and to wither from indifference, has always been held up as a dreadful cautionary example by American critics who want to argue that art should never, ever, have any truck with politics.

This is an old American habit. The denial of the *engagé* artist was not invented yesterday by Hilton Kramer. It goes back to the belief, stronger here than anywhere else in the world, that art is morally therapeutic, inherently spiritual, and above politics. The roots of this belief are entwined with America's sense of cultural identity as it developed between the Revolution and the Civil War. They lie in an obsessive conflation of the moral with the aesthetic, of art with religion, whose net result was to exaggerate the powers of art while banishing politics from its area of discourse.

This moralizing came in part from provincialism. Almost all Americans before 1820 lived in a very thin aesthetic atmosphere. America in 1830 still looked more like Dogpatch than Colonial Williamsburg. Great paintings hardly existed, great buildings were few and far between. The intelligent American abroad could therefore find the whole direction of his taste changed by a single monument of antiquity, as Jefferson's was by the sight of the Maison Carrée at Nîmes. The raw son of the young republic arrived unprepared in Europe. The impact of the authoritative past on him was traumatic. To the culturally starved Yankee it seemed like an admission to heaven—five weeks of misery and vomiting, and then Chartres. "It is as though," one New Yorker wrote in 1845, "we had always lived in a world where our eyes, though open, saw but a blank, and were then brought into another, where they were saluted by grace and beauty."

That is one reason why the literature of art in America between the first presidency of Monroe and the death of Lincoln got the odd tone it did: rapturously pietistic, evangelizing, and full of a breathless conviction that the visual arts could change the moral dimension of life.

One sees it in the weekly editorials in *Crayon*, New York's main art magazine of the 1850s—the equivalent of *Artforum* in the late sixties or *Art in America* today. *Crayon* was the voice of the American artist's profession and in 1855 it bluntly stated that "the enjoyment of Beauty is dependent on, and in ratio with, the moral excellence of the individual. We have assumed that Art is an elevating power, that it has *in itself* a spirit of morality."

This proposition, one may be fairly sure, would have been news to most artists—let alone patrons—of the Renaissance. We know, in our hearts, that the idea that people are morally ennobled by contact with works of art is a pious fiction. The Rothko on the wall does not turn its lucky owner into Bambi. But America saw the morally regenerative power of art as a given fact.

Hence the first form of the artist as American culture-hero is a preacher. His social meaning lies in his moralizing powers. If you wanted to talk about the uplift given by art you cast it in religious, rather than sensory, terms. Benefit, idealization, conversion, refinement, sublimation, and unification. The presiding metaphor, every time, was that of God as the supreme artist. And from this it was only a short step to the idea that artists were seers or saints.

Transatlantic visitors to Europe did not value the realist impulse much: they could get enough of the commonplace in America. They were looking for peak experiences, authoritative icons of memory. They wanted Raphael and Fra Angelico, not the horrors of war or visual tracts on the condition of workers. Their taste for the indefinite reflected their taste for religious mystery. Hence the language of Abstract Expressionism seems to have been already installed and running before the Civil War. Consider Herman Melville's extraordinary passage in *Moby-Dick,* where Ishmael sees the picture in the Spouter Inn:

> Such unaccountable masses of shades and shadows, that at first you almost thought some ambitious young artist had endeavoured to delineate chaos bewitched. . . . But what most puzzled and confounded you was a long, limber, portentous black mass of something hovering in the center over three blue, dim, perpendicular lines floating in a nameless yeast. A boggy, soggy, squitchy picture truly, enough to drive a nervous man distracted. Yet there was a sort of indefinite, half-attained, unimaginable sublimity about it that fairly froze you to it, till you involuntarily took an oath with yourself to find out what that marvellous painting meant.

So Rothko and Still had got to the Spouter Inn before Ishmael and Queequeg. But the marvelous anxiety of this imagined painting belong to Melville, not to the painters who were his American contemporaries. It is very much not the mood of Frederick Church and Albert Bierstadt, who gave their audience all the traits of Romantic art in the grand manner—size, virtuosity, engulfment, the view of Nature as prodigy—except for one: anxiety. The immense wilderness, for these theophantic American artists, never makes you feel insecure. Its God is an American God whose gospel is Manifest Destiny. It dovetailed beautifully with the pieties of its time.

After the Civil War, and particularly from the 1880s on, cultivated Americans began to look on art less as a form of moral instruction than as a personal or social therapy. Few things in nineteenth-century American culture are more remarkable than the complete failure, the absolute refusal, of painters to deal in any explicit way with the supreme historical trauma of the Civil War. The sense of the sorrow and the pity, the tragedy, the waste, the frustration, and the impotence in the face of a nation dismembering itself is confined to literature—to the writings of Walt Whitman, for instance, after his work as a military nurse, or Stephen Crane's novel *The Red Badge of Courage.* In the 1870s Americans expected art to help them forget all this, to pretend it hadn't happened, to establish Utopia as Arcadia. Art was still a surrogate religion – but a religion of beauty, the voice of the comforting Madonna rather than the implacable Father. Instead of sternly ennobling, it calmed the soul. It provided the anxious American superego with a relief from the disciplines of getting and spending, from female neurasthenia and male power-hunger. American collectors wanted art to do just what Henri Matisse, in 1908, said it ought to do: "to be for every mental worker, be he businessman or writer, like an appeasing influence, like a mental soother, something like a good armchair in which to rest from physical fatigue."

The so-called Robber Barons – and baronesses – who were busily applying the suction of their immense capital to old Europe at the end of the century were not doing so from simple greed. One or two were, of course, but the typical figures like Charles Freer and Isabella Stewart Gardner looked to art to cure their nervous afflictions and thought it could do the same for the less fortunate. The aims of the American museum, in those early days, were not always distinguishable from those of the American hospital. They were partly founded on the desire to cure a pathology of social resentment. The public museum would soothe the working man. The great art of the past would alleviate his resentments at his own poverty. William James caught the idea very well when he went to the public opening of Isabella Stewart Gardner's private museum in Boston, Fenway Court, in 1903. Visiting such a place, he wrote, would give harried, self-conscious Americans the opportunity to forget themselves, to become like children again, immersed in wonder.

The most powerful instrument for this was the *religious* art of earlier and other cultures. Profiting from the Dynamo, Americans turned to the Virgin, whose images proliferated with astonishing fecundity in the most unlikely haunts of Protestantism. Dorothy Parker summed it up when she noticed a large terra cotta by Andrea della Robbia over the entrance to Marion Davies's bedroom at San Simeon, and wrote:

Upon my honor
I saw a Madonna
Standing within a niche
Above the door
Of the private whore
Of the world's worst son of a bitch.

No other country had sharper cultural contrasts. On one hand, the raw, booming, hustling, ruthless, Promethean character of American capitalism, the war of all against all; and its corollary, the athletic vitalism that Teddy Roosevelt and his Rough Riders symbolized. On the other, the obsessive cultivation of a kind of religious fairy tale embodied in art, the idealized Middle Ages and Renaissance that Bernard Berenson and Joseph Duveen unloaded on the American rich. They were locked together, because one promised relief from the anxieties of the other.

We know that the American public did not embrace modernist painting as soon as it appeared at the Armory and in the 291 Gallery in the 1910s. The usual explanation is that public and critics alike were savagely hostile to any kind of abstraction or distortion: that they wanted to preserve a static reign of late, academic realism. This is true up to a point, but it misses the real crux of the matter, which is that cultivated American taste rejected modernism because, in its disjunctiveness and apparent violence to syntax, it seemed not spiritual enough. It couldn't deliver on the inherited promise of art, which was to provide avenues of transcendental or therapeutic escape from the harsh environment of *industrial* modernism.

And that, I would suggest, is why the early defenders of American modernism, such as Alfred Stieglitz or the Steins or the redoubtable Dr. Barnes of Philadelphia, put such emphasis on the spiritual powers of art. It may help explain why the paradisiacal and oceanic Matisse was more popular in America than the harsh, anxious Picasso. It certainly tells us why the Museum of Non-Objective Art, the ancestor of the Guggenheim, should have been founded by Hilla Rebay, the batty mittel-European mistress of Solomon Guggenheim, on the fog of Theosophy. It may also throw a sidelight on just why the Marxist artists of the thirties so indignantly maintained that abstraction was a tool of class: it claimed a "spiritual" content which was identified as the sanatorium, the Magic Mountain of capital. American modernists of all stripes and colors, through the twenties and thirties, gave much more than lip service to the idea of modernist transcendence; they paid it passionate homages. But the first to reap the real benefits were the Abstract Expressionists, whose domination of American and then world painting in the fifties was greatly helped by the way an exclusive pantheon was constructed around the fountain of transcendentalist rhetoric they and their critics emitted.

For there had been a shift in the political wind. In the thirties and early forties, modernism was regularly attacked for being politically and racially suspect. These attacks went on all over the world. The

virulence of denunciation in the States, however, was even fiercer, because native anti-Semitism was also joined by the fear of Bolshevism;
the rhetoric of modern art, full of appeals to revolutionary instinct,
fueled that. What changed this situation in the broad eye of the public
was the realization that though modernity was unfamiliar, it was the
enemy's enemy. Hitler had purged the German museums of modernist work. After 1945 it became clear, as the Cold War began, that
Stalin hated it too–including the modern art of Russia twenty-five
years before, the work of Tatlin and Lissitzky, Kandinsky and Malevich which, by one of those nasty ironies with which our century is
splattered, was so largely inspired by the promise of the October
Revolution. It followed that if Stalin and Hitler were out to persecute
any art that smacked of modernism, then modernism must be worth
encouraging as an emblem of free speech. And the proof of its freedom was its apolitical, nonideological nature.

Hence the policy of the State Department in the fifties of sending
shows of modern American art to England, continental Europe, and
even the Pacific Basin, as samples of freedom of democratic expression. And thus the media got on the side of modernism. Naturally,
this situation favored apolitical art.

I am inclined to think that America's traditional preference for the
therapeutic and the sublime as against the anxious and the critical had
deep effects on its ordering of art-historical priorities, where modernism was concerned. Thus there has always been a tendency to play up
the pictorial achievements of the School of Paris as against those of
northern Europe, and Germany in particular. No one can scan the
history of that Kremlin of American modernism, the Museum of
Modern Art, without being struck by this. Obviously, Alfred Barr was
not unsympathetic to either Russian Constructivism or German
Dadaism, and certainly not to the work of great social painters like
Max Beckmann. But in the general policy of most American museums, when it came to drawing didactic schemes of modernist culture,
you always knew where the basic allegiances lay. In all fields but architecture, the Weimar Republic was viewed as the merest appendage
to Paris. Not until the early eighties would an American museum attempt a historical survey of Neue Sachlichkeit painting. You would
see ten Matisses for every Beckmann. You would hear little about the
socially critical content of either Expressionism or Surrealism. And
when the time came for rehabilitating women artists, it is surely
significant that Hannah Höch, whose acrid collages in the early twenties were the first works of art to touch critically on the basic themes

of the industrialization of femininity, the mass-marketing of specious objects of desire and sexual diversion, should have been consistently ignored even by feminist critics. Unlike some writers to my left, I do not see this as the result of a conscious plot. It is more a matter of an ingrained attitude toward the expression of political anxiety in art, one which has attended American culture for a very long time. The crass persecutions of Hitler and Stalin, forty years ago, enabled Americans to admire apolitical modernist painting with the same zeal that is brought to the cult of the dissident Soviet writer today. The left's allegiance to Stalinism, right through to the mid-fifties, would have made it impossible to give the same homage to its politically critical art—even if the artists concerned had been as good as de Kooning or Gorky, which they were not. The impulse toward protest got squeezed into a narrow corridor of left-wing humanism, usually with an ethnic Jewish flavor, as with Ben Shahn. This corridor was supposed to lead nowhere special in the palace of modernism.

When I came to America sixteen years ago the idea of political art in an activist sense was thought quite passé. When people did think of it, they remembered huge murals in Mexico City of noble peons with ferocious mustaches. Abstract painting had made that kind of thing culturally improper. The radical was absorbed by mass culture. Women bought cartridge belts in Bloomingdale's and wore them to parties on the Upper East Side. The time was saturated in protest; how did you make art that responded to it? To most painters this was not an interesting question. As with the Civil War, so with Vietnam. As the American political conscience was going through its worst and most bitterly divisive turmoil in a century, the most favored artistic utterance of the period was pastel stripes on unprimed duck. However, it was not uncommon for leading artists to make political actions within the art world, in the hope that their cultural standing would cause the leaders of America to repent of their sins.

Robert Morris at the Whitney Museum, about to open an exhibition –styrofoam planks–maximal in size and length of catalogue essay, fairly minimal in actual content.

Soon before opening, bombing of Cambodia began. Morris's response: to send the museum an ultimatum to its trustees, whom he believed collectively responsible for U.S. policy in Vietnam. If the bombing didn't stop, he would cancel his show.

The bombing didn't stop.

He cancelled the show.

Still the bombing went on; evidently Nixon and Kissinger had weighed the risk that their electorate would be denied the sight of some minimal sculpture and had gone on, undeterred in their wickedness.

However, the happy ending is that a few years later, in a renewed period of the expressive and the figurative, Morris has indeed managed to connect his impulses of political criticism to his art in a way that makes full sense; his altarpiece-like paintings of nuclear disaster do have great intensity both as art and as political utterance.

It will be interesting to see how museums over the next ten years will deal with the spate of political art that has been released in the age of Reagan. From Leon Golub and Nancy Spero to Robert Arneson and Hans Haacke, there has been an outpouring of political imagery; it finds a wider audience than it did in the sixties or seventies; some of the institutions of American culture will have to respond to it. There is, of course, an enormous amount of boiler plate as well: neo-Marxist exhortations, deconstructionist sermons, impenetrable glosses on the hegemony of the mass media, lumpen-feminist diatribes, angrily failed conceptual art of every kind. It is quite possible, and some of my colleagues—particularly those of the neo-conservative persuasion, like Hilton Kramer—find it necessary, to denounce all efforts at political discourse because they risk this kind of complacent opacity. I don't think we should. For who are we critics to say that artists should exclude the political from their thought, and thus their work? If we don't think about how the social environment can be made fairer and more equitable, if we don't wish to make moral judgments, then we really have no strong claim to call ourselves civilized.

To say an artist can't call himself political unless his images have power in the real world is like saying you can't have opinions on anything that you don't actually control . . . a grossly repressive idea.

Art is the mole. It works below the surface of social structures. Its effects come up long after it has been seen. It cannot set crowds marching—we know that now. But its great claim to attention is that it can give us a mode of discussing experience which is specific, responsive, and free from the corporate generalizations of visual mass media, mainly TV. It is done for us, not to us. No painting ever saved the life of a single Jew or a single Cambodian; but in a more circuitous way, art can still be said to create models of dissent, not collectively, but individually. It cannot coerce; it can persuade, through irony, indirection, intelligence, and grace. As long as it can induce people to ask questions about why images are presented to them and in what form, art can still be said to have a political role – if only because it may help us tell a truth from a lie.

---

Robert Hughes presented "Art and Politics" as a public lecture in conjunction with *Human Rights / Human Wrongs: Art and Social Change* on April 20, 1986, at The University of Iowa. The lecture was sponsored by the Raphael Club of Iowa City, the University of Iowa School of Art and Art History, the Communication Studies Department, University Vice-Presidents Philip Hubbard, Richard Remington, and D. C. Spriestersbach, the Museum of Art, and the Iowa Department of Public Instruction.

*Dudley Andrew*          *Karin E. Becker*          *Richard M. Caplan*

## Notes on Contributors

DUDLEY ANDREW is the author of *Film in the Aura of Art* (Princeton University Press, 1984), *Concepts in Film Theory* (Oxford University Press, 1984), and many other articles and books on film theory and on the cinema of Europe and the United States. He is the founder of the Film and Literature Section of the Midwest Modern Language Association.

KARIN E. BECKER is the author of many articles and books on photography and photojournalism, including "Forming a Profession: Ethical Implications of Photo-journalistic Practice on German Picture Magazines, 1926–1933," in *Studies in Visual Communication* (1985). Her photographs illustrated *The Strip: An American Place* (University of Nebraska Press, 1985). She is currently working on a book on the rise of photojournalism in Weimar Germany, England, and the United States.

RICHARD M. CAPLAN is the author of more than 100 articles and book chapters dealing with dermatology, medical education, and the medical humanities. He is the coeditor of *Continuing Education for the Health Professional* (Aspen, 1985) and the editor of *Exploring the Concept of Mind* (University of Iowa Press, 1986).

*Antonio R. Damasio*        *Jorie Graham*        *David Hamilton*

ANTONIO R. DAMASIO is the author of more than 140 publications on anatomical aspects of higher brain function, parkinsonism, and dementia. Most of his research focuses on understanding the cerebral basis of vision, language, and memory and on applying scientific advances in those areas to the diagnosis and treatment of such diseases as Alzheimer's. Currently he is chairman of the board of Governors of the Academy of Aphasia and president of the Behavior Neurology Society.

JORIE GRAHAM is the author of *Hybrids of Plants and of Ghosts* (Princeton, 1980), *Erosion* (Princeton, 1983), and, forthcoming in 1987, *The End of Beauty* (Ecco Press).

DAVID HAMILTON edits *The Iowa Review,* a magazine of contemporary writing. His several publications include "King Lear, Inc.," in *Business Ethics* (Iowa Humanities Board, 1986); "On Certain Slants of Light Slipping, 'Zippy Zappy,' from Williams," in *The Missouri Review* (Winter, 1981–82); "Interdisciplinary Writing," *College English* (March, 1980); and "Andreas and Beowulf: Placing the Hero," in *Anglo-Saxon Poetry: Essays in Appreciation for John C. MacGalliard* (Notre Dame, Ind., 1975).

*Barbara J. Hill*    *Robert Hughes*    *Rudolf E. Kuenzli*

BARBARA J. HILL is the author of an article in the *Journal of Conflict Resolution* and coauthor of two articles in edited volumes, and she has presented numerous papers at regional and national professional conferences. Her current research interests include the investigation of different forms of international conflict resolution techniques, and the development and analysis of a game-theoretic model of international conflict dynamics.

ROBERT HUGHES, art critic for *Time,* has twice won the Frank Jewett Mather award given by the College Art Association for outstanding art criticism. He wrote and narrated the BBC/Time-Life television series *Shock of the New,* which was published by Knopf (1981) in an expanded book version. He is currently at work on *American Eye,* a television series on American art from 1700 to 1980.

RUDOLF E. KUENZLI directs the International Dada Archive at The University of Iowa. He is the coauthor of *Dada Artifacts* (University of Iowa Museum of Art, 1978), coeditor of *Dada Spectrum: The Dialectics of Revolt* (Iowa, 1979), editor and coauthor of *New York Dada* (1986), and coeditor of the journal *Dada/Surrealism.*

John S. Nelson                    Geoffrey Waite

JOHN S. NELSON has served on the editorial boards of *The American Journal of Political Science* and *The Journal of Politics*. His books include *Tradition, Science, and Interpretation, The Rhetoric of the Human Sciences,* and *What Should Political Theory Be Now?* Among his current projects are extended essays on political mythmaking in science fiction, horror stories, and adult fantasies.

GEOFFREY WAITE has written on Nietzsche, Hölderlin, the aesthetics of the nineteenth and early twentieth centuries, theories of protest literature and art, and seventeenth-century Spanish painting. His current work includes a book on visual ideology.

Robert Hobbs          Fredrick Woodard

ROBERT HOBBS is the author of *Robert Longo: Dis-Illusions* (University of Iowa Museum of Art, 1985); editor of "Earthworks: Past and Present," *College Art Journal* (Fall 1982); the author and curator of *Robert Smithson: A Retrospective View* (U.S. entry, 1982 Venice Biennale), and the coauthor of *Abstract Expressionism: The Formative Years* (Whitney Museum of American Art, 1978). He is currently writing a book on Edward Hopper, and he is co-curator of an exhibition on the art of the Mesquakie.

FREDRICK WOODARD has served as coeditor of *The Iowa Review,* has edited several poetry anthologies, and is himself a published poet. He has written extensively on Afro-American literature, and his current projects include a biography of W. E. B. DuBois.